Debating Public Diplomacy

Debating Public Diplomacy

Now and Next

Edited by

Jan Melissen
Jian Wang

BRILL
NIJHOFF

LEIDEN | BOSTON

Originally published as Volume 14, Nos. 1-2 (2019) pp. 1-197 in Brill's journal *The Hague Journal of Diplomacy*.

The Library of Congress Cataloging-in-Publication Data is available online at http://catalog.loc.gov
LC record available at http://lccn.loc.gov/2019025232

Typeface for the Latin, Greek, and Cyrillic scripts: "Brill". See and download: brill.com/brill-typeface.

ISBN 978-90-04-40992-7 (paperback)
ISBN 978-90-04-41082-4 (e-book)

Copyright 2019 by Koninklijke Brill NV, Leiden, The Netherlands.
Koninklijke Brill NV incorporates the imprints Brill, Brill Hes & De Graaf, Brill Nijhoff, Brill Rodopi,
Brill Sense, Hotei Publishing, mentis Verlag, Verlag Ferdinand Schöningh and Wilhelm Fink Verlag.
All rights reserved. No part of this publication may be reproduced, translated, stored in a retrieval system,
or transmitted in any form or by any means, electronic, mechanical, photocopying, recording or otherwise,
without prior written permission from the publisher.
Authorization to photocopy items for internal or personal use is granted by Koninklijke Brill NV provided
that the appropriate fees are paid directly to The Copyright Clearance Center, 222 Rosewood Drive,
Suite 910, Danvers, MA 01923, USA. Fees are subject to change.

This book is printed on acid-free paper and produced in a sustainable manner.

Contents

Introduction: Debating Public Diplomacy   1
  Jan Melissen and Jian Wang

Soft Power and Public Diplomacy Revisited   7
  Joseph S. Nye, Jr

The Tightrope to Tomorrow: Reputational Security, Collective Vision and
the Future of Public Diplomacy   21
  Nicholas J. Cull

Adapting Public Diplomacy to the Populist Challenge   36
  Andrew F. Cooper

Diasporas and Public Diplomacy: Distinctions and Future Prospects   51
  Jennifer M. Brinkerhoff

The Psychology of State-Sponsored Disinformation Campaigns and
Implications for Public Diplomacy   65
  Erik C. Nisbet and Olga Kamenchuk

Public Diplomacy in the Digital Age   83
  Corneliu Bjola, Jennifer Cassidy and Ilan Manor

Digital Diplomacy: Emotion and Identity in the Public Realm   102
  Constance Duncombe

Culture, Cultural Diversity and Humanity-centred Diplomacies   117
  R.S. Zaharna

Public Diplomacy and Hostile Nations   134
  Geoffrey Wiseman

US Public Diplomacy and the Terrorism Challenge   154
  Philip Seib

The China Model of Public Diplomacy and Its Future   169
   Kejin Zhao

Political Leaders and Public Diplomacy in the Contested Indo-Pacific   182
   Caitlin Byrne

Index   199

Introduction: Debating Public Diplomacy

Jan Melissen
Institute of Security and Global Affairs, Leiden University, 2511 DP The
Hague, The Netherlands; Netherlands Institute of International Relations
'Clingendael', 2597 VH The Hague, The Netherlands; University of Antwerp,
2000 Antwerp, Belgium
j.melissen@fgga.leidenuniv.nl

Jian Wang
Center on Public Diplomacy, University of Southern California, Los Angeles,
CA 90089-0281, United States
wangjian@usc.edu

As its title — *Debating Public Diplomacy* — indicates, this collection from
The Hague Journal of Diplomacy (*HJD*) is more debate-focused than *HJD*'s
previous thematic issues, which form a hallmark of the journal. It intends to
stimulate new thinking on public diplomacy in our turbulent world. There are
many definitions of public diplomacy, which, for the purposes of this collection, we generally describe as a country's efforts to create and maintain relationships with publics in other societies to advance policies and actions. The
twelve essays collected in this volume seek to reflect on recent developments
in the global information sphere that present new challenges for public diplomacy practitioners and, indeed, for academic analysis in the years ahead. If
any consensus exists among the authors, it is that the present state of affairs
across the globe constitutes a crisis, which is above all fomented by resurgent
geopolitical rivalry and technological change impacting on international politics and state-society relations — and hence on the practice of public diplomacy. The chapters are more argumentative than regular research papers; they
are shorter and forward-looking.

We have commissioned the essays in this collection from thought-leaders,
senior scholars and up-and-coming writers in the field, and we have pressed
the authors to consider observable trends affecting public diplomacy strategies and practices. The analyses look at public diplomacy from multiple thematic angles, and this volume includes the *sui generis* case study of China as
the world's most prominent emerging power. China's perspective serves as an

© KONINKLIJKE BRILL NV, LEIDEN, 2019 | DOI:10.1163/9789004410824_002

important reminder that not all states see public diplomacy and state-society relations as a practice governed by the same principles or even aiming at comparable goals. References to Russian practices in this volume also suggest that public diplomacy is unfolding in different ways in different places, and explains how this factor is complicating international relationships in a much more citizen-centric world. Making sense of what is going on *now,* and what may be *next* in public diplomacy, is as relevant for rising powers as it is for declining states. It matters to powers big and small, and those in the middle or occupying policy niches, as it does to an array of non-state actors. Complex, transnational state-society dynamics confront all and challenge public diplomacy strategists as much as coalface practitioners. Still, in a broad sense, we believe that this collection provides a better sense of where public diplomacy is going. It also gives the informed reader sufficient food for thought to upgrade a broadly shared understanding of public diplomacy that dates back to the 'new public diplomacy' literature of the first decade of this century.

One corollary of diplomacy's progressive societisation, in terms of the issues on the diplomatic agenda and the requirements of contemporary diplomatic practice involving multiple stakeholders, is that public diplomacy, also when it goes under another name, is becoming a more rather than less relevant component of diplomacy. This is not to be confused with an argument in favour of public diplomacy, which would be tantamount to being for, or against, the weather: academic students of public diplomacy have no evangelical cause. There are equally good analytical reasons for not conflating the practice of public diplomacy and academic analysis. Put simply, the articulation of policy problems in the minds of officials is different from the formulation of questions for research. The intrinsic motivation for studying public diplomacy cannot be reduced to the consultants' mission of making organisations robust and resilient. Many researchers have nevertheless drawn inspiration from the prospect of change in practice and better policies and strategies, and social relevance can therefore be an important driver for research.

Public diplomacy, also when called by a different name, requires a reconceptualisation of diplomatic practices to keep up with evolving models of public-private collaboration and communicative behaviours in the increasingly distributed system of states and global society. The progressive mainstreaming of principles of public diplomacy within governments and their foreign services, and the growing sense that this kind of diplomacy is regarded as the 'new conventional', have turned it into a practice that is harder to localise within departments with circumscribed communication tasks. Generally speaking, there is less and less diplomacy without at least an element of public diplomacy, thus making the challenge of identifying its boundaries less relevant. For early 21st century foreign ministries at the centre of national diplomatic systems, doing public diplomacy well has necessitated greater familiarity with key communication principles and techniques. It also implies the considerable and continuing task of successfully incorporating a variety of actors in their external relations, and understanding and meeting the requirements of engagement with not just foreign, but also domestic and 'in-between' diaspora publics. For other actors of growing consequence in the global system — including subnational actors, international institutions, multinational businesses and civil society organisations — public diplomacy principles and tools provide a valuable framework for their international interactions.

In order to move the research agenda forwards, but falling outside the scope of this collection, we believe that the study of public diplomacy is in need of methodological precision, more theory, and that it would benefit from engagement with debates in disciplines and fields such as political science and international relations (IR), and others such as sociology, psychology, or communication studies. More cumulative, theory-oriented research on public diplomacy is a condition for analytical rigour and academic legitimacy. Yet the papers in this collection have another objective. They aim at an expanded understanding of the practice of public diplomacy against the backdrop of current social, political and technological trends and some of the most salient trends in the global informational sphere.

The fifteenth anniversary in 2018 of the Center on Public Diplomacy (CPD) at the University of Southern California was one of two factors that prompted the initiative to compile this collection. It has been CPD's aim throughout this period to service the field through professional education, policy analysis and scholarly research. Another incentive was our impression that, ten years after the 2008 publication of the influential volume dedicated to public diplomacy of *The Annals of the American Academy of Political and Social Science*, there is a need for highlighting some of the best thinking on public diplomacy. Like the 2008 *Annals* volume, our selection for this volume is comprised largely of articles written in the English-speaking world, with North America exerting considerable influence on the transnational market of ideas. The observation that other cultural perspectives enrich global public diplomacy scholarship, also in this volume, may seem obvious, but remains an important argument to make — in favour of intellectual diversity and to compensate for the forces that facilitate US and anglophone dominance in the study of international relations. Such considerations aside, other developments suggest that public diplomacy studies should be more diverse and less parochial. These include critiques on the relative importance of soft power or sharp-power practices challenging openness as a norm in public diplomacy and undermining democratic procedure.

This collection ranges from a fundamental discussion of soft power (Nye) and public diplomacy principles (Cull), to the challenge of deep-rooted Westphalian perspectives on culture (Zaharna). It includes re-examinations of public diplomacy's contribution to countering extremist violence (Seib), and relations with hostile non-democracies (Wiseman), as well as an argument on human behaviour driving the sharp-power campaigns that are turning traditional public diplomacy practices upside down (Nisbet and Kamenchuk). Two contributions aim to offer a better grasp of the impact of new technologies on state-society relations, organisational processes and diplomatic conduct (Bjola, Cassidy and Manor; Duncombe). Two other essays introduce novel concepts and new thinking, with an appreciation of the important widening of social and political communities beyond state boundaries (Brinkerhoff) and attention for the effects of the populist turn in contemporary politics (Cooper). One essay reflects on the role of Indo-Pacific leaders in public diplomacy (Byrne) and, as mentioned above, the chapter on China (Zhao) shows how it can be top-down and, going against the conventional wisdom in the literature, emphasising telling rather than listening as one of its key principles. As guest editors, our aim is to offer authoritative, thought-provoking papers. Simultaneously, we would like to underscore our argument by building a more robust corpus of knowledge, including theoretical tools and attention for the variety of public diplomacy practices outside the Western world, of which we still have too patchy a picture.

All of the following essays have been written by academics, therefore looking from the outside-in, rather than reflecting or extrapolating from personal experience. The perspectives in this collection build on accumulated knowledge since the turn of the century. As this volume is looking forward rather than backward, it does not make a balance sheet of the early 21st-century evolution of public diplomacy. Nevertheless, there are numerous 'lessons learned' in the spheres of soft power and public diplomacy, many of which are summarised in the two scene-setting contributions. Essential soft-power features and core principles of public diplomacy, Nye and Cull suggest, remain valid and of significance in a world facing new crises.

The abstracts at the beginning of each essay provide a short summary of the main arguments. Their conclusions maintain an eye for policy implications. This volume will hopefully inspire new research and provide stimulus for debate on what is one of the most remarkable early 21st century developments in diplomacy and one, for that matter, that has challenged practitioners as much as theorists of diplomacy.

Jan Melissen
is co-Editor-in-Chief of *The Hague Journal of Diplomacy,* a Senior Fellow at Leiden University's Institute of Security and Global Affairs and at the Clingendael Institute, both in The Hague, and Professor of Diplomacy at the University of Antwerp. He is a non-resident Senior Fellow with the Center on Public Diplomacy, University of Southern California, Los Angeles, and with the Charhar Institute in Beijing.

Jian Wang
is Director of the Center on Public Diplomacy, and an Associate Professor at the Annenberg School for Communication and Journalism of the University of Southern California, Los Angeles.

Soft Power and Public Diplomacy Revisited

Joseph S. Nye, Jr
Harvard Kennedy School, Harvard University, Cambridge, MA 02138,
United States
joseph_nye@hks.harvard.edu

Received: 27 June 2018; revised: 27 September 2018; accepted: 17 December 2019

Summary

Soft power is the ability to affect others to obtain the outcomes one wants through attraction and persuasion rather than coercion or payment. A country's soft power rests on its resources of culture, values and policies. A smart-power strategy combines hard- and soft-power resources. Public diplomacy has a long history as a means of promoting a country's soft power, and soft power was essential in winning the Cold War. Smart public diplomacy requires an understanding of the roles of credibility, self-criticism and civil society in generating soft power. As authoritarian states today use new cyber technologies and other means to disrupt political processes in democracies, questions arise about the boundaries of soft power and the appropriate policies for public diplomacy.

Keywords

soft power – public diplomacy – sharp power – fake news – social media – information revolution – internet – strategic communication

Introduction

Power is the ability to affect others to obtain the outcomes you want. You can affect their behaviour in three main ways: threats of coercion ('sticks'); inducements or payments ('carrots'); and attraction and persuasion that makes others want what you want. A country may often obtain preferred outcomes in world politics because other countries want to follow it, admiring its values, emulating its example, and aspiring to its level of prosperity and openness. While many real-world situations involve all three types of power, and soft power alone is rarely sufficient, its presence can be a force-multiplier. It is important to be able to set the agenda and attract others in world politics, and not only to force them to change through the threat or use of military or economic weapons. This soft power — getting others to want the outcomes that you want — co-opts people rather than coerces them. If you have soft power, you can economize on your use of carrots and sticks. As US President Dwight Eisenhower once noted, leadership is the ability to get others to do what you want, not only because you tell them to do so and enforce your orders, but because they instinctively want to do it for you.[1]

Of course, soft power has its limitations. Much of a country's soft power is produced by its civil society, and that makes it more difficult for governments to wield. Policy-makers can give orders to their military forces, but at least in democracies, it is harder for them to direct artists, universities and foundations. Moreover, soft power usually takes longer to show results. Swords are swifter than words, but over the long term, words can change the minds behind the swords. The Berlin Wall collapsed not under an artillery barrage, but from hammers and bulldozers wielded by people whose minds had been affected by ideas that had penetrated the Iron Curtain over the preceding decades. The Roman Empire rested on the success of its legions, but its longevity also depended on the attraction of its culture. The current impatience of populist governments and reluctance to fund soft-power instruments reflects their narrow time horizons rather than a secular decline in the importance of soft power. Ironically, authoritarian governments such as China that have longer time horizons have not curtailed their investments in soft power.

Soft power rests on the ability to shape the preferences of others. It is not the possession of any one country, nor only of countries. For example, companies invest heavily in their brands, and non-governmental activists often attack company brands to press them to change their practices. Non-profit organizations manage their images to increase their soft power. In international politics, the soft power of a country rests primarily on three resources: its culture (in places where it is attractive to others); its political values (when it lives up to them at home and abroad); and its foreign policies (when they are seen as legitimate and having moral authority.) Soft power is ubiquitous at all levels of human behaviour from individuals to nations, and it is likely to become

---

1   Alan Axelrod, *Eisenhower on Leadership* (San Francisco, CA: Jossey-Bass, 2006), p. 120.

increasingly important because of the information revolution that we are living through.[2]

The Information Revolution and Soft Power

Information revolutions are not new — witness the dramatic effects of Gutenberg's printing press in the sixteenth century. Yet the current information revolution is changing the nature of power and increasing its diffusion. One can date the current information revolution from 'Moore's Law' in Silicon Valley in the 1960s — the number of transistors on a computer chip doubling every couple of years. As a result, computing power increased dramatically, and by the beginning of the twenty-first century it cost one-thousandth of what it had in the early 1970s. In 1993, there were about 50 websites in the world; by 2000, that number surpassed five million. Today, more than three and a half billion people are online; by 2020 that is projected to grow to five or six billion people, and the 'Internet of Things' will also connect tens of billions of devices.

The key characteristic of this information revolution is not the *speed* of communications: for a century and a half, instantaneous communication by telegraph has been possible between Europe and North America. The crucial change is the enormous reduction in the *cost* of transmitting and storing information. If the price of an automobile had declined as rapidly as the price of computing power, one could buy a car today for the same price as a cheap lunch. When the price of a technology declines so rapidly, it becomes widely accessible and barriers to entry are reduced. For all practical purposes, the amount of information that can be transmitted worldwide is effectively infinite. And the costs of information storage have also declined dramatically, making possible the current era of big data. Information that once would fill a warehouse now fits in your shirt pocket. In the middle of the twentieth century, people feared that the computers and communications of the current information revolution would create central governmental control, as dramatized in George Orwell's dystopian novel *1984*. Instead, as computing power has decreased in cost, and computers have shrunk to the size of smart phones, watches and other portable devices, their decentralizing effects have outweighed their centralizing effects. Yet ironically, this technological trend has also decentralized surveillance, so most people now voluntarily carry a tracking device in their pocket that continually violates their privacy as it searches

---

2 The discussion draws on Joseph S. Nye, *The Future of Power* (New York, NY: PublicAffairs, 2011).

for cell towers. And ubiquitous social media create new transnational groups and open opportunities for manipulation by governments and others.

Information provides power, and more people have access to more information than ever before — for good and for ill. That power can be used not only by governments, but also by non-state actors ranging from large corporations to non-profits to criminals to terrorists to informal ad-hoc groups. This role of non-state actors does not mean the end of the nation-state. Governments remain the most powerful actors on the global stage, but the stage has become more crowded. Moreover, many of those other actors can compete effectively in the realm of soft power. A powerful navy is important in controlling sea lanes, but it does not provide much help on the internet. In nineteenth-century Europe, the mark of a great power was the ability to prevail in war, but as John Arquilla notes, in today's global information age, victory may sometimes depend not on whose army wins, but on whose story wins.[3]

Public diplomacy and the power to attract and persuade become increasingly important, but public diplomacy is changing. Long gone are the days when 'small teams of American foreign service officers drove Jeeps to the hinterlands of Latin America and other remote regions of the world to show reel-to-reel movies to isolated audiences'.[4] Technological advances have led to a dramatic reduction in the cost of processing and transmitting information. The result is an explosion of information, and that has produced a 'paradox of plenty'.[5] Plenty of information leads to scarcity of attention. When people are overwhelmed with the volume of information confronting them, it is hard to know where to focus. Attention, rather than information, becomes the scarce resource. Reputation becomes even more important than in the past, and political struggles occur over the creation and destruction of credibility, which is affected by social and political affinities.

Social media have added a new complication. These so-called 'free' services are based on a profit model in which the user or customer is actually the product, with their information and attention being sold to advertisers. Big data allows micro targeting of advertisements and messages to narrowly selected audiences. Algorithms are designed to learn what keeps users engaged, so that they can be served more advertisements. Emotions such as outrage stimulate

---

3 John Arquilla and David Ronfeldt, *The Emergence of Neopolitik: Toward an American Information Strategy* (Santa Monica, CA: RAND, 1999).

4 Christopher Ross, 'Public Diplomacy Comes of Age', in A.T.J. Lennon (ed.), *The Battle for Hearts and Minds: Using Soft Power to Undermine Terrorist Networks*, special issue of *Washington Quarterly* (Pittsburgh, PA: MIT Press, 2003), p. 252.

5 Herbert A. Simon, 'Information 101: It's Not What You Know, It's How You Know It', *Journal for Quality and Participation* (July-August 1998), pp. 30-33.

SOFT POWER AND PUBLIC DIPLOMACY REVISITED

engagement, and false news that is outrageous has been shown to engage more viewers than accurate news. A 2018 study of demonstrations in Germany, for example, found that 'YouTube's algorithm systematically directs users toward extremist content [...] It looks like reality, but deforms reality because it is biased toward watch time'.[6] Fact checking by conventional news media is often unable to keep up in the race for attention. As we shall see below, the nature of this profit model has also been exploited as a weapon by Russia and non-state actors.

Reputation has always mattered in world politics, but the role of credibility becomes an even more important power resource. Information that appears to be propaganda may not only be scorned; it may also turn out to be counter-productive if it undermines a country's reputation for credibility. During the Iraq War, the treatment of prisoners at Abu Ghraib and Guantanamo — in a manner inconsistent with American values — led to perceptions of hypocrisy that could not be reversed by broadcasting pictures of Muslims living well in the United States. Presidential claims that prove to be demonstrably false undercut American credibility and reduce US soft power. The effectiveness of public diplomacy is measured by minds changed (as measured by interviews or polls), not dollars spent. It is interesting to note that polls and the consultancy Portland's index of the *Soft Power 30* show a decline in US soft power since the beginning of the Trump administration.[7] Tweets can help to set the global agenda, but they do not produce soft power if they are not credible.

Public Diplomacy

Edmund Gullion is sometimes credited with coining the term 'public diplomacy' in 1965, but as Eytan Gilboa points out, public diplomacy is not new, and its essence is 'the good impression that a country seeks to make on the public of another country'.[8] It is an effort to appear attractive and to create soft power. Some cynics dismiss it as simply propaganda, but such cynicism misunderstands that simple propaganda often lacks credibility and thus fails to attract, although it can have other effects. For example, a study of recent

---

6 Max Fisher and Katrin Bennhold, 'As Germans Seek News, YouTube Delivers Far-Right Tirades', *The New York Times* (8 September 2018), p. A4.

7 Pew Research Center, *Spring 2017 Global Attitudes Survey* (Washington, DC: Pew Research Center, 2017); and Portland, *The Soft Power 30: A Global Ranking of Soft Power* (London: Portland Communications, 2018).

8 Eytan Gilboa, 'Public Diplomacy', in Gianpietro Mazzoleni *et al.* (eds), *The International Encyclopedia of Political Communication* (New York, NY: Wiley, 2015).

Russian media messages in Ukraine found them persuasive only to those already predisposed in Russia's favour. But even though it did not change minds, it did polarize its audience.[9] Nor is public diplomacy merely public relations campaigns. Selling a positive image is part of it, but public diplomacy also involves building long-term relationships that create an enabling environment for government policies.

In terms of time horizons, Mark Leonard has distinguished three important aspects of public diplomacy.[10] The first and most immediate dimension is daily communication, which involves explaining the context of domestic and foreign policy decisions. After making decisions, government officials in modern democracies usually devote a good deal of attention to what and how to tell the press. But they generally focus on the domestic press. In the age of the internet and social media, it is often difficult to distinguish domestic and foreign press, or to be clear about what constitutes 'the press'. In dealing with crises and breaking news, a rapid-response capability means that false charges or misleading information must be answered immediately. After dramatic events such as a mass shooting, for instance, different groups flood social media with interpretations, some of which are deliberately false but designed to create trends for algorithms that skew the ensuing debate. The need to monitor social media and to respond quickly enough is often a difficult skill for bureaucracies to master.

The second dimension is strategic communication, which develops a set of simple themes, much as a political or advertising campaign does. The campaign plans symbolic events and communications over the course of the next year or so to reinforce central themes or to advance a particular government policy. Special themes focus on particular policy initiatives. For example, after the Reagan administration decided to implement NATO's two-track decision of deploying missiles while negotiating to remove existing Soviet intermediate-range missiles, former US Secretary of State George Shultz concluded:

> I don't think we could have pulled it off if it hadn't been for a very active program of public diplomacy. Because the Soviets were very active all through 1983 [...] with peace movements and all kinds of efforts to dissuade our friends in Europe from deploying.[11]

---

9   Leonid Peisakhin and Arturas Rozenas, 'When Does Russian Propaganda Work — And When Does It Backfire?', *The Washington Post* (3 April 2018).

10   Mark Leonard, *Public Diplomacy* (London: Foreign Policy Centre, 2002).

11   Hans N. Tuch, *Communicating with the World: US Public Diplomacy Overseas* (New York, NY: St Martin's Press, 1990), chapter 12.

More recently, as the Bush and Obama administration sought to counter radical jihadists, the US State Department developed a campaign to attract Muslims by demonstrating tolerance and hospitality, albeit with mixed results.

A third dimension of public diplomacy has a longer time horizon and involves the development of lasting relationships with key individuals over many years through scholarships, exchanges, training, seminars, conferences and access to media channels. Each year, nearly one million foreign students study in the United States, and hundreds of thousands — including several hundred heads of governments — have participated in American cultural and academic exchanges. These exchanges have helped to educate world leaders including Anwar Sadat, Helmut Schmidt and Margaret Thatcher. Unfortunately, in promoting the hard-power nature of its approach, the Trump administration tried to slash many of these exchange programmes.

Each of these three aspects of public diplomacy plays an important role in helping to create an attractive image of a country that can improve its prospects of obtaining its desired outcomes. Yet even the best advertising cannot sell an unpopular product. Policies that appear to be narrowly self-serving or arrogantly presented are unlikely to produce soft power. At best, long-standing friendly relationships may lead others to be slightly more tolerant in their responses. Friends will sometimes give you the benefit of the doubt and this is what is meant by an enabling or a disabling environment for policy. A communications strategy cannot work if it cuts against the grain of policy. Actions speak louder than words. As former US Senator Charles Hagel noted, many people in Washington DC after 9/11 were suddenly talking about the need for renewed public diplomacy to 'get our message out'. Yet, as he went on to say,

> Madison Avenue-style packaging cannot market a contradictory or confusing message. We need to reassess the fundamentals of our diplomatic approach [...] Policy and diplomacy must match, or marketing becomes a confusing and transparent barrage of mixed messages.[12]

This remains as true for Twitter and Facebook campaigns as for broadcasts.

The most effective public diplomacy is a two-way street that involves listening as well as talking. Attraction is about the minds of others, and we need to understand better what is going on there and what values we share. This is why exchanges are often more effective than mere broadcasting. By definition, soft power means getting others to want the same outcomes you want, and that

---

12 US Senator Chuck Hagel, 'Challenges of World Leadership', speech to the National Press Club, Washington, DC (19 June 2003).

requires an understanding of how they are hearing your messages and adapting accordingly. Unlike hard power, soft power depends on what is happening in the minds of the beholders. It is crucial to understand the target audience. Yet research on foreign public opinion is woefully under-funded.

All information goes through cultural filters, and what we think are clear statements are rarely heard as intended. Telling is far less influential than actions and symbols that show as well as tell. This is why the Bush administration's initiatives on increasing development assistance or combating HIV/AIDS were so important and why the current administration's cuts are damaging US soft power. It is interesting that the provision of tsunami relief to Indonesia in 2004 helped to reverse in part the precipitous slide in the United States' standing in Indonesian polls that began after the Iraq War. And US efforts to support public health, including the efforts to combat the Ebola virus in West Africa during the Obama administration, were important in helping to restore US soft power.

Broadcasting remains important and many people rely on television for their news. Increasingly, however, younger generations get their news via social media and the internet. About 47 per cent of Americans report getting news from social media often or sometimes, with Facebook the dominant source.[13] Overseas, mobile telephones have now made such media available to people who previously could not afford a computer. Moreover, the developments in computing power, cheap storage and artificial intelligence have allowed the development of low-cost, flexible micro-messaging that allows for the targeting of messages to particular groups and individuals. A combination of personal visits and internet resources can create both virtual and real networks of young people who want to learn about each other's cultures, or diasporas that maintain transnational contacts, as well as affinity groups that are susceptible to fake news.[14]

Not only do actions need to reinforce words; it is important to remember that the same words and images that are most successful in communicating to a domestic audience may have negative effects on a foreign audience. When President Bush used the term 'axis of evil' to refer to Iraq, Iran and North Korea in his 2002 State of the Union address, it was well received domestically. However, foreigners reacted against lumping together disparate diplomatic situations under a moralistic label. Similarly, while President Trump's advisors

---

13   Jeffrey Gottfried and Elisa Shearer, 'News Use Across Social Media Platforms 2017' (Washington, DC: Pew Research Center, 2017).

14   Jan Melissen, 'Fake News and What (Not) to Do About It' (January 2018), available online at https://www.clingendael.org/publication/fake-news-and-what-not-do-about-it.

have tried to explain that his slogan 'America First' does not mean 'America Alone', many foreign audiences heard a message that their interests were devalued and secondary.

Even when policy and communications are 'in sync', wielding soft-power resources in an information age is difficult. For one thing, government communications and public diplomacy are only a small fraction of the total communications among societies in an age that is awash in information. Hollywood movies that offend religious fundamentalists in other countries or activities by American missionaries that appear to devalue Islam will always be outside the control of government. Some sceptics have concluded that Americans should accept the inevitable and allow market forces to take care of the presentation of the United States' culture and image to foreigners. Why pour money into Voice of America (VOA) when CNN, MSNBC or Fox can do the work for free? But such a conclusion is too facile. Market forces portray only the profitable mass dimensions of American culture, thus reinforcing foreign images of a one-dimensional country. The role for public diplomacy remains. Developing long-term relationships is not always profitable in the short term, and thus leaving it simply to the market may lead to under-investment. While higher education may pay for itself, and non-profit organizations can help, many exchange programmes would shrink without government support.

At the same time, post-modern publics are generally sceptical of authority, and governments are often mistrusted. Thus, it often behooves governments to keep in the background and to work with private actors. Some non-governmental organizations (NGOs) enjoy more trust than governments do, and although they are difficult to control, they can be useful channels of communication. US foundations and NGOs played important roles in the consolidation of democracy in Eastern Europe after the end of the Cold War. Similarly, for countries like Britain and the United States, which enjoy significant immigrant populations, such diasporas can provide culturally sensitive and linguistically skilled connections. Building relationships among political parties in different countries was pioneered by Germany, where the major parties have foundations for foreign contacts that are partly supported by government funds. During the Reagan administration, the United States followed suit when it established the National Endowment for Democracy, which provided funds for the National Democratic Institute and the International Republican Institute, as well as trade unions and chambers of commerce, to promote democracy and civil society overseas. In the eyes of the West, this was open public diplomacy carried out by quasi-governmental instruments, but in the eyes of some authoritarian governments, these instruments were designed for regime change and subversion.

Indirect public diplomacy has the benefit that it is often able to take more risks in presenting a range of views. It is sometimes domestically difficult for governments to support the presentation of views that are critical of their own policies. Yet such criticism is often the most effective way of establishing credibility. Part of US soft power grows out of the openness of the United States' society and polity and the fact that a free press, Congress and the courts can criticize and correct policies. When government instruments avoid such criticism, they not only diminish their own credibility, but also fail to capitalize on an important source of attraction for foreign elites (even when they are fiercely critical of government policies). In fact, some observers believe that US civil society — including Hollywood, television, foundations and universities — does more to create soft power than does the government.

Even the military can sometimes play a role in the generation of soft power. In addition to the aura of power that is generated by its hard-power capabilities, the military has a broad range of officer exchanges, joint training and assistance programmes with other countries in peacetime. The US Pentagon's international military and educational training programmes include sessions on democracy and human rights along with military training. In wartime, military psychological operations ('PSYOPS') are an important way to influence foreign behaviour. An enemy outpost, for example, can be destroyed by a cruise missile or captured by ground forces, or enemy soldiers can be convinced to desert and leave the post undefended. Such PSYOPS often involve deception and disinformation that is effective in war but counterproductive in peace. The dangers of a military role in public diplomacy arise when the military tries to apply wartime tactics in ambiguous situations. This is particularly tempting in the current ill-defined war on terrorism that blurs the distinction between normal civilian activities and traditional war. Russian theories of 'hybrid war' increasingly use a variety of measures short of open kinetic force wielded by formal armies. The net result of such efforts is to undercut rather than create soft power. Information warfare may involve intangibles, but that does not make it soft power.

The Authoritarian Challenge and Sharp Power

Over the past decade, Russia and China have spent tens of billions of dollars to shape public perceptions and behaviour around the world, using tools that exploit the asymmetry of openness between their own restrictive systems and democratic societies. The effects are global, but in the United States, concern has focused on Russian interference in the 2016 presidential election and on

Chinese efforts to control the discussion of sensitive topics in American publications, movies and classrooms.[15] In a report for the National Endowment for Democracy, Christopher Walker and Jessica Ludwig have labelled these efforts at manipulation as 'sharp power' and argue that the expansion and refinement of Chinese and Russian sharp power should prompt policy-makers in democracies to respond.[16] They contrast 'sharp power, which pierces, penetrates, or perforates the political and information environments in the targeted countries', with soft power, which harnesses the allure of culture and values to enhance a country's strength. They argue that democracies must not just 'inoculate themselves against malign authoritarian influence', but also 'take a far more assertive posture on behalf of their own principles'. The challenge posed by Chinese and Russian information warfare is real, but at the same time democratic societies should avoid changing public diplomacy to imitate their adversaries. To do so would be to weaken their soft power. Although soft power can be used for bad ends, its means depend on voluntarism, which is preferable from the point of view of human autonomy. Hard power, by contrast, rests on inducements by payment or coercion by threat. If someone puts a gun to your head and demands your wallet, it does not matter what you want or think. That is hard power. If the person is trying to persuade you to give up your wallet freely, everything depends on what you want or think. That is soft power. Sharp power — the deceptive use of information for hostile purposes — is a type of hard power.

The manipulation of ideas, political perceptions and electoral processes has a long history. Both the United States and the Soviet Union resorted to such methods during the Cold War. Authoritarian governments have long tried to use fake news and social disruption to reduce the attractiveness of democracy. In the 1980s, the Soviet Union's KGB seeded the rumour that AIDS was the product of the US government's experiments with biological weapons; the rumour started with an anonymous letter to a small New Delhi newspaper and then was propagated globally by widespread reproduction and constant repetition. In 2016, an updated version of the same technique was used to create 'Pizzagate', the false rumour that Hillary Clinton's campaign manager had abused children in a Washington restaurant. What is new is not the basic model; it is the speed with which such disinformation can spread and the low cost of spreading it in the current information environment. Electrons are cheaper, faster, safer and more deniable than spies. With its armies of paid

---

15   'Sharp Power', *The Economist* (16 December 2017).

16   Christopher Walker and Jessica Ludwig, *Sharp Power: Rising Authoritarian Influence* (Washington, DC: National Endowment for Democracy, 2017).

trolls and botnets, along with outlets such as *Russia Today* (*RT*) and *Sputnik*, Russian intelligence, after hacking into the emails of the Democratic National Committee and senior Clinton campaign officials, could distract and disrupt news cycles week after week. While it is impossible to say whether Russian efforts swayed the outcome of an over-determined event like the 2016 US election, Russia's efforts to discredit US democracy led to a widespread backlash in American attitudes towards Russia.

Although sharp power disrupted Western democratic processes, it has done little to enhance the soft power of its perpetrators — and in some cases it has done the opposite. China wants both the soft power of attraction and the coercive sharp power of disruption and censorship, but these two are hard to combine. In Australia, for example, public approval of China was growing, until accounts of its use of sharp-power tools, including meddling in Australian politics, set it back considerably. According to David Shambaugh, China spends US\$ 10 billion a year on its soft-power instruments, but it has received minimal return on its investment.[17] The *Soft Power 30* index ranks China as 25th (and Russia 26th) out of 30 countries assessed.[18]

Sharp power and soft power work in very different ways, although the fact that they both use intangible information sometimes make them at first appear similar. All persuasion involves choices about how to frame information. When that framing shades into deception, which limits the subject's voluntary choices, it crosses the line into coercion. Openness and limits on deliberate deception distinguish soft from sharp power and should remain the hallmark of democratic public diplomacy. When Moscow's *RT* or Beijing's *Xinhua* broadcast openly in other countries, they are employing soft power, which should be accepted as legitimate public diplomacy even if the message is unwelcome. When they covertly back radio stations in other countries, or establish fake accounts on social media, they cross the line into sharp power, which should be exposed. Without proper disclosure, the principle of voluntarism has been breached. (The distinction applies to US diplomacy as well: during the Cold War, secret funding for anti-communist parties in the 1948 Italian election and the US Central Intelligence Agency's covert support to the anti-communist cultural foundation the Congress for Cultural Freedom were examples of sharp power, not soft power.)

Today's information technology introduces additional complications. In the 1960s, the broadcaster Edward R. Murrow noted that the most important part of international communications was not the ten thousand miles of

---

17   David Shambaugh, *China Goes Global* (Oxford: Oxford University Press, 2013).
18   Portland Communications, *The Soft Power 30*.

electronics, but the final three feet of personal contact. In a world of social media, 'Friends' are a click away, and fake friends are easy to fabricate; they can propagate fake news generated by paid trolls and mechanical bots. Fake news has been defined as 'fabricated information that mimics news media content in form but not in organizational process or intent'.[19] Discerning the dividing line between soft and sharp power online is a task not only for governments and the press, but also for the private sector. During US Congressional hearings in 2018, Facebook's CEO was pressed by legislators to outline policies to do so.

As democracies respond to sharp power, they have to be careful not to over-react, so as not to undercut their own soft power. Much of this soft power comes from civil societies — in the case of Washington, Hollywood, universities and foundations more than official public diplomacy efforts — and closing down access or ending openness would waste this crucial asset. Authoritarian countries such as China and Russia have trouble generating their own soft power precisely because of their unwillingness to free the vast talents of their civil societies. Shutting down legitimate Chinese and Russian soft-power tools would be counterproductive. Like any form of power, soft power is often used for competitive zero-sum purposes, but it can also have positive-sum effects. For example, if China and the United States wish to avoid conflict, exchange programmes that increase American attraction to China, and vice versa, can be good for both countries. And on transnational challenges such as climate change, soft power can help to build the trust and networks that make co-operation possible. Yet as much as it would be a mistake to prohibit Chinese soft-power efforts simply because they sometimes shade into sharp power, it is important to monitor the dividing line carefully. Take the 500 Confucius Institutes and 1,000 Confucius classrooms that China supports in universities and schools around the world to teach Chinese language and culture. Government backing does not mean they are necessarily a sharp-power threat. The BBC also gets government backing, but is independent enough to remain a credible soft-power instrument. Only when a Confucius Institute crosses the line and tries to infringe on academic freedom (as has occurred in some instances) should it be treated as sharp power.[20]

Democracies should be careful about offensive actions. Information warfare can play a useful tactical role on the battlefield, as in the war against the (self-proclaimed) Islamic State. But it would be a mistake to launch major programmes of covert information warfare. Such actions would not stay covert

---

19 David Lazer *et al.*, 'The Science of Fake News', *Science*, vol. 359 (9 March 2018), p. 1094.
20 Josh Rogin, 'China's Foreign Influence Operations are Causing Alarm in Washington', *The Washington Post* (10 December 2017).

for long and, when revealed, would undercut soft power. Western public diplomacy will do best if it remembers the importance of credibility to soft power. In the realm of defensive measures, meanwhile, there are some steps that democratic governments can take to counter the authoritarians' aggressive information warfare techniques. Democracies have to develop better strategies for deterrence and resilience. In the 1980s, the Reagan administration developed an inter-agency Active Measures Working Group, chaired by a State Department official, that exposed Soviet plots such as the false AIDS rumour; and in France in 2017, Emmanuel Macron's election campaign was successful in exposing Russian interference in the presidential election. Openness remains the best defence. Faced with the current challenge, the press, academics, civic organizations, government and the private sector should focus on exposing information-warfare techniques, inoculating the public by exposure and avoiding the temptation to turn our public diplomacy into a sharp-power competition. Openness is a key source of democracies' ability to attract and persuade. Democracies can afford to practise open public diplomacy, despite the new information environment, because that openness provides them the ultimate advantage of soft power.

Joseph S. Nye Jr
is the University Distinguished Service Professor Emeritus and former Dean of Harvard's Kennedy School of Government. He received his bachelor's degree summa cum laude from Princeton University, won a Rhodes Scholarship to Oxford and earned a Ph.D. in political science from Harvard. He has served as the US Assistant Secretary of Defense for International Security Affairs, Chair of the National Intelligence Council and a Deputy Under-Secretary of State. His most recent books include *The Powers to Lead, The Future of Power* and *Presidential Leadership and the Creation of the American Era*. He is a fellow of the American Academy of Arts and Sciences, the British Academy and the American Academy of Diplomacy. In a recent survey of international relations scholars, he was ranked as the most influential scholar on American foreign policy, and in 2011, *Foreign Policy* named him one of the top 100 Global Thinkers. In 2014, Japan awarded him the Order of the Rising Sun.

The Tightrope to Tomorrow: Reputational Security, Collective Vision and the Future of Public Diplomacy

Nicholas J. Cull[1]

USC Annenberg School for Communication and Journalism, University of Southern California, Los Angeles, CA 90089, United States
cull@usc.edu

Received: 27 July 2018; revised: 12 December 2018; accepted: 24 January 2019

Summary

A global crisis exists today, driven by a toxic mix of populist politics and disruptive social media. For public diplomacy to respond, it must remain true to its core principles: 1) begin by listening; 2) connect to policy; 3) do not perform for domestic consumption; 4) look for credibility and partnership; as 5) the most credible voice is not your own. 6) Public diplomacy is not always 'about you'; but 7) is everyone's business. These core principles must now be supplemented by the following future needs: 1) reframing soft power as a new category of reputational security, relevant to the survival of vulnerable states; 2) contest disinformation and engage in information disarmament; 3) counter victim narratives; and 4) articulate a compelling vision of the future. This article refuses to abandon an element of optimism and continues to see hope in the ability of humans to connect effectively with one another.

Keywords

public diplomacy – digital diplomacy – soft power – reputational security – listening – visions of the future – response to propaganda

---

1   This article is an expansion of material prepared for the conclusion of Nicholas Cull, *Public Diplomacy: Foundations for Global Engagement in the Digital Age* (Cambridge: Polity, 2019). The author acknowledges the input of the anonymous peer reviewers and editorial team at *The Hague Journal of Diplomacy* in preparing this piece for publication.

© KONINKLIJKE BRILL NV, LEIDEN, 2019 | DOI:10.1163/9789004410824_004

Introduction

There is a pattern to the arrival of new technologies in this world. Someone will seize on them with public hope and predict that the mechanism will deliver Utopia. Someone will seize on them with private avarice and set about finding a way to exploit the mechanism to defraud their neighbour, service humanity's basest desires, or advance the dominion of one over another. Thus the railways and steam ships that the Manchester School of the 1840s believed would bind the world together if the laws allowed free trade became the sinews of exploitative nineteenth-century empires; the radio and newsreel of the inter-war years, which were supposed to educate one and all, became the staple tools of the dictator; and the digital technologies so vaunted a decade ago by writers like Clay Shirky have proven themselves to be potentially damaging to democracy, as well as potentially redemptive.[2] The warning bell against an overly optimistic interpretation of internet platforms was sounded by Evgeny Morozov in a piece for *Boston Review* in 2009 titled 'Texting toward Utopia'.[3] Morozov developed his warning fully in his book *The Net Delusion: The Dark Side of Internet Freedom*, predicting that the internet would be a boon for tyrants.[4] While the debate over the inherent good or ill of social media is set to run on, all accept that there is a question with two sides.

A decade ago, scholars of public diplomacy were among the most enthusiastic about the potential of new technology.[5] Innovations such as Twitter press conferences, virtual exchanges, and embassies on platforms such as Second Life were vaunted as ushering in a new era. The need to think in terms of networks as an extension of the digital revolution was a core insight of writing on the new public diplomacy.[6] Yet scholars of the practice of digital diplomacy,

---

2 Clay Shirky, *Here Comes Everybody: The Power of Organizing without Organizations* (New York, NY: Penguin, 2008).

3 Evgeny Morozov, 'Texting toward Utopia: Does the Internet spread Democracy?', *Boston Review* (1 March 2009), available at http://bostonreview.net/evgeny-morozov-texting-toward-utopia-internet-democracy.

4 Evgeny Morozov, *The Net Delusion: The Dark Side of Internet Freedom* (New York, NY: PublicAffairs, 2011).

5 For works engaging the early evolution of digital engagement, see Amelia Arsenault, 'Public Diplomacy 2.0', in Philip Seib (ed.), *Toward a New Public Diplomacy: Redirecting US Foreign Policy* (New York, NY: Palgrave Macmillan, 2009), pp. 135-153; and Lina Khatib, William Dutton and Michael Thelwall, 'Public Diplomacy 2.0: A Case Study of the US Digital Outreach Team', *Middle East Journal*, vol. 66, no. 3 (2012), pp. 453-472.

6 For an overview of the New Public Diplomacy and the emergence of networked paradigms, see Jan Melissen (ed.), *The New Public Diplomacy: Soft Power in International Relations* (New York, NY: Palgrave, 2005); James Pamment, *New Public Diplomacy: A Comparative Study of*

THE TIGHTROPE TO TOMORROW 23

such as Corneliu Bjola and Ilan Manor, soon noted the difficulty in finding genuine relationship-based examples in government practice.[7] Governments tended to look to digital and social media as just another mechanism to push out the message. The need for real interconnection remains. Today the world stands in a precarious place: a tightrope walker balancing on the wire that was supposed to deliver our collective salvation. Can public diplomacy be part of a way forward, or is it just one more part of the problem?[8]

Any discussion of the future of public diplomacy must be grounded in an understanding of the present. While most observers perceive a moment of crisis today, there is a range of views on its exact extent. Certainly, one element is the return to great-power rivalry as a central element in international relations. There is also the challenge to the communication order associated with the rise of fake news, disinformation, paid trolls and bots.

The two issues broke simultaneously in 2014 with Russia's intervention in Ukraine and simultaneous disruption of media. The world was unprepared for a nation-state lying point blank about deployment of its armed forces in the territory of another, or diluting the debate around a controversial incident by pushing out multiple accounts of it, as if weaponizing not just information, but the condition of post-modernity. The cocktail of military and media excess was swiftly labelled 'hybrid warfare'.[9]

Yet the present crisis is deeper than the need to respond to a single rogue state undermining international media, or even the crisis of multiple states seeking to assert themselves through aggressive use of media, recently dubbed 'sharp power'.[10] The crisis is a symptom as much as a disease in its own right; it speaks of a world in which many states are using foreign policy as a mechanism

---

     Policy and Practice (Abingdon: Routledge, 2013); and R.S. Zaharna, *Amelia Arsenault* and *Ali Fisher* (eds), *Relational, Networked and Collaborative Approaches to Public Diplomacy: The Connective Mindshift* (Abingdon: Routledge, 2014).

7   Corneliu Bjola and Marcus Holmes (eds), *Digital Diplomacy: Theory and Practice* (Abingdon: Routledge, 2015); Romit Kampf, Ilan Manor and Elad Segev, 'Digital Diplomacy 2.0? A Cross-National Comparison of Public Engagement in Facebook and Twitter', *The Hague Journal of Diplomacy*, vol. 10, no. 4 (2015), pp. 331-362. See also Brian Hocking and Jan Melissen, *Diplomacy in the Digital Age*, Clingendael Report (The Hague: Netherlands Institute of International Relations Clingendael, July 2015); and, for a historical perspective, Nicholas Cull, 'The Long Road to Public Diplomacy 2.0: The Internet in US Public Diplomacy', *International Studies Review*, vol. 15, no. 1 (March 2013), pp. 123-139.

8   For a full exploration of this question, see Cull, *Public Diplomacy*.

9   The term was coined in András Rácz, *Russia's Hybrid War in Ukraine: Breaking the Enemy's Ability to Resist*, FIIA Report no. 43 (Helsinki: Finnish Institute for International Affairs, 2015).

10   Christopher Walker and Jessica Ludwig, 'The meaning of Sharp Power: How Authoritarian States Project Influence', *Foreign Affairs.com* (16 November 2017), available online at

to rally domestic support and are demonizing their neighbours. Leaders of the new populism around the world are promising to make their respective countries great again, to withdraw from old alliances, rebuild walls and settle old scores. The situation has not been good for public diplomacy. Rising authoritarians have frequently sought to limit the operation of exchanges and the activities of external non-governmental organizations in their territory.

Some have even demonized them as a source of national ills. Consider Russian President Vladimir Putin's condemnation of the work of the National Endowment for Democracy in Russia, or Hungarian Prime Minister Viktor Orbán's vendetta against that great institution of educational diplomacy and democratization: Central European University. Conversely, but no less harmfully for the optimal practice of public diplomacy today, some nations have embraced the tools of public diplomacy as a mechanism for projecting their narrow national image and agenda, without embracing the underlying implications of exchange: that we all need to listen to and learn from each other.

The coincidence of the same kind of politics in multiple locations speaks to the ubiquity of the context: the aftermath of the economic downturn of 2008; the failure of globalization to deliver prosperity evenly; and dislocation in the realm of communication coming from the new technologies, which both dilute the authoritative and often moderating voice of the legacy media and elevate the more extreme views associated with online communities looping round on themselves. And yet there is no alternative to cooperation. The problems we face — with climate change as the foremost — are simply too great for any one country. The time for using or asserting independence has passed. The world needs to acknowledge its interdependence and use the mechanisms of public diplomacy to see what can be learned across national boundaries to address our collective challenges. The crisis of our times demands specific responses, which *should* be part of a healthy future of public diplomacy, but before addressing those it is important not to lose sight of the underlying lessons of public diplomacy practice thus far.[11]

The best guide to the future of public diplomacy is the trends that are gaining momentum in our own time. The general trends most likely to continue include: 1) the proliferation of actors in the international space, each seeking to engage foreign publics to accomplish their goals, including cities, regions,

---

https://www.foreignaffairs.com/articles/china/2017-11-16/meaning-sharp-power?cid=int-fls&pgtype=hpg.

11　These seven core points were first presented in 2008 in Nicholas Cull, 'Public Diplomacy: Seven Lessons for its Future from its Past', in Jolyon Welsh and Daniel Fearn (eds), *Engagement: Public Diplomacy in a Globalized World* (London: Foreign & Commonwealth Office Books, 2008), pp. 16-29.

THE TIGHTROPE TO TOMORROW

non-governmental and corporate actors and actors originating in, or developing on, social networks; 2) the reduction of budgets owing to national-level economic difficulties; 3) an increased emphasis on partnership and collaboration as a necessity for tackling transnational problems; and 4) increased use of technology in public diplomacy, including immersive technology. Against this backdrop, it is important to remember core principles that were part of the discourse a decade ago, but that have even greater significance in our current era of crisis.[12]

Principle One: Public Diplomacy Begins with Listening

Global public engagement must begin with listening: systematically collecting and analysing the opinions of foreign publics. Listening must be done and must be seen to be done. It should be open-ended and unhindered by preconceived categories.[13] New technology has made listening easier, in that software can monitor blogs and Twitter feeds in real time, but practitioners must remember that technology may also place new distance between them and their audience. In public diplomacy, relationships remain paramount.

Principle Two: Public Diplomacy Must Be Connected to Policy

The golden rule of public diplomacy is that what counts is not what you say, but what you do. There is no substitute for sound policy, and actors with a

---

12   For the diversification of actors that the literature includes: on corporate diplomacy, see Enric Ordeix-Rigo and João Duarte, 'From Public Diplomacy to Corporate Diplomacy: Increasing Corporation's Legitimacy and Influence', *American Behavioral Scientist*, vol. 53, no. 4 (2009), pp. 549-564; on the regional approach, see Ellen Huijgh, 'The Public Diplomacy of Federated Entities: Examining the Quebec model', *The Hague Journal of Diplomacy*, vol. 5, no. 1 (2010), pp. 125-150; and on city diplomacy, see Benjamin Barber, *If Mayors Ruled the World: Dysfunctional Nations, Rising Cities* (New Haven, CT: Yale University Press, 2013).

13   For a discussion of approaches to listening, see Andrew Dobson, *Listening for Democracy: Recognition, Representation, Reconciliation* (Oxford: Oxford University Press, 2014); and for models of good practice (recognized by Dobson), see Leonard Waks, 'Listening and Questioning: The Apophatic/Cataphatic Distinction Revisited', *Learning Inquiry*, vol. 1, no. 2 (2007), pp. 153-161; and Leonard Waks, 'Two Types of Interpersonal Listening', *Teachers College Record*, vol. 112, no. 11 (2010), pp. 2743-2762. On clinical best practice, see Sheila Shipley, 'Listening: A Concept Analysis', *Nursing Forum*, vol. 45, no. 2 (2010), pp. 2833-2849.

reputation for sound policy will find their power in the world enhanced. By extension, the most important link in any public engagement structure is that which connects 'listening' to policy-making and ensures that foreign opinion is weighed in the foreign policy process. Once sound policies have been identified, they should be publicized by or coordinated with public diplomacy. There is, in addition, a need to coordinate with those partners whose role could be considered 'engagement by deed'. Conversely, actors should remember that in the wired world, a major policy error is seen globally.

Principle Three: Public Diplomacy Must Not Become a Performance for Domestic Consumption

One of the major problems facing public diplomats today is the tendency of some governments to conceive of their work not as a means to engage international publics, but rather as a mechanism to impress domestic audiences. These governments are keen to show their own people all that they are doing to educate the world or to correct 'ignorant' foreigners' misperceptions. They conduct public diplomacy overseas for the purposes of propaganda at home, hoping to give their own people the gift of the world's admiration. Today, the political context of much foreign public engagement requires that it yield measurable results, which in turn threatens to create bias towards those elements of public diplomacy that can most easily show short-term effectiveness. This bias has placed culture and exchange — with their longer horizons — at a disadvantage. If public diplomacy is to retain a mission beyond winning short-term political gain, it will require restraint and vision on the part of leaders.

Principle Four: Effective Public Diplomacy Requires Credibility

The value of credibility has been proverbial since the day when Aesop's shepherd boy first cried 'Wolf!' The problem is that the ways of achieving credibility differ from one element of public diplomacy to another and are harmed if too closely associated with each other. Listeners and advocates need to be close to power; cultural diplomats need to be close to art and the people; exchanges must be mutual to be credible; while international broadcasters are judged by professional journalistic mores. There is a clear advantage to the Anglo-German model of separating elements of public engagement into firewalled units such as the British Council, British Broadcasting Corporation (BBC) World Service, Goethe Institute or Deutsche Welle (DW), coordinated

THE TIGHTROPE TO TOMORROW   27

at the highest level, rather than corralling them all within a foreign ministry. Credibility remains the foundation of all effective public diplomacy, and social networks provide even greater scope for that credibility to resonate. As the volume of information available over the internet grows, the provenance of that information becomes ever more significant. Public diplomacy has its own brands — the BBC, Voice of America (VOA), DW and so forth — and information provided under those brands can have special authority and is more likely to be voluntarily passed by one internet user to a peer, so long as the credibility of those brands is upheld.

Principle Five: Sometimes the Most Credible Voice Is Not Your Own

The desire to be seen to be effective has been one of the factors that have historically pushed actors to place themselves at centre stage in their public diplomacy, regardless of whether their voice is best suited to advance the cause that they wish to help. Some of the most effective cases of foreign public engagement have occurred when actors have empowered others to tell their story. National public diplomacy does well to privilege voices from its regions and minorities. All actors do well to seek out partners who are credible to their audiences. As the survey data collected by the Edelman Trust Barometer has shown, in the era of peer-to-peer technology, the ultimate credibility rests with similarity.[14] This means that effective public diplomacy will be that which enrols 'people like me' and provides them with information that they can pass to their peers. The corresponding conceptualization of engagement is that of a mechanism not for making single communications to a target audience, but for introducing a reproducible idea into a network so that it can be passed among a target group.

Principle Six: Public Diplomacy Is Not Always 'About You'

Public diplomacy is about advancing foreign policy, and that foreign policy may not necessarily concern the image of an actor: it may be directed at engineering improvement of the international environment, or empowering local voices within a target state or states. Once liberated from a narrow obsession with national image, foreign public engagement holds the potential to

---

14   For early comment on the trend, see http://www.edelman.com/trust/2008/prior/2006/ FullSupplement_final.pdf.

address a wide range of global issues. It is one of the few tools available to an international actor wishing to engage the international public, who hold the fate of the earth in their hands as never before. More than this, with public diplomacy now aimed at shared issues and using networks, old models of success are redundant. Some governments still have a narrow idea of success in international affairs. They understand the value of networks and relationships, but look for a unilateral advantage at the end of the process. This is untenable. One cannot win one's relationships. Relationships have to be based on mutual interest. The desire to win one's relationships is a symptom of psychosis.

Principle Seven: Public Diplomacy Is Everyone's Business

It is tempting to compartmentalize foreign public engagement as the exclusive preserve of those who draw salaries for working in the field, but this is to ignore both the contribution of 'citizen diplomats' and the 'people-to-people' public diplomacy carried out through formal work like town twinning and myriad positive connections across frontiers. Arguably, the greatest achievement of public diplomacy in the last half century has been the reconciliation between Germany and France, but a process in which local town-to-town exchanges existed for fifteen years before the nationally organized exchange schemes of the 1963 Élysée Treaty.[15]

No less significantly, the citizen plays a role in promoting the message or image that the public diplomat is seeking to project to the world. Just as public diplomacy is vulnerable to bad policy, so it is vulnerable to bad people. If a nation fails to uphold its 'brand', any messaging will be undermined. A small number of people can cause a great deal of damage. Sometimes the key battle in engaging a foreign public lies not in projecting a reputation overseas, but rather in persuading the population at home to live up to a reputation that they already have. It is a task equivalent to that of 'quality control' in manufacturing.[16]

Today, government-sponsored messages are only one mechanism by which to communicate across frontiers. Opinion is also built from the direct experience of individuals meeting. A country's image can be shaped as much by the experience of a returning migrant, or the fate of an asylum seeker, as well

---

15   For one of the Élysée Treaty institutions, see https://www.fgyo.org/.
16   Cases focused on improving or maintaining domestic behaviour include that of South Korea, which included work to make its public more globally minded within its portfolio of nation-branding activities in the run-up to hosting Expo 2012 in Yeosu.

THE TIGHTROPE TO TOMORROW   29

as by the words of its highest-ranking officials. Images will always be judged against experience. Citizens of diasporas are a resource for public diplomacy partnerships for their country of origin as well as their country of residence; they are also an important audience.[17] For a society to prosper in the international marketplace of ideas, it is necessary not only to strive to say the right thing, but actually to be what it claims to be. This emphasis on reality in the national contribution underpins Simon Anholt's extension of his work measuring the relative strength of nation brands in the global imagination through the Anholt GfK Nation Brands Index, to provocatively attempt to chart the reality of national contributions to the global good, adjusted by GDP in the Good Country Index.[18] In September 2018, Anholt took his idea to the next level and announced the formation of the Good Country as a country in its own right, with the idea that it could welcome internationally and collaboratively minded citizens from any and all countries and serve as a launch pad for policies that aim at the collective well-being.[19]

Beyond these seven core principles, four future needs have emerged from the present international difficulties.

Future Need 1: Build Reputational Security

The crisis of our moment has raised serious issues about the international order. For example, if parts of Ukraine can be swallowed by a neighbour with relative impunity, who is safe? The fate of Ukraine raises the possibility that public diplomacy, soft power and nation-branding may have been conceptualized in the wrong way. These concepts are often seen as luxuries of the wealthiest and best-known countries. The reality is that, at the other end of the spectrum, smaller or newer countries need to engage to establish reputational security. Reputational security is a place on the high ground of the global imagination. Once established, it means that when a challenge comes — whether

---

17   For work on diasporas as a part of international broadcasting, see Marie Gillespie and Alban Webb (eds), *Diasporas and Diplomacy: Cosmopolitan Contact Zones at the BBC World Service (1932-2012)* (Abingdon: Routledge, 2012).

18   For the Good Country Index, see http://goodcountry.org. The Index may be seen as a kind of public diplomacy in its own right — 'index diplomacy' perhaps — and the opening salvo in a discussion over what a country should really do to improve its standing in the world.

19   On the 'Good Country' as a country, see https://goodcountry.org/wp-content/uploads/2018/09/The-Good-Country.pdf. In February 2019 Anholt wound down the "Good Country" project.

from a neighbour contesting sovereignty, internal secession, or a natural threat like rising sea levels — the world cares. Ukraine plainly lacked reputational security. Despite such public diplomacy gambits as co-hosting the European Football Championship in 2012, it was simply not understood as sufficiently distinct from Russia by international audiences to provoke the same kind of reaction as, for example, the Soviet threat to Polish sovereignty, which the West read into the declaration of martial law in Poland in 1981.

Reputation has long figured in international relations. As Jonathan Mercer pointed out in his prize-winning study from 1996 (*Reputation and International Politics*), from the days of Thucydides onwards, leaders of nations have seen the need to preserve reputation as a vital interest and even a justification for war. Yet the scholarship of reputation has focused on the reputation of leaders for resolution or irresolution and the contribution of reputation to the world of deterrence.[20] My argument locates security not in the perception of a national leader as being sufficiently resolute to resist encroachment, but in the perception of an entire state or society as being sufficiently relevant to an international audience for its preservation or continued integrity to be considered a priority. Czechoslovakia in 1938 lacked reputational security and so its dismemberment seemed an acceptable concession to Hitler at the Munich Conference. Part of Britain's success in communicating its war effort to the United States in the vital period of 1939-1941 could be understood as reframing its reputation away from an old emphasis on empire, class and tradition and instead emphasizing the nobility of its suffering — the democratic values of a country engaged in a 'People's War' with a reputation for honesty.[21] It was an image for which the United States was willing to risk war to support and defend. Reputational security had been achieved, and just in the nick of time.

The quest for reputational security helps to explain the national branding efforts of Kosovo, its attempts to win diplomatic recognition and its work to be present in international cultural platforms such as the Venice Biennale of art and architecture. Reputational security concerns also seem to be a driver of Taiwan's engagement of foreign publics. Nation-branding is simply too relaxed

---

20 Jonathan Mercer, *Reputation and International Politics* (Ithaca, NY: Cornell University Press, 1996), especially p. 228. Mercer showed the limits of assumptions around reputation in leadership, arguing that 'fighting to create a reputation for resolution with adversaries is unnecessary and fighting to create a reputation for resolution with allies is unwise'. Interestingly, Mercer suggests that whether for resolution or irresolution, reputations are seldom malleable. This is consistent with data on national reputation at the level of brand, collected over time by researchers such as Anholt.

21 For a sustained study of this campaign, see Nicholas Cull, *Selling War: British Propaganda and American Neutrality in World War II* (New York, NY: Oxford University Press, 1995).

THE TIGHTROPE TO TOMORROW   31

a frame for the reality of the goal. Similarly, Kazakhstan's hard work to build a reputation in its first 30 years of independence are not solely about attracting investment, but reflect a deeper need to be relevant beyond its borders. Hence the government of Kazakhstan's President Nursultan Nazarbayev hosted Expo 2017, initiated a cycle of inter-faith conferences, launched its Astana Film Festival and invested in an externally oriented university sector. The model is that of Singapore rather than Dubai. The hope is to be both relevant and better connected.

Aids to this connectivity include the use of English as the language of instruction for all science, technology, engineering and mathematics (STEM) education and the decision to abandon the Cyrillic alphabet of the Soviet era and adopt the Latin alphabet going forward. The desire to be known is such that even virtual slanders like the 2006 comedy film *Borat: Cultural Learnings of America for Make Benefit Glorious Nation of Kazakhstan* are understood as 'gifts' by some Kazakh officials. Being known as the 'Borat country' gives Kazakhstan a place on the mental map of Western audiences, which Tajikistan, Uzbekistan, Turkmenistan and Kyrgyzstan lack. It is a starting point from which more accurate knowledge and an awareness of the country's relevance can be built. Without meaning something to the world, there is much less at stake should a rapacious neighbour decide to compromise Kazakh sovereignty. Foreign public engagement is one way to build reputational security.

Future Need 2: Effectively Contest Disinformation

The surge in disinformation requires a response to return stability to the international environment. While it is tempting to respond to fake news in kind, the collective response of the North Atlantic Treaty Organization (NATO) to the crisis has avoided compromise to established news values. Western media should be careful not to demonize the Russian people while attacking their leaders, and might do well to adopt the same strategy as historian Alban Webb found in the BBC Russian Service in the 1950s: focus criticism on issues rather than personalities.[22] Western countries should certainly be careful not to conform to the stereotypes promulgated by their enemies. Thus far the Western allies have worked to *expose* disinformation and distortion where it is happening. Support for the famous Ukrainian fact-checking website StopFake and other activities,

---

22   Alban Webb, *London Calling: Britain, the BBC World Service and the Cold War* (London: Bloomsbury, 2012), pp. 60 and 130.

such as the European Union External Action Service's Disinformation Review, are part of this.[23]

Yet this is not enough. It is also crucial that Western allies *engage* audiences that are under pressure from disinformation and hybrid threats through the established channels of public diplomacy, including cultural relations, exchange and international broadcasting, to assist in the construction of resilient societies that are better able to cope with such threats. There is a need to *enhance* indigenous media — a public diplomacy of empowerment to support the local creation of reliable news depicting the world authoritatively from the location under threat. In a city like Narva, the Russian-speaking border town in Estonia, the answer to a 'one-size-fits-all' message from Moscow is not a 'one-size-fits-all' message from Washington, DC, but instead to work to provide media that fits the complexities of that particular community, which seeks to be simultaneously Russian-speaking, Estonian and European. Finally, it is worth remembering that the answer to a communication problem may not necessarily lie in the field of communication. Perhaps weaponized information needs an information disarmament process; certainly that was part of the solution to the media challenge of the Cold War in the late 1980s. The clearest example of this is the way in which the US government successfully pressed the Soviet Union to stop claiming that AIDS was a US-made bio weapon, by threatening to suspend all US–Soviet scientific cooperation.[24]

Future Need 3: Effectively Counter Victim Narratives

In the marketplace of ideas, the meme of the victim narrative has become the fat little cuckoo chick pushing other ideas out of the nest. The victim narrative is an ideal message to resonate in the self-obsessed closed loops of social media. It tells the audience that its community has a special story of suffering and needs to be attended to before the needs of others can be considered. Such narratives kept communities apart in the 1990s and — with symmetrical embrace — fuelled the decade's ugliest disputes, including Israel/Palestine and the break-up of Yugoslavia. In the first decade of the twenty-first century, they drove recruitment to the global jihad. In the second decade they are fuelling

---

23   On StopFake, see http://www.stopfake.org/en. The homepage of the EU's counter-disinformation effort is https://euvsdisinfo.eu/.

24   Nicholas Cull, *The Cold War and the United States Information Agency: American Propaganda and Public Diplomacy, 1989-2001* (Cambridge: Cambridge University Press, 2008), pp. 467 and 474.

the new populism. Public diplomacy needs to consider how victim narratives of the past were diffused and to look for ways to overcome them using the kind of resources that were devoted to countering violent extremism in recent years. We have been here before. Victim narratives and mutual fear were part of the antipathy underpinning the great struggles of the twentieth century. These struggles were not simply overcome by force of arms, but by communicating a vision. The challenge for our generation is to achieve the same result without the trial by fire.

Future Need 4: Articulate a Compelling Collective Vision of the Future

The best way to overcome negative and divisive messaging is to circulate a truly compelling alternative. The answer in the United States to the intracommunity resentments that were released during the early years of the Second World War was a greater vision of national cohesion. In California, the answer to resistance to vaccination was a greater vision of child health, which placed vaccination in context as a component in a desirable whole.[25] In the case of our present international system, the ultimate answer to narrow narratives of national suffering must be an inclusive vision of the future.

Consider the tightrope walker evoked in the second paragraph of this article. Tightrope walkers have a simple secret. In order to stay stable on the high wire they fix their eyes on their destination: the far end of the wire. If they cannot see the end they turn around and focus on their point of origin. If they are looking at neither, they will wobble and fall. Much the same is true for nations. Stability requires either a clear sense of a future destination or a vision of the past. The crisis of our moment is based on so many leaders around the world drawing their stability from visions of the past. Beyond simply trying to correct the mutually antithetical visions of the past, our collective public diplomacy should also consider ways to turn the tightrope walker around and articulate compelling visions of the future. The history of public diplomacy suggests that such turnarounds are possible; indeed they are the chief way in which the great international crises of the past were solved. Consider the Great War, the Second World War and the Cold War. The road beyond these

---

25   On the role of the 'vision' in counter propaganda, see Nicholas Cull, *Counter Propaganda: Cases from US Public Diplomacy and Beyond* (London: Legatum Institute, 2015), available online at https://www.li.com/activities/publications/counter-propaganda-cases-from-us -public-diplomacy-and-beyond.

conflicts required the articulation of a vision of the future so attractive that not only allies found it compelling, but adversaries also. The visions sprang from many places and defied any one country's attempt to claim ownership; however, US presidents were essential to their dissemination. Woodrow Wilson, Franklin D. Roosevelt, John F. Kennedy and Ronald Reagan were all masters of presenting collective visions of the future. Yet they did not speak alone. Their messages were carried by the public diplomacy apparatus of their respective era, and participants from many nations shaped the presentation. The greatest communicators of the era were part of the process. During the Great War, for example, when the British government realized that it needed to present a vision of the future to the German public, it hired the man best known for his writing about the subject: H.G. Wells.[26] The problem in that case was not the lack of the vision's plausibility, but the failure of the post-war settlement to live up to wartime promises.

Despite the current obsession with hurts and glories of the past, some public diplomacy actors are already articulating visions of the future. The United Nations, for example, has rallied member states behind its seventeen Sustainable Development Goals (SDGs) to be achieved by 2030.[27] Positive visions of the future were part of Expo 2017 in Astana and underpin plans for the Dubai Expo in 2020.[28] Other projects focusing on the future include a remarkable project by the City of Oslo to demonstrate its commitment to the future by building a library of the future. Designed by Scottish artist Katie Paterson, this is not simply an eco-friendly new space, but a collection of books commissioned from and delivered by one major author each year, which will not be published until 2114. Participating writers announced so far include Canadian Nobel laureate Margaret Atwood and *Cloud Atlas* author David Mitchell. The library has also planted a forest of 1,000 trees to provide paper for the pages when the time comes.[29] A like-minded project from 2015 by film director Robert Rodriguez and actor John Malkovich produced, in association with a cognac company, a feature film called *100 Years*, which will not be released until 2115.[30] In a similar vein, a team affiliated with the Hebrew University in

---

26   On H.G. Wells' war propaganda work, see J. Lee Thompson, *Politicians, Press and Propaganda: Lord Northcliffe and the Great War, 1914-1919* (Kent, OH: Kent State University Press, 1999).

27   See https://sustainabledevelopment.un.org/post2015/transformingourworld.

28   Nicholas Cull, 'Soft Power's Next Steppe: National Projection at the Astana EXPO, 2017', *Place Branding and Public Diplomacy*, vol. 13, no. 4 (2017), pp. 269-272.

29   For information on the Future Library, see https://www.futurelibrary.no/.

30   On *100 Years*, see https://variety.com/2015/film/news/john-malkovich-robert-rodriguez -100-years-1201644846/. I owe this reference to Alexander Cull.

Jerusalem has chosen to mark the centenary of Einstein's theory of relativity not by looking back or reiterating his achievement, but by seeking out one hundred visions from visionary thinkers in our own time and anthologizing them in a way that can inspire the next generation in the way that Einstein fired our parents and grandparents.[31]

The era of social media has opened up fresh possibilities, but it has not erased the relevance of the rich history of public diplomacy or the knowledge of seasoned practitioners. On the contrary, the lessons of our collective experience seem even more relevant in an age in which communications play an unprecedented role. Whether the communications travel electronically at the speed of light or in hand-delivered notes written with quills and spread at the speed of a horse, the underlying foundations remain as valid today as they were when the term 'public diplomacy' was coined in the 1960s, or in previous centuries when generations practised the art oblivious to its name. We have seen that people can be driven apart by fear, but they can also be drawn together by hope. Public diplomacy can be the mechanism for communicating that hope, but still more importantly, when given the right vision and the right interconnection, public diplomacy can be part of the process by which the publics themselves become the hope.

Nicholas J. Cull

is Professor of Public Diplomacy at the University of Southern California, where he is the founding Director of the Master's Program in Public Diplomacy. He is a prolific writer in the field of public diplomacy and the media aspects of international relations and international history. His works include the introductory text: *Public Diplomacy: Foundations for Global Engagement in a Digital Age* (Cambridge: Polity, April 2019). He has lectured widely in foreign ministries and diplomatic academies around the world, including those of the United States, United Kingdom, Armenia, Canada, Chile, India, Mexico, South Africa and Switzerland, and has also served as a consultant, working with the Foreign & Commonwealth Office in London, Japan Foundation and Internet Corporation on Assigned Names and Numbers, among others. His current work is an examination of public diplomacy around the issue of apartheid in South Africa.

---

31   For Genius 100 visions, see http://genius100visions.com/.

Adapting Public Diplomacy to the Populist Challenge

Andrew F. Cooper
Balsillie School of International Affairs, University of Waterloo, Waterloo,
ON N2L 6C2, Canada
acooper@uwaterloo.ca

Received: 25 June 2018; revised: 4 October 2018; accepted: 30 November 2018

Summary

Public diplomacy has been externally directed via a strategy of assertive reputation-building. In an era of insurgent populism, this model faces strong backlash, driven by the image of public diplomacy being disconnected from domestic publics. Under these conditions, an opportunistic set of ascendant political leaders — even those located at the international system's core — have considerable incentive to diminish 'their' own diplomats as part of a wider campaign to stigmatize the traditional establishment. While more attention needs to be directed to the causes of this disconnection between diplomats and public, this article highlights a number of key ingredients in a menu of adaptation to the populist challenge. Above all, the focus of engagement in public diplomacy should be broadened to include domestic as well as foreign audiences. Disruption, it must be emphasized, does not mean the end of public diplomacy. Rather, public diplomacy must take a domestic turn.

Keywords

public diplomacy – anti-diplomatic impulses – populist challenge – domestic turn – Donald Trump – Brexit

© KONINKLIJKE BRILL NV, LEIDEN, 2019 | DOI:10.1163/9789004410824_005

Introduction[1]

Public diplomacy has until recently been framed through a number of inter-related progressive lenses. As a model, public diplomacy is interpreted as an advance on traditional statecraft associated with a closed culture. Rather than an exclusively inter-state approach, ample space is allowed for engagement with numerous publics. Shared concerns, instead of the promotion of national interests, are showcased. Network, not club, diplomacy is privileged.[2] From an ideational perspective, public diplomacy has been judged to be a positive development, especially — albeit not exclusively — in liberal Western democracies. It not only promoted democratization in the machinery of diplomacy, but placed enhanced value on the normatively oriented status of an actor. Only through the measure of attractiveness, via a strategy of assertive reputation-building, can authentic public diplomacy be implemented. Here, the contrast between public diplomacy and disinformation or propaganda campaigns still remains instructive.[3]

In anticipating future trends, however, it is the severe contestation facing public diplomacy in a newly disruptive political environment that jumps out. This predicament is largely because of the externalized focus of the model. Viewed through mainstream lenses, the orientation of public diplomacy has been directed beyond the borders of the state. From the time of Woodrow Wilson, US-based public diplomacy was premised on 'the belief that it was possible to apply to the conduct of *external* affairs, the ideas and practices which, in the conduct of *internal* affairs, had for generations been regarded as the essentials of liberal democracy'.[4] In similar fashion, the cornerstone of European Union (EU) public diplomacy has been 'improving the reputation of the EU to the external public', with emphasis on a brand that underscores the concepts of 'peace, abundance, prosperity, democracy and freedom'.[5]

---

1   The author wishes to thank Marcus Holmes, Jan Melissen, Jay Wang and Jérémie Cornut, as well as three anonymous reviews for their helpful comments on earlier drafts of this article. Research support was provided by SSHRC Connection Grant 611-2015-0359.

2   See, for example, Nancy E. Snow and Philip M. Taylor (eds), *Routledge Handbook of Public Diplomacy* (Abingdon: Routledge, 2008); Jan Melissen (ed.), *The New Public Diplomacy: Soft Power in International Relations* (Basingstoke: Palgrave Macmillan, 2008); Mark Leonard, *Public Diplomacy* (London: Foreign Policy Centre, 2002).

3   Ilya Yablokov, 'Conspiracy Theories as a Russian Public Diplomacy Tool: The Case of Russia Today (RT)', *Politics*, vol. 35, nos. 3-4 (2015), pp. 301-315.

4   Harold Nicolson, *Diplomacy* (London: Thornton Butterworth, 1939), p. 113.

5   European Union, *Shared Vision, Common Action: A Stronger Europe* (June 2016), available at https://europa.eu/globalstrategy/sites/globalstrategy/files/pages/files/eugs_review_web.pdf.

Although viable and valuable in the past, this model faces strong backlash in an era of insurgent populism, driven by the image of public diplomacy as disconnected from domestic publics. If, as Nicholas Cull suggests, the 'best public diplomacy begins with listening', a major weakness of the traditional approach has been that the listening process only started 'beyond the water's edge'.[6] Indeed, this external/internal disconnect has been acknowledged by sophisticated observers. As Jan Melissen has remarked, 'many scholars today regard public diplomacy's domestic dimension as alien territory, or even an oxymoron'.[7] An important exception, however, is Ellen Huijgh, who has pointed to the need 'to involve domestic citizens in broader (public) diplomacy projects and to see them as part of the concept, or public diplomacy's domestic dimension'.[8]

Populism and Anti-diplomatic Impulses

Such a disconnect plays into the hands of those political forces deeply suspicious of diplomats and diplomatic culture. At the moment — and most likely stretching into the future — these anti-diplomatic impulses are on the rise again through a widespread populist challenge. In a markedly different way than nationalists, populists contest the international system as well as diplomacy and diplomats as constraining forces, part of a self-serving and controlling technocracy.[9] From the theoretical tradition associated with Ernesto Laclau, the populist logic may be contrasted from nationalists in a fundamental dimension.[10] Whereas nationalists differentiate horizontally between those inside and outside (that is, the 'other') the nation state, populists differentiate on a down/up basis with antagonism between the elite and 'the people' as underdogs.

---

6   Nicholas J. Cull, *Public Diplomacy: Lessons from the Past*, CPD Perspectives on Public Diplomacy (Los Angeles, CA: Figueroa, 2009), available at http://kamudiplomasisi.org/pdf/kitaplar/PDPerspectivesLessons.pdf.

7   Jan Melissen, 'Public Diplomacy', in Pauline Kerr and Geoffrey Wiseman (eds), *Diplomacy in a Globalizing World* (New York, NY: Oxford University Press, 2018), p. 211.

8   Ellen Huijgh, 'Public Diplomacy's Domestic Dimension in the European Union', in Mai'a K. Davis Cross and Jan Melissen (eds), *European Public Diplomacy: Soft Power at Work* (London: Palgrave, 2013); see also Ellen Huijgh, 'Public Diplomacy in Flux: Introducing the Domestic Dimension', *The Hague Journal of Diplomacy*, vol. 7, no. 4 (2012), pp. 359-367.

9   Christopher Bickerton and Carlo Invernizzi Accetti, 'Populism and Technocracy', in Cristóbal Rovira Kaltwasser, Paul Taggart, Paulina Ochoa Espejo and Pierre Ostiguy (eds), *The Oxford Handbook of Populism* (Oxford: Oxford University Press, 2017), chapter 17.

10   Ernesto Laclau, 'Populism: What's in a Name?', in Francisco Panizza (ed.), *Populism and the Mirror of Democracy* (London: Verso, 2005), pp. 32-49.

ADAPTING PUBLIC DIPLOMACY TO THE POPULIST CHALLENGE

With this challenge in mind, a wide number of commentators have scrutinized about how anti-systemic pressures have shifted from one with an exclusively external locus to one that has an important internal dimension. Ulrich Speck, for example, highlights the stresses coming from inside liberal democracies, 'where populist politicians are pushing back against open borders and open societies'.[11] This is not to say, of course, that such impulses are completely novel. Illustrations of populist challenges to diplomacy — and diplomats — have been widespread within much of the Global South for generations. To give just one recent illustration, Venezuela under President Hugo Chávez (1999-2013) celebrated the disruption of orthodox practices through the mixture of charismatic leadership and so-called 'diplomacy of the peoples' (*diplomácia de los pueblos*). The difference under current conditions is that the populist challenge has moved from the periphery to parts within the centre of the system. No less than in Venezuela, where Elsa Cardozo highlighted the deterioration of professional diplomacy in favour of personalism and the 'diplomacy of microphones',[12] the disruption of accepted ways in practice is attractive to many constituencies in foundational domains of liberal democratic culture.

In looking more closely at the disconnect between the 'elite' and the 'people', two themes are highly salient in weakening the model of public diplomacy. As reviewed above, the first relates to the divide between an external and internal orientation. In both ideational and material terms, the focus of attention on the part of diplomats has been looking outward to the international community or society. By way of contrast, the focus of attention on the part of the aroused publics that constitute the populist base is intensely localistic. For diplomats, the practice of public diplomacy — as with other activities — is contingent on the key tenets of two-way dialogue and the building of transnational connections. For the populist base, national interest and identity begin (and end) at home, reflective of a spatial enclosed and aggressively self-absorbed mindset.

Moreover, the second theme is the distance between a public diplomacy that is predicated on inducing change of 'others' and the value placed by the populist base on the hold of continuity among themselves. At the core of the public diplomacy model are enthusiasm and confidence about the firm link between public diplomacy and an ambitious transformation in governance

---

11   Ulrich Speck, 'The Crisis of Liberal Order', *The American Interest* (12 September 2016), available at https://www.the-american-interest.com/2016/09/12/the-crisis-of-liberal-order/.

12   Elsa Cardozo, 'La política exterior del gobierno bolivariano y sus implicaciones en el plano doméstico, ildis' (2010), available at http://library.fes.de/pdf-files/bueros/caracas/08796 .pdf.

practices. Michael McFaul, a prominent scholar in the field of democratization and the former US Ambassador to Russia, for example, claimed in the post-9/11 context that democracy as a constitutive norm of the West was stronger than ever before and remained equally important for the foreign policy of Western states on both sides of the Atlantic.[13] Such an ambitious agenda was anathema to populists. In part this attitude came to be wrapped up in an increasingly cynical attitude towards diplomacy, as captured by Joseph Nye, caught up in the wider problem of publics that are 'sceptical of authority'.[14] Yet these sentiments go much deeper among populists, because of their visceral opposition to globalization, cosmopolitan values, transnational connections, and specific initiatives including global corporate social responsibility and global/regional trade arrangements.

The Implications for Public Diplomacy of the Anti-diplomatic Impulses

It is one thing in terms of the implications for diplomacy (and diplomats) to have populism in ascendancy on the margins of the international system; it is another thing to have these political forces presenting a challenge at the core. Populism in Venezuela, or for that matter in the Philippines with Rodrigo Duterte, built on significant national cultures, but it is not an upsurge in populism in these sites that is systematically important. Nor for that matter is populism still dominant in all its traditional sites. On the contrary, in many of the legacy 'homes' of populism in the Global South, the trend has been completely different. In Argentina, for instance, President Mauricio Macri has pushed back against the tradition, stating that 'Argentina suffered a lot because of populism'.[15]

What merits greater attention is the rise of populism in systemically important states, as exhibited by Narendra Modi in India and Jair Bolsonaro in Brazil. Yet even with these salient examples, it is unlikely that the challenge of populism would be treated with the seriousness that it merits without the spread of disruptive forces in many parts of the EU (including Hungary and

---

13   Michael McFaul, 'Democracy Promotion as a World Value', *Washington Quarterly*, vol. 28, no. 1 (2004-2005), p. 148.

14   Joseph S. Nye, *Soft Power: The Means to Success in World Politics* (New York, NY: Public Affairs, 2004), p. 127.

15   César Calero, 'Mauricio Macri: Argentina sufrió mucho por el populismo', El Mundo (18 February 2017), available at http://www.elmundo.es/internacional/2017/02/18/58a754 afe5fdeac57c8b45fe.html.

Poland), within the United Kingdom (UK), and especially with the election of President Donald Trump in the United States. A common theme throughout these contexts is that the progressive model of public diplomacy is interpreted as a constraining force, part of an entrenched repertoire of a self-serving and controlling establishment

This anti-diplomatic/anti-foreign ministry sentiment is most noticeable in the aversion towards insiders and communities of identity and interest beyond the national. A case in point is the comment by the former UK Independence Party (UKIP) leader Nigel Farage, on the resignation of Sir Ivan Rogers (the permanent representative of the UK to the EU), that: 'it would be appropriate if a lot more people in that position, British ambassadors, left. The world has changed, [which] the political establishment in this country and the diplomatic service just doesn't accept'.[16]

What is more, this type of anti-system, anti-diplomatic sentiment can be located over multiple sites beyond the classic ones in the Global South. To give another illustration, Marine Le Pen, leader of the French National Rally (formerly known as the National Front), conflates diplomacy with other key considerations for the 'total failure' of the EU: 'It's a social failure, it's an economic failure, it's a failure in terms of power, it's a diplomatic failure'.[17]

On top of all this, of course, is the serious threat to contemporary diplomatic culture that US President Donald Trump presents. In contradistinction to the progressive diplomatic culture symbolized by former US President Barack Obama's administration, Trump's operational style is focused on personalism, the use of bilateral one-on-ones, constant surprises, and direct and highly targeted communication with 'his' domestic supporters. At its core is a winner-take-all approach to any external engagement, in which asymmetrical structural advantages are translated into transactional leverage. The goal is not to stabilize institutions or to enhance followership or goodwill among strategic allies or commercial partners, but to extract material advantages on a self-help basis. The audience is exclusively domestic communities, with a great onus on publicizing successful outcomes (or 'wins') with their interests in mind.

Looking back to the early 1990s, some experienced diplomatic practitioners warned of the rise of this type of domestic threat, even as they considered diplomacy to have had a positive external record in the post-Cold War era.

---

16   Quoted in 'Farage Says "A Lot More" Diplomats Should Follow Rogers and Resign', *The Guardian* (3 January 2017), available at https://www.theguardian.com/politics/video/2017/jan/03/nigel-farage-calls-for-more-resignations-after-sir-ivan-rogers-quits-video.

17   Interview, Vivienne Walt, *Time Magazine* (28 June 2016), available at http://time.com/4386695/brexit-france-q-and-a-marine-le-pen-national-front/.

A generalized concern was expressed, particularly about a potential backlash 'by constituents who have felt over-constrained by excessive paternalism, been empowered by information technology, and stirred to act by the apparent lack of accountability in the institutions that they entrusted with their affairs'.[18] In detailing in a more retrospective manner the specific sources of the US divide between perceived elites and the people, Geoffrey Wiseman points to how the forces of isolation in early American history built on a culture of distrust about diplomacy.[19] To be sure, notable American politicians prior to Donald Trump echoed these sentiments.[20]

Yet notwithstanding these warnings, diplomats have been placed in a tenuous situation in an era of rising populism. This fragility is particularly evident in the United States, but it extends well beyond American exceptionalism. It has long been assumed, with some validity, that public diplomacy facilitates mediation, but in other ways, public diplomacy has promoted a disintermediation dilemma. Disintermediation showcases the disconnect between the priorities defined by a worldly elite as opposed to a localistic public. To exacerbate the dilemma, the effect of disintermediation is felt more pervasively because of the array of avenues and means by which citizens can go around established institutions.

Another route that accentuates this dynamic, paradoxically given the anti-elitist bias of populism, is via the proliferation of hyper-empowered individuals who become the champions of 'the people'. Personalism is no longer restricted to the leaders of distinctive political parties. The cult of celebrity, free of loyalty to established ways of doing things, comes into play.[21] Even the most cynical citizens are drawn to the aura of these hyper individuals, allowing them to speak for the 'people' even if this interpretation is at odds with what diplomatic culture — based on an understanding of the national interest — represents. Making the challenge even more formidable is the ability of these hyper-empowered individuals to represent themselves as flagbearers for the frustrations of ordinary and often left-behind citizens through free-wheeling

---

18   George Haynal, 'Diplomacy on the Ascendant in the Age of Disintermediation', Weatherhead Center for International Affairs, Harvard University (2001-2002), available at https://scholarsprogram.wcfia.harvard.edu/files/fellows/files/haynal.pdf.

19   Geoffrey Wiseman, 'Distinctive Characteristics of American Diplomacy', *The Hague Journal of Diplomacy*, vol. 6, nos. 3-4 (2011), pp. 235-259.

20   Wiseman cites, for example, Newt Gingrich, 'Rogue State Department', *Foreign Policy* (July-August 2003), pp. 42-48; and from a scholarly account, S.W. Hook, 'Domestic Obstacles to International Affairs: The State Department under Fire at Home', *PS: Political Science and Politics* (2003), pp. 23-29.

21   See, for example, Andrew F. Cooper, *Celebrity Diplomacy* (Boulder, CO: Paradigm Publishing, 2007); and *Diplomatic Afterlives* (Cambridge: Polity, 2014).

tactics stretching from the use of referenda, social media, and 'soft-entry' institutions including the EU Parliament. The common theme in each of these vehicles is loose networking as outsiders, rather than the use of insiders' closed clubs.

Given the power of the disintermediation dilemma, an opportunistic set of ascendant political leaders — even those located at the core of the international system — have considerable incentives to diminish 'their' own diplomats as part of a wider campaign to stigmatize the traditional establishment. Difference in messaging is not tolerated, as witnessed in the US case by the firing of Steve Goldstein, the US State Department's Under-Secretary for Public Diplomacy and Public Affairs, when he contradicted the White House's account of US Secretary of State Rex Tillerson's departure.[22] Significantly, Goldstein was replaced by Heather Nauert, a former anchor at Fox and Friends, a television programme that acts as a key conduit between President Trump and his base.

Facing up to the Challenge of Populism: A Menu for the Future

While the challenge of populism should not be conflated out of proportion, it should not be ignored. What is required is a recalibrated model of public diplomacy that builds on the strengths of the current public diplomacy model, while compensating for its weaknesses. In terms of a menu of adaptation to the populist challenge, a number of key ingredients come to the fore. *First, the generalized focus of engagement must be relocated.* That is to say, the revised framework of public diplomacy needs to be directed towards domestic as well as towards foreign audiences. At every opportunity, diplomacy and diplomats should counter the image of 'denationati[zation]' — originally put forward as a concern by Sir Harold Nicolson in the inter-war years,[23] but a concept that in the context of the populist challenge underscores the disconnect between the practitioners of public diplomacy and a localistic-oriented public. In common

---

22   Eliza Reiman, 'Trump Fired a Top State Department Official who Contradicted the White House's Account of Tillerson's Firing', *Business Insider* (13 March 2018), available at https://www.businessinsider.com/trump-fires-steve-goldstein-state-department-after-tillerson-2018-3.

23   Derek Drinkwater, *Sir Harold Nicolson and International Relations* (Oxford: Oxford University Press, 2005), p. 96.

with creative proposals for rebuilding trust in other institutions,[24] diplomacy needs to draw on the knowledge of a wider set of domestic publics.

Second, we must accept that into the future the personalistic public diplomatic brand of leaders will be just as important as the brand of a country. Given the prominence of hyper-empowered individuals in the populist challenge, it is the response of anti-populist leaders that is salient at the apex of a reconfigured public diplomacy. With President Trump's massive Twitter presence, US diplomacy and diplomats will be faced by constant surprises from the White House to which they will have to react. As one commentator, an advisor to the Obama administration, put it: 'how to follow the lead of a president who seems uninterested in consistency, protocol and nuance?'[25] By way of contrast, it is contingent on anti-populist leaders to utilize a different style of communication and substantive narrative.

One interesting illustration of a leader who is willing and ready to provide an explicit anti-populist form of public diplomacy is Canada's prime minister, Justin Trudeau. In terms of communication, Trudeau has provided a more systemic approach to rebranding Canada: not through random tweets, but a relatively consistent stream of political 'moments', especially so as they are sharable — via 'hugs, hand-on-the-heart gestures, selfies, and Twitter town halls'.[26] In terms of substance, the emphasis is on promoting Canada as an open, progressive country.

Trudeau's celebrity status gives him impressive visibility in the US media market, including CBS's *60 Minutes*, and the cover of *GQ* magazine, access embellished by his role as a 'Viral PM'. It also links him to other sources of non-state soft-power influence such as Canadian rapper/musical artist Drake and the closely related 'We The North' campaign.

Although the Trudeau approach showcases a different form of identity politics, the focus of public diplomacy from a wider number of countries is to try to temper the challenge of populism that is manifested in protectionist and self-help measures in the economic and security domain. Some of these efforts

---

24 An excellent example comes from central banking; see Andrew G Haldane, 'Folk Wisdom', speech on the 100th Anniversary of the Bank of Estonia, Tallinn, Estonia (19 September 2018), available at https://www.bankofengland.co.uk/-/media/boe/files/speech/2018/folk -wisdom-speech-by-andy-haldane.pdf?la=en&hash=DA3CC381EAC763701787B79E68013 BE7BB2D2C52.

25 Shamila N. Chaudhary, 'Why the State Department Is Worried About Donald Trump and His Tweets', *Politico* (20 December 2016), available at http://www.politico.com/magazine/ story/2016/12/donald-trump-state-department-tweets-worried-214538.

26 Evan Solomon, 'The Soft Power of Justin Trudeau, Canada's Viral PM', *Maclean's* (9 March 2016), available at http://www.macleans.ca/politics/ottawa/the-soft-power-of -justin-trudeau-canadas-viral-pm/.

will have a traditional air about them, such as the use of golf by Japan's Prime Minister Shinzō Abe as a means of interacting on a leader-to-leader basis with Donald Trump.

This type of approach, however, anticipates the use of greater personality profiling in future public diplomacy. As it is, several countries have used psychology experts in an attempt to interpret Donald Trump.[27] Still, the results of this preparation have been mixed. The early February 2017 visit to the United States by Abe (with five meals, five hours of golf, a number of rides in the presidential limousine and several meetings with President Trump) showed positive signs. During their summit, Abe discussed the extended pattern of investment and job creation by Japanese automotive companies in the United States. Trump, who had earlier complained that the Japan–US auto trade relationship was 'not fair', welcomed the continued production of Japanese automakers within the United States. Nonetheless, the impact of Abe's charm offensive has subsequently stalled. Instead of listening to his Japanese counterpart, Trump has listened to his domestic political base on issues such as the Trans-Pacific Partnership (TPP). In consequence, at least one Japanese expert argues that 'the concept of "public diplomacy" is getting more ambiguous and problematic' in an age of populist backlash.[28]

Despite these setbacks, it is more likely that a variety of countries will continue to refine the personalistic approach to public diplomacy. One indication of what will become accepted practice in the future was the April 2018 state visit of Emmanuel Macron to the United States. While Trump's anti-globalist instincts biased him towards Macron's main opponent, the hard-populist Marine Le Pen, Macron has been able to cut through the differences and build a strong personal relationship with the US president. Gérard Araud, the French Ambassador to Washington, in acknowledging the contrasts between the worldviews and personalities of the two presidents, argued that there were strong bonds between them. On the one hand, both were 'disruptors' whose elections had surprised and challenged the old political order in their countries; and on the other hand, both spoke their mind: 'Donald Trump has never

---

27   According to the *Nikkei Asian Review*, the assessment could be reduced to: 'After you hear him speak, say "yes" first. Do not disagree', and 'He strongly dislikes being told what he does not know'; see Koya Jibiki and Ken Moriyasu, 'Abe Scores Big in "Fairway Diplomacy" with Trump', *Nikkei Asian Review* (16 February 2017), available at https://asia.nikkei.com/Politics/Abe-scores-big-in-fairway-diplomacy-with-Trump.

28   Yasushi Watanabe, 'Public Diplomacy and the Evolution of US–Japan Relations' (March 2018), available at https://www.wilsoncenter.org/sites/default/files/public_diplomacy_and_the_evolution_of_u.s.-japan_relations_watanabe.pdf.

hidden what he thinks, and Emmanuel Macron is the same — so they have built a dialogue'.[29]

What cannot be overlooked is that at least in the case of the Trump administration, public diplomacy is unlikely to be successful with only a symbolic dimension. Accordingly, *a third ingredient for future public diplomacy should be a greater transactional component*. As Japan found out, a charm offensive directed exclusively at the United States can only get you so far without some substantive trade-offs. Nicholas Cull, for example, has argued in his historical analysis of public diplomacy that 'what counts is not what you say but what you do'.[30] The difference from the past is that under current conditions this approach must be directed at showcasing why US allies such as Japan need to push initiatives that go around the United States, such as the push for the Comprehensive and Progressive Trans-Pacific Partnership as an alternative to the TPP. The priority of public diplomacy needs to be to sell this type of alternative — and still contested — initiative in a manner that targets localized interests.

Notwithstanding all of this turbulence, *a fourth ingredient of future public diplomacy should be the revitalization of some traditional components of public diplomacy*. This will be most visible in cultural exchanges and other related techniques of soft power. To some considerable extent, this trend relates to the insertion of not only a symbolic but an instrumental dynamic into public diplomacy. If there are some clear red lines in the Trump–Macron relationship, it is clear that the mobilization of the enormous capacity of French soft power in terms of inviting Trump to the Bastille Day celebration in July 2017 was effective in two different ways. On the one hand, there was an emulation effect in that Trump pushed for a ceremony along similar lines. On the other hand, Macron achieved a prime objective in receiving a reciprocal invitation, with a state visit to the United States in April 2018.

A similar transactional component could well emerge through a renewed US cultural offensive in the future. As is well known, among the Trump administration's many demands on China has been on China's use of tools such as the Confucius Institutes, with increased US oversight and a demand for reciprocity in cultural exchanges.[31] As argued in a *SinoInsider* article, one scenario that

---

29   Angelique Chrisafis, 'Macron to Put "Trump Whisperer" Skills to Test on State Visit', *The Guardian* (2 April 2018), available at https://www.theguardian.com/world/2018/apr/23/macron-trump-whisperer-state-visit.

30   Cull, *Public Diplomacy*.

31   Don Tse and Larry Ong, 'Are Cultural Exchanges Next in Trump's Push to Get China to Play Fair?', *SinoInsider* (19 April 2018), available at https://sinoinsider.com/2018/04/are-cultural-exchanges-next-in-trumps-push-to-get-china-to-play-fair/.

administrations could entertain in years to come is a push for more cultural exchanges with China as a form of re-engagement. Administrations could, for example, encourage the Chinese government to allow more American centres to be set up in China (there are currently only three) and to relax restrictions on importing 'Made in USA' culture and entertainment.

Although initiated by instrumental motivations and means, the attractions of a revitalized public diplomacy based on the lure of popular culture has some sustained appeal, despite the weakened condition of the US State Department, with many positions unfilled and a stream of departures (including from the Bureau of Educational and Cultural Affairs). To give just one example, if public diplomacy is intended at its core 'to reinforce the American narrative as the "incubator of people's dreams", highlighting American values',[32] the role of athletes has immense value. Support for this scenario came with the February 2018 trip of Ivanka Trump, President Trump's 'first' daughter, to the PyeongChang Winter Olympics, where she not only met with South Korea's President Moon Jae-in, but cheered on American competitors. However, in an era of Black Lives Matter, the mobilization of a much more diverse set of athletes generally and African-American athletes specifically would present added value.

Finally, *a fifth ingredient of future public diplomacy should be to convey positive narratives of how diplomacy and diplomats support the activities of domestic citizens.* Through an inward-looking lens, a number of devices can be used as part of a concerted effort to demonstrate value on an instrumental basis. Already happening in some countries, 'reunions' of ambassadors and consuls could take place on an annual basis, not only on a fixed/closed basis (meetings in the capital city) but on a more diversified geographical/functional basis. This mechanism is not only valuable in connecting diplomats to domestic policy, but can pinpoint specific features of regional interest. Of value in breaking down the sense of disconnect between diplomats and citizens is the establishment of 'local' offices, with an array of activities from investment to passports. Such activities could be supplemented by the extension of features such as award ceremonies showcasing creativity, innovation and dedication to serving the public. Of particular importance here is an amplification of consular services, as witnessed by Mexico's extensive web of activities in the United States.[33] As elaborated in an earlier special issue of *The Hague Journal*

---

32   The Aspen Institute, *The Dialogue on Diplomacy and Technology* (2014), available at http://csreports.aspeninstitute.org/documents/ADDTech14%20Report.pdf.

33   Andrés Rozental and Alicia Buenrosto, 'Bilateral Diplomacy', in Andrew A. Cooper, Jorge Heine and Ramesh Thakur (eds), *The Oxford Handbook of Modern Diplomacy* (Oxford: Oxford University Press, 2013), pp. 229-247.

of Diplomacy, this trend is connected to the impulse towards the 'duty of care' that is moving to the centre of diplomatic practice.[34]

Even if implemented on a differentiated basis, this type of response offers a platform to demonstrate the capacity of national diplomats at multiple sites 'on the frontlines' across a wide spectrum, whether negotiating and mediating on the ground, promoting investment and trade across a wide spectrum of area, providing emergency assistance to distressed travellers, or managing consular issues.[35] Attention to the frontlines shifts the image of diplomacy in various ways, most importantly with a focus on how the balance of reward and risk has been altered. In previous eras, diplomacy abroad could be separated from political dynamics at home. This is no longer the case as commercial, disaster, humanitarian diplomacy, and even individual consular cases, attract close scrutiny.

The rewards of showcasing this citizen-support function are particularly important in the case of post-Brexit UK. While excessive privileging of a rejuvenated 'Global Britain' by populist politicians may be highly inflated, this should not detract attention away from the need to concentrate on a range of deliverables, from enhanced trade and investment opportunities to protecting the interests of UK expatriates. Still, the obstacles in the way of building support for this type of approach are formidable. For one thing, it will depend on a substantive redeployment of personnel and assets to facilitate well-staffed, well-resourced missions around the world. For another thing, it is premised on the assumption that 'good' narratives will outweigh the 'bad', not a foregone conclusion if poor performance on the front lines or unattractive features in policy application make media headlines. As with the other ingredients, this component of the menu of a revitalized public diplomacy requires a wide degree of backing by domestic publics.

Conclusion: An Accentuated and Responsive Domestic Turn

Under the weight of the changing conditions of the twenty-first century, many traditional pillars of strength with respect to public diplomacy face severe

---

34   Jan Melissen and Maaike Okano-Heijmans, 'Introduction: Diplomacy and the Duty of Care', *The Hague Journal of Diplomacy*, vol. 13, no. 2 (2018), pp. 137-145.

35   Andrew F. Cooper, 'The Changing Nature of Diplomacy', in Andrew A. Cooper, Jorge Heine and Ramesh Thakur (eds), *The Oxford Handbook of Modern Diplomacy* (Oxford: Oxford University Press, 2013), pp. 35-53.

tests. Not only has the strategic model come up against operational contestation from increasingly confident authoritarian forces in the external domain, but the legitimacy of public diplomacy has been cut into by the antagonism of anti-establishment domestic forces at the heart of the populist challenge. While the geopolitical backlash from the outside had been increasingly visible for over a decade, the disruptive societal impulses from inside came to the fore as part of a worldwide debate only with the largely unexpected success of the Trump presidential victory and the Brexit referendum success.

Still, the shift in the sources of pressure was not altogether unanticipated. In the post-Cold War environment, the advance of state-based public diplomacy has been to a great extent in sync with normatively progressive global-oriented societal forces, both in civil society and corporate constituencies. In contradistinction, the scenario that domestic publics could be both inward-looking and illiberal, with important constraining effects for the promotion of the established model of public diplomacy, was largely ignored.

The effects of the disruptive populist challenge mean that many of the accepted mantras about the future of public diplomacy were turned on their head. Disruption, it must be emphasized, does not mean eradication. As the potential adaptive menu showcased above signals, public diplomacy is far from being condemned to disappear. On the contrary, albeit in a highly uneven and messy manner, it looks to be re-energized.

Disruption has brought with it a new emphasis on instrumentality as well, in keeping with the goal of getting results for a wider set of constituents. There is clearly a huge downside in the animation of this approach, in terms of a narrow form of accountability and the downgrading of reciprocity as a means of engagement. Yet although full of potential risks, there can be a type of output legitimacy attached to this form of transactional style. Here, the emphasis placed by Trump and the Brexiteers on hard tangible results, accompanied by a self-congratulatory performance style, sets a very distinctive standard.

Above all, the disruption caused by the challenge of populism highlights the paradox of diplomacy under threat as an elite, outward-oriented activity. As long as public diplomacy is viewed as a strategic model without the 'people' in mind — and a larger domestic footprint in place — it will come under intense inward-oriented pressure. Yet, paradoxically, the position of responsibility for diplomacy and diplomats is enhanced. Furthermore, while this challenge in its populist form is highly problematic in a myriad of ways, not the least because of the complete downgrading of the normative component of public diplomacy, there is a menu by which diplomacy and diplomats can weather the challenge now and into the future. Simply put, no longer can the purpose of public diplomacy be regarded as simply affecting the 'policies, dispositions and actions of other states'.[36] Public diplomacy must embrace an accentuated and responsive domestic turn that puts an onus on practical and visible delivery in terms of different strata of society.

Andrew F. Cooper
is Professor at the Balsillie School of International Affairs and the Department of Political Science, University of Waterloo, Canada. From 2003 to 2010 he was Associate Director at the Centre for International Governance Innovation (CIGI). Cooper is the author most recently of *BRICS VSI* (Oxford: Oxford University Press, 2016); *Diplomatic Afterlives* (Cambridge: Polity, 2014); and *Internet Gambling Offshore* (Basingstoke: Palgrave Macmillan, 2011). He is also the co-editor of the *Oxford Handbook of Modern Diplomacy* (Oxford: Oxford University Press, 2013). His scholarly publications have appeared in a number of prestigious journals, including *International Organization, International Affairs, World Development* and *International Studies Review*.

---

36   Alan K. Henrikson, *What Can Public Diplomacy Achieve?*, Discussion Papers in Diplomacy, no. 4 (The Hague: Netherlands Institute for International Relations 'Clingendael', 2006), p. 8, available at https://www.clingendael.org/publication/what-can -public-diplomacy-achieve.

Diasporas and Public Diplomacy: Distinctions and Future Prospects

Jennifer M. Brinkerhoff
Elliott School of International Affairs, George Washington University,
Washington, DC 20052, United States
jbrink@gwu.edu

Received: 27 June 2018; revised: 18 October 2018; accepted: 16 January 2019

Summary

Diaspora diplomacy encompasses diasporas as: agents in their own right; instruments of other's diplomatic agendas; and/or intentional or accidental partners with other actors pursuing shared interests. Diaspora diplomacy is not territorially bound, and agendas are fluid. Three important features of diaspora diplomacy distinguish it from public diplomacy more generally. First, the diaspora identity results in specific applications of diplomacy for which diasporans may play a unique role. Second, diasporans' responses to global crises of identity and inequity yield particular motivations and targets of engagement. Third, diasporans may have an in-between advantage for public diplomacy. The complexity of diaspora diplomacy is likely to increase because of circular migration, layered identities, and continued improvements and access to telecommunications. Researchers and policy-makers should focus attention on how to integrate diasporas into existing efforts to account for the complexity of transnational relations.

Keywords

public diplomacy – diasporas – diplomacy

© KONINKLIJKE BRILL NV, LEIDEN, 2019 | DOI:10.1163/9789004410824_006

Introduction

Public diplomacy and diaspora diplomacy are inextricably linked. Former US Secretary of State Hillary Clinton summed it up nicely. In her remarks to the first ever US State Department-organized Global Diaspora Forum, she stated:

> You have the potential to be the most powerful people-to-people asset we can bring to the world's table. Because of your familiarity with cultural norms, your own motivations, your own special skills and leadership, you are, frankly, our Peace Corps, our USAID, our OPIC [the Overseas Private Investment Corporation], our State Department all rolled into one.[1]

This is high praise indeed. And it encompasses lofty expectations. Are they warranted? What role do diasporas actually play in public diplomacy? What might we expect from diaspora public diplomacy in the future? Following an overview of diaspora diplomacy, this article examines how diaspora diplomacy can be defined, what makes it different from other forms of public diplomacy, and what to expect in the future. The article concludes with implications for our conceptualizations of diaspora and public diplomacy.

The Scope of Diaspora Diplomacy

Both independently and in conjunction with other actors, including state officials, diaspora diplomacy can contribute to a range of objectives. Many of these are embodied in the largest, most known and historically enduring diasporas. The Chinese diaspora, for example, has long facilitated business networks throughout South-East Asia and beyond. One is hard pressed to find a country that does not host Chinese restaurants — an indicator of cultural diffusion. And, more recently, Chinese migration to Africa coincides with, and arguably supports, Chinese foreign policy related to accessing Africa's natural resources.[2] For its part, the Israeli diaspora benefits enormously from the historic dispersion of the Jewish people. In modern times, the Israeli state has strategically cultivated its diaspora, for example through programmes such as Birthright Israel, which provides free organized trips to Israel for Jewish adolescents.

---

1 Hillary Clinton, 'Keynote Address' at Global Diaspora Forum (17 May 2011), available online at http://www.diasporaalliance.org/2011-global-diaspora-forum/.
2 See, for example, Emmanuel Ma Mung, 'Chinese Migration and China's Foreign Policy in Africa', *Journal of Chinese Overseas*, vol. 4, no. 1 (2008), pp. 91-109.

DIASPORAS AND PUBLIC DIPLOMACY

The American Jewish Committee seeks to capitalize on its extensive diaspora-engaged experience to train US-based diasporans from Latin America and Africa through institutes, representing unique multi-pronged, non-state-based public diplomacy. Both the Chinese and Israeli/Jewish diasporas encompass public diplomacy objectives to: improve the image of their country of origin (COO); secure the support of their country of residence (COR) for policies or interventions targeted to their COO; influence perceptions of their COR within the COO; facilitate material exchanges between the COO and the COR; and support the settlement and integration of their compatriots in the COR.

Through the many cultural associations that they form, diasporas can proactively improve the image of their COO in their COR or internationally. State and private-sector officials in the COO may also target them for this purpose. The Irish diaspora in the United States, for example, has established a plethora of cultural organizations (such as the American Irish Historical Society, The Friendly Sons of St Patrick, and clubs for hurling and Gaelic football), alongside philanthropic organizations such as the American Ireland Fund. St Patrick's Day celebrations have arguably become a uniquely American tradition. These cultural celebrations directly impact the consumption of all things Irish. IrishCentral, a global website for the Irish diaspora, encourages Irish companies to market their products directly to the US-based Irish diaspora, promoting it as easy and cost-effective.

Diasporas may also seek support for a policy or intervention targeted to the COO. This is an enduring feature of US international relations historically.[3] Diasporas are important listening channels for states to gain a better understanding of 'foreign' public opinion. Diasporas may provide these perspectives through direct advocacy, as well as their own representation efforts and actions in the public sphere. Diasporas' influence on COR foreign policy is most effective when it corresponds with the COR's national interest and values — in this case, their American identity.[4] For example, the US Copts Association has worked to promote awareness of the plight of Coptic Christians in Egypt. Its advocacy efforts have been reflected in the US State Department's Religious Freedom Reports, where instances of discrimination, violence and repressive laws are identified. These advocacy efforts align well with freedom of religion,

---

3 Tony Smith, 'Convergence and Divergence Yesterday and Today in Diaspora–National Government Relations', in Josh DeWind and Renata Segura (eds), *Diaspora Lobbies and the US Government: Convergence and Divergence in Making Foreign Policy* (New York, NY: Social Science Research Council and New York University Press, 2014), pp. 239-268.

4 Yossi Shain, *Marketing the American Creed Abroad: Diasporas in the US and Their Homelands* (Cambridge: Cambridge University Press, 1999); see also Nadejda K. Marinova, *Ask What You Can Do for Your (New) Country* (New York, NY: Oxford University Press, 2017).

and the US Copts Association has appealed to the broader Christian community accordingly.

Alternatively, diasporans may oppose a COR foreign policy targeted to their COO, even when it is welcomed in the COO. Polling shows, for example, that American Jews are much less supportive of the US Embassy's recent move to Jerusalem than are Israelis.[5]

Diaspora diplomacy may also aim to influence perceptions of the COR within the COO, often promoting diplomatic agendas of COR state actors, whether intentionally or not. The US Peace Corps is the most obvious example of such state-sponsored public diplomacy. Indicorps exemplifies Secretary Clinton's assertion that diasporas are 'our Peace Corps'. For over ten years, Indicorps provided fellowships to people of Indian heritage, enabling them to 'reconnect with India and with the means to contribute to its development, while fostering a new generation of socially-conscious global leaders'.[6] Fellows were intentionally assigned to regions other than their family heritage in order to foster a pan-Indian global identity.[7]

Diasporas are increasingly recognized for their potential to facilitate and contribute to material exchanges between the COO and the COR. Beyond the much-touted remittances they contribute, the diaspora phenomenon is now viewed as a potential brain gain as opposed to a brain drain. Diasporans participate in short- and long-term knowledge-transfer activities, such as through the United Nations Development Programme's (UNDP) Transfer of Knowledge through Expatriate Nationals (TOKTEN) (most recently in Sudan and the Palestinian Territory); invest in their COOs; facilitate investment in their COO by other actors, including their multinational corporation (MNC) employers;[8] and organize and deliver philanthropic programming and humanitarian assistance. The Haitian diaspora, for example, has long contributed philanthropic aid and initiatives in Haiti. Following the 2010 earthquake, the Haitian diaspora's contributions escalated and were officially recognized by state actors, such as when the Haitian diaspora gained a representative seat on the Interim Haiti Recovery Commission.[9] Haitian diasporans were also included among

---

5   'Geographic Divide: Taking the Pulse of Jews in America and Israel', Editorial, *Jerusalem Post* (14 June 2018).

6   Indicorps website: http://www.indicorps.org/#default.

7   Roopal Shah (co-founder of Indicorps), Remarks to the IRG Discussion Forum on Rethinking the Diaspora: Financial Capital Flows, Washington, DC (22 June 2007).

8   See Benjamin A.T. Graham, *Investing in the Homeland: The Political Economy of Diaspora Direct Investment* (Ann Arbor, MI: University of Michigan Press, 2019).

9   Daniel P. Erikson, 'The Haitian Diaspora: Building Bridges After Catastrophe', in Josh DeWind and Renata Segura (eds), *Diaspora Lobbies and the US Government: Convergence*

DIASPORAS AND PUBLIC DIPLOMACY

the state officials involved — for example, Foreign Service Officer Jean Pierre-Louis served on loan as Senior Program Manager of the Clinton–Bush Haiti Fund from 2010-2012. When working in tandem with official actors, diasporas may enhance relevance, representativeness and responsiveness of development and aid efforts.[10]

Finally, diaspora efforts can more internally focus within the COR to support the reception of compatriot newcomers. New Coptic immigrants flooded into the United States following the Arab Spring and its aftermath. The Los Angeles Diocese of the Coptic Orthodox Church developed an elaborate support system, including linking new Coptic immigrants to public social services available from other sources. The Diocese also provides cultural education programmes to support new immigrants' integration into American society, addressing intermarriage and 'Bridging the Gap' between parents and their children who have no memory or experience of living in Egypt. US state-sponsored internal diplomatic mechanisms were launched at the city level, supported under the Obama administration through the Building Welcoming Communities Campaign. The city of Pittsburgh launched the '30 Neighbors in 30 Days' project, where immigrants of diverse backgrounds share their stories, broadcasted broadly through social media. The project addresses the perceived need to combat fear of refugees following the 11 September 2001 attacks.

Diaspora Diplomacy Defined

Efforts to define diaspora diplomacy are often case specific (such as the Philippine diaspora),[11] function specific (for example, influencing COR foreign policy),[12] or role specific (such as the functions of an ambassador).[13] Elaine Ho

---

and Divergence in Making Foreign Policy (New York, NY: Social Science Research Council and New York University Press, 2014), pp. 185-211.

10 Jennifer M. Brinkerhoff, 'Digital Diasporas and International Development: Afghan-Americans and the Reconstruction of Afghanistan', *Public Administration and Development*, vol. 24, no. 5 (December 2004), pp. 397-413.

11 Joaquin Jay Gonzalez, III, *Diaspora Diplomacy: Philippine Migration and its Soft Power Influences* (Minneapolis, MN: Mill City Press, 2012).

12 Josh DeWind and Renata Segura, 'Diaspora–Government Relations in Forging US Foreign Policy', in Josh DeWind and Renata Segura (eds), *Diaspora Lobbies and the US Government: Convergence and Divergence in Making Foreign Policy* (New York, NY: Social Science Research Council and New York University Press, 2014), pp. 3-27.

13 C. Jovenir, 'Diaspora Diplomacy: Functions, Duties, and Challenges of an Ambassador', paper for the *Understanding Diaspora Diplomacy* series (June 2013), available online at http://www.academia.edu/13397113/Diaspora_Diplomacy (accessed 19 December 2018).

and Fiona McConnell,[14] whose work offers the most comprehensive treatment to date, provide a useful starting point for understanding and further refining diaspora diplomacy definitions. Below, I offer several amendments.

Ho and McConnell focus on 'the role of diasporas in shaping diplomacy's core functions of representation, communication and mediation'.[15] They provide a much-needed expansion of reductionist definitions of diaspora diplomacy. Taking a spatial approach, they move beyond individual nation-states in their analysis, challenging simplistic interpretations of this complex phenomenon. They aptly recognize that diaspora diplomacy extends beyond the territories and targets of nation-states and their governments.

They distinguish diplomacy *by* diaspora (an agency perspective) and diplomacy *through* diaspora (an instrumental orientation). I argue that diasporas play three general roles in public diplomacy, as: agents; instruments of others' diplomatic agendas; and intentional or accidental partners with other actors through uncoordinated efforts in pursuit of common interests. These roles are illustrated in the examples above. Diasporas endeavour to influence public opinion and the opinion of targeted non-state actors and collectives; they also engage directly with governments and international organizations; and they may be used by these to advance state objectives.

Diasporans may be represented among 'official' state diplomats. They may even be selected for particular duties because of their diaspora identity, as in the above example of the Haitian-American US Foreign Service Officer. Diasporans may move in and out of official and public roles and positions. For example, Geneive Brown Metzger was a prominent organizer and leader of the Jamaican diaspora in the United States before she was invited by the government of Jamaica to become the Jamaican Consul General for New York. She rescinded her US citizenship to do so and served in that capacity from 2008-2012. She continues to live in New York City and refers to herself as a 'diaspora strategist', working with US-based Jamaicans who want to give back to their country of origin.[16]

---

14   Elaine L.E. Ho and Fiona McConnell, 'Conceptualizing "Diaspora Diplomacy": Territory and Populations betwixt the Domestic and Foreign', *Progress in Human Geography* (2017), pp. 1-21, available online at https://journals.sagepub.com/doi/abs/10.1177/030913251774021 7?journalCode=phgb.

15   Ho and McConnell, 'Conceptualizing "Diaspora Diplomacy"', p. 3.

16   See Laura Joseph Mogul, 'For Former Jamaican Consul General, Cortlandt Manor Is Now Home', *Westchester Magazine* (15 July 2015).

DIASPORAS AND PUBLIC DIPLOMACY   57

As these and other examples attest, diaspora diplomacy is not the exclusive domain of collectives, as Ho and McConnell argue.[17] Individuals matter, and they may act decisively, and independently. Ho and McConnell privilege organized groups without sufficiently examining the changing interface between individuals and the groups they organize or whence they emerge, and related activist agendas. For example, individual diaspora leaders from former Zaire mobilized an advocacy campaign for political change in their COO, specifically for support to (targeting the United States) or non-interference in (targeting France) Laurent Kabila's march to Kinshasa to overthrow Mobutu Sese Seko. They later separated from their diaspora organization to pursue opportunities to serve as individuals in Kabila's government. The example is similar to Ahmad Chalabi's influence on US engagement in Iraq.[18] Members of Kabila's government — including some of these diasporans — were not as welcoming of democracy as the United States had been led to believe. The potential for an individual to have a significant impact on diplomacy, including but not limited to their ability to mobilize like-minded diasporans and others, is too obvious to ignore.

What Makes Diaspora Diplomacy Different?

Three important features of diaspora diplomacy distinguish it from public diplomacy more generally. First, the diaspora identity results in specific applications of diplomacy for which diasporans may play a unique role. Second, diasporans' responses to two global political crises that affect the institutions of governance — crises of identity and inequity[19] — yield particular motivations and targets of engagement. Third, diasporans may have a particular in-between advantage[20] for public diplomacy.

---

17   Ho and McConnell, 'Conceptualizing "Diaspora Diplomacy"'.
18   Ahmed Chalabi convinced US policy-makers that Iraqis would welcome the 2003 US invasion of Iraq with great enthusiasm and that he enjoyed broad legitimacy from the Iraqi people.
19   Manuel Castells, 'The New Public Sphere: Global Civil Society, Communication Networks, and Global Governance', *The Annals of the American Academy of Political and Social Science*, vol. 616, no. 1 (2008), pp. 78-93.
20   Jennifer M. Brinkerhoff, *Institutional Reform and Diaspora Entrepreneurs: The In-Between Advantage* (New York, NY: Oxford University Press, 2016).

Diaspora Identity

A fundamental difference between diasporans and other public diplomacy actors is that diasporans' everyday existence, alone, is an act of public diplomacy. Diaspora identity is neither completely one nor the other, but a mix of characteristics from the country of origin, the country of residence and lived experience. This mix is precisely the foundation on which modern societies have flourished, incorporating diversity along with shared values and aspirations.[21] Diasporans may be uniquely capable of bridging the people-to-people understandings that are often the subject of public diplomacy. These identity features are a key component of the in-between advantage discussed below.

The lived experience of diasporans leads to significant public diplomacy — whether intentionally or not. Diasporans are compelled — either for identity expression or social obligation — to remain in contact with their places of origin. Manuel Orozco classifies related engagements as the 'Five Ts': transportation; tourism; telecommunications; transfer (remittances, investment and philanthropy); and nostalgic trade.[22] Former US Under-Secretary of State for Democracy and Global Affairs Maria Otero perhaps put it best: 'what the State Department might call diplomacy is what you might think of as a phone call home. For those of us who come from a different country, "foreign relations" is family relations'.[23]

Many diasporans have a sense of not fully belonging in any one territory or affinity group — neither their COO culture nor their adopted country's culture. This identity challenge may compel them to engage in diaspora diplomacy activities that bridge the divide. In the words of a Dutch-Ethiopian who helped to create a coffee project in Ethiopia: 'Sometimes I feel schizophrenic. I don't know who I am. Through this project I know who I am. It has helped me to be myself. [...] I don't have to choose'.[24] Mobilization around identity is different from mobilization prompted by material interests. Identity is likely to generate

---

21   Jennifer M. Brinkerhoff, 'Diaspora Identity and the Potential for Violence: Toward an Identity-Mobilization Framework', *Identity: An International Journal of Theory and Research*, vol. 8, no. 1 (January 2008), pp. 67-88.

22   Manuel Orozco, *Migrant Remittances and Development in the Global Economy* (Boulder, CO: Lynne Rienner, 2013).

23   Maria Otero, Remarks to the Global Diaspora Forum (17 May 2011).

24   Malugetah Asmallash, Remarks on the Dir Foundation Coffee project in Ethiopia, Policy Seminar on Migration and Development: Diasporas and Policy Dialogue, African Development Policy Centre (with support from the Dutch Ministry of Foreign Affairs), Institute of Social Studies, The Hague (24 October 2007).

DIASPORAS AND PUBLIC DIPLOMACY

greater passion and staying power, and it may include sacrifice and voluntary efforts without obvious material rewards.

Diasporans' potential responses to identity challenges are difficult to predict. The COO-related aspects of their identity may be latent; emerging, for example, only when their COO experiences a crisis that propels it to the world stage, or when an element of that identity is directly challenged, compelling a defensive response. After 9/11, some Afghan-Americans mobilized around an Afghan identity for the first time. Diasporans are known to be extremely generous in their response to natural disasters in their country of origin, and this extends beyond financial donations. They mobilize voluntary efforts to respond to immediate needs, and sometimes these efforts may evolve into formal organizations that move beyond relief to promote more sustainable economic development (as seen in Haiti following the devastating earthquake in 2010).

Safeguarding one's heritage can be a powerful mobilizer of latent diasporans. Diasporas may be particularly important and potent for place branding, influencing thoughts, feelings and associations with a place.[25] Ethiopian diasporans organized a campaign to protect Ethiopia's geographic coffee branding from Starbucks' efforts to usurp these powerful cultural symbols for profit.[26] Accomplished diasporan professionals with broad networks and a deep understanding of American society, government and business led the campaign. They assisted the Ethiopian Intellectual Property Office and Oxfam America to mobilize 100,000 petitioners against Starbucks. Starbucks eventually signed voluntary trademark licensing agreements and the US Patent Trade Office ultimately legalized them.

Diasporas' Response to Global Political Crises

Manuel Castells describes global political crises that impact governance institutions.[27] Two are relevant to diasporas' distinctions in public diplomacy. In a crisis of identity, people see 'their nation and their culture increasingly disjointed from the mechanisms of political decision-making'. For diasporans, 'nation' and 'culture' transcend a particular nation-state. Rather than leading them to a resistance identity, as Castells argues, diasporans may mobilize their cultural identity through diverse networks, potentially implicating two or more nation-states, non-governmental organizations (NGOs), global civil

---

25   Peter Van Ham, 'Place Branding: The State of the Art', *The Annals of the American Academy of Political and Social Science*, vol. 616, no. 1 (2008), pp. 126-149.

26   Brinkerhoff, *Institutional Reform and Diaspora Entrepreneurs*.

27   Castells, 'The New Public Sphere', pp. 78-93.

society, or international organizations, etc. They may sense potential efficacy *vis-à-vis* more than one mechanism or source of political decision-making, and feel empowered. The US-based Chadian diaspora organized the *Groupe de Réflexions et d'Analyses d'Intérêts Tchadiens* (GRANIT), a think tank to address 'the paucity of reflective analysis benefiting the Chadian interest'.[28] GRANIT partnered with an international NGO and engaged in numerous international-level policy and advocacy efforts, including crafting policy recommendations to the European Union, US President Barack Obama's administration and the United Nations.

Castells also describes a crisis of equity, where 'the process of globalization [...] often increases inequality between countries and between social groups within countries'.[29] Diasporans often suffer direct, personal experience with these inequities. They may enjoy a quality of life that is inaccessible to most of their compatriots in the COO, including family members. Alternatively, they may provide so much support to family and friends at 'home' that they are unable to enjoy the quality of life of those surrounding them in the COR. This visceral understanding spawns their direct interventions, which may bypass governing institutions. They may take the form of individuals or hometown associations directly supporting other individuals and communities through remittances and philanthropy. Diasporans may ask why their family, friends and compatriots do not have access to the same opportunities and institutions and why that lack should be inevitable. They may engage in more targeted advocacy, or institutional interventions, such as knowledge transfer and investment.

In-between Advantage
These identity characteristics and motivations contribute to diasporas' potential in-between advantage for public diplomacy. These include the back-with-the-future effect and psycho-social and operational advantages.[30] Diasporans know what the future can be for their COO, because they have already lived it as diaspora. They have direct understanding and experience, and they may be positioned to 'translate' new ideas in local culturally appropriate ways. They may be uniquely able to persuade their COO actors (both official and general publics) to adopt new ideas, as they may be able to connect these ideas to local circumstances with which they may have emotional and socio-cognitive experience.

---

28   Brinkerhoff, *Institutional Reform and Diaspora Entrepreneurs*.
29   Castells, 'The New Public Sphere', p. 78.
30   See Brinkerhoff, *Institutional Reform and Diaspora Entrepreneurs*.

DIASPORAS AND PUBLIC DIPLOMACY

They may employ socio-cognitive advantages as well as operational ones. They may have the opportunity to operate by exception, since they are not wholly of one culture or the other. And they may use this to their advantage by hedging their identities. They can engage in potentially culturally inappropriate ways while claiming their American selves, including skirting expectations to practise favouritism that reinforces inequitable systems. For example, rather than make promises that she knows she will not want to keep, Nermien Riad, founder of Coptic Orphans, can respond '*insha'Allah*' (God willing). She operates by exception in Egypt as a woman who is not wealthy, but nevertheless can gain an audience with the Coptic Orthodox Pope.

Operationally, diasporans can connect various sources of resources, both material (funding, expertise and network extensions) and non-material (legitimacy, moral support and authority). They may be well positioned to develop multi-polar influence efforts. They may speak the language of both the coo and the cor; and they may speak the cultural language of different sets of actors, official and unofficial, local and international. For example, Ethiopian diasporan (living in the United States) and economist Eleni Gabre-Madhin was able to do so when she negotiated for donor support — with the Ethiopian prime minister's blessing — to create the Ethiopian Commodities Exchange.[31]

What Lies Ahead?

The future of diasporas' engagement in public diplomacy is likely to reflect increasing complexity. Its features include layered identities that motivate engagement differently, at different times. We have not resolved conceptually or practically how to classify 'returned' diasporans and especially those who engage in circular migration — keeping a toehold in more than one country simultaneously or sequentially. Returned Ethiopian diaspora entrepreneurs migrate back and forth between, for example, Ethiopia and the United States. The founding partners of Ernst & Young Ethiopia — returned diaspora entrepreneurs — aspired to serve as much of Africa as possible. The firm's successful restructuring of Ethiopia Airlines enabled them to specialize in airline restructuring continent-wide.

What might we expect in the future? First, we will see more issue-based diplomacy. Territory of citizenship will likely become less relevant and state power will increasingly become a multi-polar target. For example, the Multicultural Network of Women Workers for Peace (mwpn) assembles women from a

---

31   See Brinkerhoff, *Institutional Reform and Diaspora Entrepreneurs.*

variety of diasporas, mostly from countries of origin experiencing conflict. In 2004, the MWPN supported an international mission of women from a variety of diasporas (then living in the Netherlands) to visit Burundi and provide training and support to women politicians to run for parliament. Diplomacy agendas are likely to focus increasingly on shared humanistic concerns and experiences. Within countries of settlement, diasporans from numerous COOs might promote and/or be enabled to come together based on shared experiences related to discrimination, integration and common foreign-policy approaches *vis-à-vis* countries of origin. This occurred in the United States as various diaspora groups united to protest the Trump administration's so-called 'Muslim ban'.

Second, these issue-based diplomatic efforts, as well as campaigns specific to particular identities and experiences, are likely to occur more frequently and with greater potential impact. The role of diasporas in public diplomacy is on the rise. Refugee diasporas are a particular case. Survivors of a concentration camp in Bosnia-Herzegovina, for example, petitioned the European Union to pressure Serbia and Bosnian Serb authorities to recognize their suffering. They also secured the support of a multinational corporation to pressure local authorities to issue a permit for building a memorial on the site, and to construct a memorial in London.[32]

Telecommunications and advancements in education and development in both the COR and other identity-based territories have facilitated the enactment of such identities. The Global North's advantage in information and communications technology (ICT) applies less and less in today's world. Diasporans have incentives to equip their family members with telecommunication devices for the purpose not only of communicating, but also for financial transfers. The Syrian diaspora, for example, has been credited with 'shaping the world's image of the Syrian uprising'.[33] Specifically, Syrian diasporans have coordinated social-media sites and internet news channels and trained citizen journalists who remain inside Syria.

Third, telecommunications are imminently manipulatable. Just as we witness a plethora of 'fake news', it may become increasingly difficult to decipher 'fake' diaspora diplomacy from well-intended and representative diaspora

---

32 Maria Koinova and Dzeneta Karabegovic., 'Diasporas and Transitional Justice: Transnational Activism from Local to Global Levels of Engagement', *Global Networks*, vol. 17, no. 2 (2017), pp. 212-233; see also Maria Koinova, 'How Refugee Diasporas Respond to Trauma', *Current History*, vol. 115, no. 784 (2016), pp. 322-324.

33 Kari Andén-Papadopoulos and Mervi Pantti, 'The Media Work of Syrian Diaspora Activists: Brokering between the Protest and Mainstream Media', *International Journal of Communication*, vol. 7 (2013), pp. 2185-2206 at p. 2185.

engagement. Misleading diaspora public diplomacy is not new. The Tamil Tigers famously produced their own media, with significant impact on both their diasporas and the general public. Information technologies broaden the tool kit for masking true intentions and maximizing impact on selected audiences.

Need for a New Paradigm?

Ho and McConnell argue that diaspora diplomacy helps to crystallize the limits of our conceptual understanding of public diplomacy. They question, 'Who has the right to speak for and represent a particular community?'[34] Public diplomacy is not a realm where we typically ask whether a particular individual or group has a *right* to engage. Rather, it behoves us to consider the diaspora connection as a potential motivating and possible explanatory factor for individuals' and groups' choice of engagement, subject matter and means. In bringing public and diaspora diplomacy together, we should not be tempted to allow the diaspora's inclusion to derail what we understand of the bedrock of public diplomacy.

The more appropriate question is whether targets of influence (such as governments and international organizations) should privilege these actors when considering response options. Diasporas are important constituents that may warrant specific outreach and engagement strategies. As with all official diplomacy, it is important to ask whether specific voices are 'legitimate' in terms of shared agendas/interests and representativeness of broader constituencies. The potential unique and advantageous features of diaspora diplomacy that are reviewed above should be approached as hypotheses for particular groups and individuals, not as givens. Diasporans are unique actors in public diplomacy in some respects, and no different in others. Diaspora diplomacy suggests a need to develop specialized knowledge. Researchers and policy-makers should focus attention on how to integrate diasporas into existing efforts to account for the complexity of transnational relations broadly. What is needed for diaspora and public diplomacy is not a new conceptual framework, but an enriched one. As global migration continues unabated, and is aided by telecommunications' innovations, public diplomacy will become increasingly diasporic, with all the opportunities and challenges that diasporas represent.

---

34   Ho and McConnell, 'Conceptualizing "Diaspora Diplomacy"', p. 15.

Jennifer M. Brinkerhoff

is Professor of Public Administration and International Affairs, and Associate Dean for Faculty Affairs and Research Initiatives, at the Elliott School of International Affairs, George Washington University. She holds a Ph.D. in Public Administration from the University of Southern California in Los Angeles. Her most recent book is *Institutional Reform and Diaspora Entrepreneurs: The In-Between Advantage* (Oxford: Oxford University Press, 2016). She won the 2016 Fred Riggs Award for Lifetime Achievement in International and Comparative Public Administration, and is an elected Fellow of the National Academy of Public Administration.

The Psychology of State-Sponsored Disinformation Campaigns and Implications for Public Diplomacy

Erik C. Nisbet
School of Communication and Political Science (by courtesy), and
Eurasian Security and Governance Program, Mershon Center for
International Security Studies, The Ohio State University, Columbus, OH
43201, United States
nisbet.5@osu.edu

Olga Kamenchuk
Eurasian Security and Governance Program, Mershon Center for
International Security Studies, The Ohio State University, Columbus, OH
43201, United States
kamenchuk.1@osu.edu

Received: 29 June 2018; revised: 13 September 2018; accepted: 26 November 2018

Summary

Policy discourse about disinformation focuses heavily on the technological dimensions of state-sponsored disinformation campaigns. Unfortunately, this myopic focus on technology has led to insufficient attention being paid to the underlying human factors driving the success of state-sponsored disinformation campaigns. Academic research on disinformation strongly suggests that belief in false or misleading information is driven more by individual emotional and cognitive responses — amplified by macro social, political and cultural trends — than specific information technologies. Thus, attention given to countering the distribution and promulgation of disinformation through specific technological platforms, at the expense of understanding the human factors at play, hampers the ability of public diplomacy efforts countering it. This article addresses this lacuna by reviewing the underlying psychology of three common types of state-sponsored disinformation campaigns and identifying lessons for designing effective public diplomacy counter-strategies in the future.

© KONINKLIJKE BRILL NV, LEIDEN, 2019 | DOI:10.1163/9789004410824_007

Keywords

public diplomacy – disinformation – misinformation – corrective strategies – adversarial information campaigns – fake news – information technology – strategic communication

Introduction

Since the Russian Federation's takeover of Crimea, and now the investigation of Russian disinformation operations targeting the 2016 US elections, understanding the spread and influence of state-sponsored disinformation — the purposeful spread of false or misleading information — has become a highly salient issue for public diplomacy scholars and practitioners alike. Although there has been a great deal of policy attention on the technical, network and organizational dynamics of disinformation campaigns (such as bots and algorithms), the social–psychological mechanisms by which disinformation strategies influence public opinion and perceptions have not received the same level of scrutiny. This technologically deterministic approach creates misperceptions about the role of information technology in promulgating belief in disinformation that may 'distract' from designing effective counter-strategies.[1] In order to design effective strategies and develop new technologies for countering disinformation, we thus first need to understand how disinformation campaigns take advantage of our *human vulnerabilities* to false or misleading information.[2]

This article attempts to fill this lacuna by reviewing the psychological mechanisms underlying common forms of disinformation campaigns and the implications for designing public diplomacy efforts to counter their influence. The three forms of disinformation campaigns discussed — *identity grievance, information gaslighting* and *incidental exposure* — are general archetypes of disinformation operations that underlie a range of state-sponsored disinformation efforts targeting foreign audiences. By unpacking the psychological

---

1 R.K. Garrett, 'The "Echo Chamber" Distraction: Disinformation Campaigns are the Problem, Not Audience Fragmentation', *Journal of Applied Research in Memory and Cognition*, vol. 6, no. 4 (2017), pp. 370-376.

2 S. Lewandowsky, U.K.H. Ecker and J. Cook, 'Beyond Misinformation: Understanding and Coping with the "Post-Truth" Era', *Journal of Applied Research in Memory and Cognition*, vol. 6, no. 4 (2017), pp. 353-369; and S. Lewandowsky, U.K.H. Ecker, C.M. Seifert, N. Schwarz and J. Cook, 'Misinformation and its Correction: Continued Influence and Successful Debiasing', *Psychological Science in the Public Interest*, vol. 13, no. 3 (2012), pp. 106-131.

THE PSYCHOLOGY OF DISINFORMATION 67

dimensions of each, we gain a better understanding of how to design corrective messaging, technology and other public diplomacy efforts to counter their
influence. The article concludes with a discussion on how public diplomacy
may best take advantage of technology to counter state-sponsored disinformation campaigns and promote resilience among target populations.

Identity-Grievance Disinformation Campaigns

'Identity-grievance' campaigns focusing on activating polarized social identities (political, ethnic, national, racial and religious, etc.), exploiting real or
perceived political, economic, religious, or cultural wrongs and/or leveraging
low institutional trust, are one of the most common forms of state-sponsored
disinformation operations. Primarily negative in tone and valence, examples
range from Russian Facebook election advertisements in the United States that
inflamed racial resentment, China's disinformation campaign undermining
political trust and amplifying partisan discord in Taiwan, and Bahrain's divisive
disinformation promoting conflict between Shi'a and Sunni Muslims.[3] These
campaigns' success has been amplified by wide-ranging, concurrent political,
social and cultural trends (including populism, economic inequality, migration, low social capital and extreme political polarization) affecting most of
the globe.[4]

Identity-grievance disinformation campaigns capitalize on two interrelat-
ed psychological mechanisms: *motivated reasoning*; and *affective polarization*.
Motivated reasoning is the desire to avoid dissonant information or beliefs and
its accompanying affective distress — which in turn leads individuals to bias
in their response to information and arguments through processes of selective exposure, attention, comprehension and recall.[5] For instance, audiences
seek out ideologically consistent information while ignoring, misinterpreting,

---

3 M.J. Cole, 'Will China's Disinformation War Destabilize Taiwan?', *The National Interest* (30
July 2017), retrieved from http://nationalinterest.org/feature/will-chinas-disinformation-war
-destabilize-taiwan-21708; N. Penzenstadler, B. Health and J. Guynn. 'We Read Every One of
the 3,517 Facebook Ads Bought by Russians: Here's What We Found', *USA Today* (11 May 2018),
retrieved from https://www.usatoday.com/story/news/2018/05/11/what-we-found-facebook-
ads-russians-accused-election-meddling/602319002/; S. Kelly, M. Truong, N. Shahbaz, M. Earp
and J. Whit, *Freedom on the Net, 2017: Manipulating Social Media to Undermine Democracy*,
Freedom of the Net project (Washington, DC: Freedom House, November 2017), retrieved
from https://freedomhouse.org/sites/default/files/FOTN_2017_Final.pdf.
4 Lewandowsky, Ecker and Cook, 'Beyond Misinformation'.
5 M. Lodge and C.S. Taber, *The Rationalizing Voter* (Cambridge: Cambridge University Press,
2013).

counter-arguing and/or derogating ideologically incongruent information.[6] In this context, emotional desires precede and bias cognitive processing in ways that result in wishful thinking, on the one hand, and stereotyping on the other.[7] In sum, our political evaluations, judgements and thinking are mostly a subsequent 'rationalization' of *how we feel*.[8]

Beliefs are a foundation of identity.[9] Claims threatening closely held social identities (political, ethnic, racial and/or religious, etc.) elicit negative emotional responses and colour assessments of new information.[10] Likewise, pre-existing negative feelings (such as dislike and distrust, etc.) towards targets of disinformation will increase an audience's readiness to believe disinformation, while positive feelings increase resistance to disinformation.[11]

Moreover, to protect a positive image of their self- and social identity, people are often inclined to resist corrective messages that contradict motivated beliefs, by ignoring them or misinterpreting their meaning, arguing against their content and/or derogating their source.[12] New information may also make people angry, which has been found to shut down further processing, short-circuit the search for new information and/or lead to strengthening their belief in the disinformation.[13]

---

6   Lewandowsky, Ecker, Seifert, Schwarz and Cook, 'Misinformation and its Correction'; and Lodge and Taber, *The Rationalizing Voter*.

7   J. Haidt, *The Righteous Mind: Why Good People Are Divided by Politics and Religion* (New York, NY: Vintage, 2013); N. Haslam, 'Dehumanization: An Integrative Review', *Personality and Social Psychology Review*, vol. 10, no. 3 (2006), pp. 252-264; and D. Kahneman, *Thinking, Fast and Slow* (New York, NY: Farrar, Straus and Giroux, 2011).

8   R.K. Garrett and M. Jeong, 'From Partisan Media to Misperception: Affective Polarization as Mediator', paper presented at the Annual meeting of the International Communication Association, San Diego (2017); and Lodge and Taber, *The Rationalizing Voter*.

9   G.L. Cohen, J. Aronson and C.M. Steele, 'When Beliefs Yield to Evidence: Reducing Biased Evaluation by Affirming the Self', *Personality and Social Psychology Bulletin*, vol. 26, no. 9 (2000), pp. 1151-1164.

10   Lodge and Taber, *The Rationalizing Voter*.

11   D.J. Flynn, B. Nyhan and J. Reifler, 'The Nature and Origins of Misperceptions: Understanding False and Unsupported Beliefs about Politics', *Advances in Political Psychology*, vol. 38, suppl. 1 (2017), pp. 127-150.

12   B.T. Johnson and A.H. Eagly, 'Effects of Involvement on Persuasion: A Meta-Analysis', *Psychological Bulletin*, vol. 106, no. 2 (September 1989), pp 290-314; Lewandowsky *et al.*, 'Misinformation and its Correction'; and E.C. Nisbet, K. Cooper and R.K. Garrett, 'The Partisan Brain: How Dissonant Science Messages Lead Conservatives and Liberals to (Dis)trust Science', *Annals of the Academy of Political and Social Science*, vol. 658, no. 1 (2015), pp. 36-66.

13   E. Halperin, A.G. Russell, C.S. Dweck and J.J. Gross, 'Anger, Hatred, and the Quest for Peace: Anger can be Constructive in the Absence of Hatred', *Journal of Conflict Resolution*, vol. 55 (2011), pp. 274-291; P.S. Hart and E.C. Nisbet, 'Boomerang Effects in

THE PSYCHOLOGY OF DISINFORMATION

While motivated reasoning may drive belief in disinformation and resistance to correction, our differentiated feelings about groups of people who are different from ourselves is also a key component of identity-grievance disinformation campaigns. Affective polarization refers to the idea that political messaging has the power to amplify the salience of closely held social identities, while increasing prejudice towards 'out-groups'.[14] Group members become 'polarized' about how negatively they feel about the other group — with greater negative affect (anger, dislike or disgust) towards the 'out-group', increasing the likelihood of adopting and promoting disinformation about it, especially if motivated to cement 'in-group' membership.[15]

In sum, identity-grievance campaigns take advantage of our emotional responses to information in order to persuade, reinforce polarization, promote sharing of disinformation and resist its correction. The largest study to date of online disinformation analysed the spread of 126,000 verified true and false news stories on Twitter between 2006 and 2017. False information 'diffused significantly farther, faster, deeper and more broadly' than accurate information — propelled by emotional reactions such as fear and disgust.[16] It is thus no surprise that a highly emotional disinformation narrative describing a three-year-old boy crucified by the Ukrainian army is endorsed by a sizeable portion of the targeted population.[17]

Science Communication: How Motivated Reasoning and Identity Cues Amplify Opinion Polarization about Climate Mitigation Policies', *Communication Research*, vol. 39, no. 6 (2012), pp. 701-723; and B. Weeks, 'Emotions, Partisanship, Misperceptions: How Anger and Anxiety Moderate the Effect of Partisan Bias on Susceptibility to Political Misinformation', *Journal of Communication*, vol. 65, no. 4 (2015), pp. 699-719.

14   S. Iyengar, G. Sood and Y. Lelkes, 'Affect, Not Ideology: A Social Identity Perspective on Polarization', *Public Opinion Quarterly*, vol. 76, no. 3 (2012), pp. 405-431, doi:10.1093/poq/nfs038; and M. Wojcieszak and R.K. Garrett 'Social Identity, Selective Exposure, and Affective Polarization: How Priming National Identity Shapes Attitudes toward Immigrants via News Selection', *Human Communication Research*, vol. 44, no. 3 (2018), pp. 247-273, doi:10.1093/hcr/hqx010.

15   D.M. Kahan, 'Ideology, Motivated Reasoning, and Cognitive Reflection: An Experimental Study', *Judgment and Decision Making*, vol. 8 (2013), pp. 407-424; and Garrett and Jeong, 'From Partisan Media to Misperception'.

16   S. Vosoughi, D. Roy and S. Aral, 'The Spread of True and False Information News Online', *Science*, vol. 359 (2018), pp. 1146-1151.

17   A. Nemtsova, 'There's No Evidence the Ukrainian Army Crucified a Child in Slovyansk', *The Daily Beast* (15 July 2014), retrieved from https://www.thedailybeast.com/theres-no-evidence-the-ukrainian-army-crucified-a-child-in-slovyansk.

Strategies for Countering Identity-Grievance Campaigns

If emotional biases make us vulnerable to disinformation campaigns that play off our identities and grievances, what type of anti-disinformation strategies should public diplomacy practitioners focus on developing in the forthcoming years? *Identity-affirmation* is one message strategy employed to counter disinformation that is tied to closely held social identities.[18] This strategy positively affirms the identity or values of the audience upon which disinformation preys. This messaging reduces biased processing and promotes positive emotional responses, while at the same time presenting corrective information. This approach, for example, is widely used in efforts to counter disinformation campaigns about climate change and has been suggested as a means to counter Russia's disinformation war on Ukraine.[19] For example, a possible message strategy would be to affirm Russian nationalist identity, while at the same time providing information or claims about the economic costs of Russia's aggressive policies and intervention in the region.

Alternatively, one could also use a *shared identities/values* approach that reduces affective polarization between groups.[20] By priming a common 'in-group' identity — for example, national identity over partisan identity — this type of messaging reduces negative affective polarization towards the 'out-group' and thus lessens vulnerability to disinformation. The caveat is that social identities are commonly defined in opposition to an 'imagined other'.[21] Thus, by priming a common 'in-group' identity to reduce polarization between two groups — for example, national identity trumping partisan polarization — one may inadvertently create affective polarization towards a third group.[22] In addition, identities themselves may be contested, with heterogeneous meaning among

---

18   D.M. Kahan, 'Fixing the Communications Failure', *Nature*, vol. 463 (2010), pp. 296-297; and Lewandowsky, Ecker, Seifert, Schwarz and Cook, 'Misinformation and its Correction'.

19   R.K. Garrett, 'Strategies for Countering False Information and Beliefs about Climate Change', in M.C. Nisbet, M. Schafer, E. Markowitz, S. Ho, S. O'Neill and J. Thaker (eds), *Oxford Research Encyclopedia of Climate Science* (Oxford: Oxford University Press, 2018); Lewandowsky, Ecker, Seifert, Schwarz and Cook, 'Misinformation and its Correction'; E. Stoycheff and E.C. Nisbet, 'Priming the Costs of Conflict? Russian Public Opinion about the 2014 Crimean Conflict', *International Journal of Public Opinion Research*, vol. 4, no. 1 (2017), pp. 657-675.

20   M.S. Levendusky, 'Americans, Not Partisans: Can Priming American National Identity Reduce Affective Polarization?', *Journal of Politics*, vol. 80, no. 1 (2017), pp. 59-69.

21   J.R. Bowen, 'Anti-Americanism as Schemas and Diacritics in France and Indonesia', in P. Katzenstein and R. Keohane (eds), *Anti-Americanisms in World Politics* (Ithaca, NY: Cornell University Press, 2006), pp. 227-250.

22   Wojcieszak and Garrett, 'Social Identity, Selective Exposure, and Affective Polarization'.

THE PSYCHOLOGY OF DISINFORMATION   71

group members, further complicating the communication of shared values that reduce negative feelings.

The other component of identity-grievance disinformation campaigns — that is, grievance — may be addressed by *solutions-efficacy messaging*.[23] Research has shown that messages focusing on effective solutions to grievances and promoting the self-efficacy of audiences to enact corrective changes induce positive emotions such as hope, while reducing fear and anger. These positive emotions increase the likelihood of corrective information being accepted and likewise reduce audiences' vulnerabilities to disinformation.

Efficacy messages have been a successful part of the new digital-platform strategy targeting Russian-speaking audiences by the United States Agency for Global Media called *Current Time*. One of its programmes, 'Unknown Russia', has been widely shared on YouTube and highlights local problems and the actions that ordinary citizens take to address them. This form of solutions-efficacy messaging, optimized for social media platforms and digital sharing, may be a means to create resilience to disinformation among target audiences — as well as build a platform for disseminating corrective messaging.

Information Gaslighting

A second major emerging disinformation strategy is 'information gaslighting', or the rapid proliferation of false or misleading information online through social media platforms, blogs, fake news, online comments, advertising and/ or online news outlets. Rather than overt persuasion, the primary goal of information flooding is one of 'strategic distraction', while sowing uncertainty among its targets.[24] Examples include Russia's disinformation about the

---

23   A. Curry, N.J. Stroud and S. McGregor, *Solutions Journalism and News Engagement* (Austin, TX: University of Texas at Austin Center for Media Engagement, 2016), retrieved from https://mediaengagement.org/research/solutions-journalism-news-engagement; L. Feldman and P.S. Hart, 'Is There Any Hope? How Climate Change News Imagery and Text Influence Audience Emotions and Support for Climate Mitigation Policies', *Risk Analysis*, vol. 38, no. 3 (2018), pp. 585-602; K. McIntyre, 'Solutions Journalism: The Effects of Including Solution Information in News Stories about Social Problems', *Journalism Practice* (online, 14 December 2017).

24   G. King, J. Pan and M.E. Roberts, 'How the Chinese Government Fabricates Social Media Posts for Strategic Distraction, Not Engaged Argument', *American Political Science Review*, vol. 111, no. 3 (2017), pp. 484-501; C. Paul and M. Matthews, *The Russian 'Firehouse of Falsehood' Propaganda Model: Why it Might Work and Options to Counter It* (Santa Monica, CA: RAND Corporation, 2016), retrieved from https://www.rand.org/pubs/perspectives/PE198.html.

so-called 'little green men' who rapidly took control of the Crimea in 2014, or China's large-scale social media operation that fabricates millions of false or misleading posts in order to demobilize its citizens.[25]

This widespread pollution of the information environment with false or misleading information substantially increases audiences' difficulty to discern truth from fiction. A successful information gaslighting campaign makes this task: 1) highly costly, if not impossible, for audiences; and 2) creates a sense of loss of control over the information environment.[26] Under these conditions, information gaslighting may lead to a feeling of 'learned helplessness' among audiences, which subsequently conditions their vulnerability and openness to disinformation.

The premise of learned helplessness is that individuals who experience prolonged exposure to difficult, uncontrollable situations, which they can neither avoid nor alleviate, will 'learn' to accept the situation as a given.[27] The individual eventually no long attempts to fix or avoid an aversive situation because they believe there is no relationship between action and outcome. Furthermore, learned helplessness may be induced vicariously by watching others experience uncontrollable adverse situations.[28]

In this sense, information gaslighting leads to a specific form of *informational learned helplessness* (ILH) that leads to cognitive exhaustion, low motivation, and anxiety when audiences process news and information.[29] This

---

25 King, Pan and Roberts, 'How the Chinese Government Fabricates Social Media Posts for Strategic Distraction, Not Engaged Argument'; S. Pifer, *Watch Out for Little Green Men* (Washington, DC: Brookings Institute, 7 July 2014), retrieved from https://www.brookings.edu/opinions/watch-out-for-little-green-men/.

26 King, Pan and Roberts, How the Chinese Government Fabricates Social Media Posts for Strategic Distraction, Not Engaged Argument'.

27 S.F Maier and M.E.P. Seligman, 'Learned Helplessness: Theory and Evidence', *Journal of Experimental Psychology: General*, vol. 105, no. 1 (1976), pp 3-46.

28 I. Brown and D.K. Inouye, 'Learned Helplessness through Modeling: The Role of Perceived Similarity in Competence', *Journal of Personality and Social Psychology*, vol. 36, no. 8 (1978), pp. 900-908.

29 L.Y. Abramson, M.E Seligman and J.D. Teasdale, 'Learned Helplessness in Humans: Critique and Reformulation', *Journal of Abnormal Psychology*, vol. 87, no. 1 (1978), pp. 49-74; Maier and Seligman, 'Learned Helplessness'; G. Sedek and M. Kofta, 'When Cognitive Exertion Does Not Yield Cognitive Gain: Toward an Informational Explanation of Learned Helplessness', *Journal of Personality and Social Psychology*, vol. 58, no. 4 (1990), pp. 729-743; Y. Amichai-Hamburgerm, M. Mikkulincer and N. Zalts, 'The Effects of Learned Helplessness on Processing of a Persuasive Message', *Current Psychology: Developmental, Learning, Personality, Social*, vol. 22, no. 1 (2003), pp. 37-46; M. Gasiorowska, 'The Effects of Learned Helplessness and Message Framing on the Processing of Verbal and Visual Information in Advertisements', in T. Marek, W. Karwoski, M. Frankowicz, J. Kantola and

THE PSYCHOLOGY OF DISINFORMATION   73

opens up audiences to persuasion across several dimensions. First, ILH leads audiences to be less deliberative when evaluating messages and more likely to focus on peripheral cues in the message, rather than the credibility, or strength, of message arguments.[30] In addition, anxiety increases vulnerability to negatively framed messages and reduces reliance on pre-existing attitudes or beliefs (such as partisanship) when processing messages.[31] The cognitive exhaustion associated with ILH may also potentially reduce reactance and counter-arguing to counter-attitudinal messages.[32] Lack of control, such as that associated with learned helplessness, has also been shown to increase belief in conspiracy theories, as individuals are motivated to create structure by seeing illusory patterns and interconnections.[33]

Those most vulnerable to ILH are individuals with low self-esteem, experiencing depression or anxiety, having a pessimistic explanatory style, or who make incorrect attributions regarding their failure.[34] Furthermore, individuals with an internal attribution for their failure to discern false from true messages (for example, 'I am not good enough') may experience greater, more constant ILH than individuals who believe an external attribution (such as being targeted by a disinformation campaign) for failure.

Strategies to Counter Gaslighting Disinformation Campaigns
Unfortunately, as a relatively new disinformation tactic, there is not much research examining what may counter ILH stemming from information

---

P. Zgaga (eds), *Human Factors of a Global Society: A System of Systems Perspective* (Boca Raton, FL: CRC Press, 2014), pp. 379-394.

30 Amichai-Hamburgerm, Mikkulincer and Zalts, 'The Effects of Learned Helplessness on Processing of a Persuasive Message'; Gasiorowska, The Effects of Learned Helplessness and Message Framing on the Processing of Verbal and Visual Information in Advertisements'.

31 Gasiorowska, 'The Effects of Learned Helplessness and Message Framing on the Processing of Verbal and Visual Information in Advertisements'; Weeks, 'Emotions, Partisanship, Misperceptions'; T. Brader, 'Striking a Responsive Chord: How Political Ads Motivate and Persuade Voters by Appealing to Emotions', *American Journal of Political Science*, vol. 49 (2005), pp. 388-405, doi:10.1111/j.0092-5853.2005.00130.x; T. Brader, 'The Political Relevance of Emotions: "Reassessing" Revisited', *Political Psychology*, vol. 32 (2011), pp. 337-346, doi:10.1111/j.1467-9221.2010.00803.x.

32 J.P. Dillard and Shen Lijiang, 'On the Nature of Reactance and its Role in Persuasive Health Communication', *Communication Monographs*, vol. 72, no. 2 (2005), pp. 144-168; J.Z. Jacks and K.A. Cameron, 'Strategies for Resisting Persuasion', *Basic and Applied Social Psychology*, vol. 25, no. 2 (2003, pp. 145-161.

33 J.A. Whitson and A.D. Galinsky, 'Lacking Control Increases Illusory Pattern Perception', *Science*, vol. 322, no. 3 (2008), pp. 115-117.

34 C. Peterson, S.F. Maier and M.E.P. Seligman, *Learned Helplessness: A Theory for the Age of Personal Control* (New York, NY: Oxford University Press, 1995).

gaslighting. Research on learned helplessness more generally, however, suggests that the most effective means for public diplomacy campaigns to counter ILH is to provide *self-affirmation* to audiences on their ability to discern accurate from inaccurate information. This self-affirmation has two important dimensions: attribution failure; and self-efficacy. For instance, if audiences believe that the reason for their inability accurately to discern and evaluate false or misleading disinformation is internal to themselves, then a public diplomacy campaign may focus on building self-confidence among targeted populations that they have the ability and skills to tell truth from fiction. Such a campaign should also simultaneously highlight the external factors/conditions that negatively influence their information environment, paired with suggested solutions that build their self-efficacy for changing such conditions.

A second strategy is 'information-discernment education' as a means to improve information literacy.[35] Information literacy intervention programmes positively affect the cognitive and emotional states of audiences and increase their ability to evaluate information critically.[36] This is the approach being taken by the Italian government to counter disinformation programmes, by creating a special curriculum on identifying online disinformation for high-school students.[37] IREX also conducted a similar programme in the Ukraine on behalf of the Canadian government in 2015 and 2016.[38] IREX's 'Learn to Discern' media literacy programme directly trained 15,000 youth and adults in Ukraine on basic media literacy skills and had secondary impacts on another 90,000. Participants in the programme were 25 per cent more likely to say that they check multiple news sources and 13 per cent more likely to identify correctly and analyse disinformation critically.

---

35   S. Lewandowsky, U.K.H. Ecker and J. Cook, 'Beyond Misinformation: Understanding and Coping with the "Post-Truth" Era', *Journal of Applied Research in Memory and Cognition*, vol. 6, no. 4 (2017), pp. 353-369.

36   G. Walton and M. Hepworth, 'A Longitudinal Study of Changes in Learners' Cognitive States During and Following an Information Literacy Teaching Intervention', *Journal of Documentation*, vol. 67 (2011), pp. 449-479; E. Vraga and L. Boyd, 'Leveraging Institutions, Educators, and Networks to Correct Misinformation: A Commentary on Lewandowsky, Ecker, and Cook', *Journal of Applied Research in Memory and Cognition*, vol. 6, no. 4 (2017), pp. 382-388.

37   J. Horowitz, 'In Italian Schools, Reading, Writing and Recognizing Fake News', *New York Times* (18 October 2017), p. A1, retrieved from https://www.nytimes.com/2017/10/18/world/europe/italy-fake-news.html.

38   E Murrock, J. Amulya, M. Druckman and T. Liubyva, *Winning the War on State-sponsored Propaganda: Gains in the Ability to Detect Disinformation a Year and a Half after Completing a Ukrainian News Media Literacy Program* (Washington, DC: IREX, 2018), retrieved from https://www.irex.org/sites/default/files/node/resource/impact-study-media-literacy-ukraine.pdf.

Incidental Exposure to Disinformation

State-sponsored disinformation campaigns may simply be banal, in that they focus on increasing foreign audience's everyday incidental exposure to false or misleading information through international state-controlled broadcast media, online news websites, blogs, or social media. Both Russia and China in recent years have substantially increased the reach of their international broadcasting that targets foreign audiences, while simultaneously developing new online news portals, such as Russia's *Sputnik*.[39] Iran has also launched several international broadcasting channels and online news websites, targeting foreign audiences in multiple languages, as platforms for disinformation.[40]

Incidental exposure to disinformation does not necessarily rely on direct exposure to state-sponsored media platforms. For example, analysis shows that most major American news outlets used information in their reporting that was originally generated by Twitter bot accounts controlled by Russia's online disinformation organization, Russian Internet Research Agency.[41] In turn, this banal exposure to disinformation may lead *unmotivated* audiences to accept and internalize the disinformation. This exposure, and acceptance, of disinformation from low-credible sources is abetted by a widespread decline of confidence in credible media organizations in many democratic countries, leading audiences to rely on alternative information sources.[42]

Beliefs are not always tied to deeply held views, and individuals do not always have deep commitments to identities or grievances. Instead, common information-processing shortcuts, or heuristics, upon which we rely influence which beliefs we adopt.[43] For example, audiences are likely to accept

---

39   G. Rawnsley, 'To Know Us Is To Love Us: Public Diplomacy and International Broadcasting in Contemporary Russia and China', *Politics*, vol. 35, nos. 3/4 (2015), pp. 273-286; I. Yablokov, 'Conspiracy Theories as Russian Public Diplomacy Tool: The Case of Russia Today (RT)', *Politics*, vol. 35, nos. 3/4 (2015), pp. 301-315.

40   E. Wastnidge, 'The Modalities of Iranian Soft Power: From Cultural Diplomacy to Soft War', *Politics*, vol. 35, nos. 3/4 (2017), pp. 364-377.

41   J. Lukito and C. Wells, 'Most Major Outlets have Used Russian Tweets as Sources for Partisan Opinion: Study', *Columbia Journalism Review* (8 March 2018), retrieved from https://www.cjr.org/analysis/tweets-russia-news.php.

42   W.L. Bennett and S. Livingston, 'The Disinformation Order: Disruptive Communication and the Decline of Democratic Institutions', *European Journal of Communication*, vol. 33, no. 2 (2018), pp. 122-139.

43   R. McDermott, *Political Psychology in International Relations* (Ann Arbor, MI: University of Michigan Press, 2004); Y.Y.I. Vertzberger, *The World in Their Minds: Information Processing, Cognition, and Perception in Foreign Policy Decision-making* (Stanford, CA: Stanford University Press, 1990).

disinformation, even disinformation with low believability, to which they are more frequently exposed. Frequent exposure increases the fluency, familiarity and accessibility of disinformation in memory.[44] This accessibility and familiarity also potentially creates 'sleeper effects', where audiences recall and believe the false information but do not remember the credibility of the original source.[45] Disinformation, especially in simple narrative formats, may also fill explanatory gaps for audiences struggling to make sense of a complex world and 'feel' their way through complex situations.[46]

Moreover, cognitive biases also make disinformation difficult to correct. Informing audiences, for instance, that their beliefs are incorrect and that they need to update them may trigger cognitive and affective reactance, leading them to hold on to those beliefs more firmly.[47] The 'continued influence effect' is another bias that may lead individuals to maintain a false belief, despite accepting that it is based upon false information.[48] This continued influence of disinformation is primarily because of our inherent need to maintain easily accessible mental cause-and-effect explanations (models) that help us to make sense of a complex world. Without new information or alternative explanations that fill the 'causal gap', the false belief will persist and continue to shape thinking.[49]

In sum, audiences need not be emotionally motivated by identity or grievance, or cognitively exhausted, to believe disinformation. Rather, simple

---

44 G. Pennycook, T.D. Cannon and D.G. Rand, 'Prior Exposure Increases Perceived Accuracy of Fake News', *Journal of Experimental Psychology: General* (forthcoming 2019); M.S. Ayers and L.M. Reder, 'A Theoretical Review of the Misinformation Effect: Predictions from an Activation-based Memory Model', *Psychonomic Bulletin & Review*, vol. 5, no. 1 (1998), pp. 1-21; and N. Schwarz, J. Sanna, I. Skurnik and C. Yoon, 'Metacognitive Experiences and the Intricacies of Setting People Straight: Implications for Debiasing and Public Information Campaigns', in M.P. Zanna (ed.), *Advances in Experimental Social Psychology*, vol. 39 (Cambridge, MA: Academic Press, 2007), pp. 127-161.

45 G.T. Kumkale and D. Albarracin, 'The Sleeper Effect in Persuasion: A Meta-Analytic Review', *Psychological Bulletin*, vol. 130, no. 1 (2004), pp. 143-172.

46 M.F. Dahlstrom, 'Using Narratives and Storytelling to Communicate Science with Non-Expert Audiences', *Proceedings of the National Academy of Sciences*, vol. 111, suppl. 4 (2014), pp. 13614-13620; R.K. Garret, E.C. Nisbet and E. Lynch, 'Undermining the Corrective Effects of Media-based Political Fact Checking? The Role of Contextual Cues and Naïve Theory', *Journal of Communication*, vol. 63, no. 4 (2013), pp. 617-637.

47 S.S. Brehm and J.W. Brehm, *Psychological Reactance: A Theory of Freedom and Control* (New York, NY: Academic Press, 2013).

48 C.M. Seifert, 'The Continued Influence of Misinformation in Memory: What Makes a Correction Effective?', in H.R. Brian (ed.), *Psychology of Learning and Motivation*, vol. 41 (Cambridge, MA: Academic Press, 2002), pp. 265-292.

49 Garrett, 'Strategies for Countering False Information and Beliefs about Climate Change'.

THE PSYCHOLOGY OF DISINFORMATION 77

repeated exposure from even low-credible sources may lead to the assimilation of false or misleading information by large segments of the population because of common cognitive biases in how we process information. Once assimilated, these same cognitive biases make disinformation, and consequential attitudes, difficult to dislodge from the minds of audiences.

Strategies for Countering Incidental Exposure to Disinformation

Among unmotivated audiences, the same cognitive biases and heuristics that lead to assimilating disinformation in the first place can also be used to good effect to counter it. One strategy is *repeated exposure* to corrective information that supplants the disinformation in the minds of targets.[50] Two key elements, however, of this strategy are: to avoid any repetition of the false or misleading information in your messaging and solely focus on the correct information in your communications with audiences; and to provide audiences with a pre-warning that they may be targets of disinformation through incidental exposure.[51]

A second strategy is communicating corrective information in clear and easily digestible *compelling formats* that increase 'information fluency', are more easily accessible in memory and less likely to induce reactance.[52] For example, one study found that presenting corrective messages in graphic formats was highly effective in correcting false beliefs about a range of issues ranging from the troop surge in Iraq to climate change.[53]

Creating and presenting *alternative narratives* or explanations is a strategy that targets audiences vulnerable to the aforementioned 'continued influence' effect.[54] The goal is to provide an alternative narrative that 'fills the gap' left in audience's mental models when correcting disinformation. This alternative narrative needs to be heavily repeated, without reinforcing the original disinformation, to ensure that it is assimilated. In general, using narrative

---

50   Schwarz, Sanna, Skurnik and Yoon, 'Metacognitive Experiences and the Intricacies of Setting People Straight'.

51   Lewandowsky, Ecker, Seifert, Schwarz and Cook, 'Misinformation and its Correction'.

52   P. Winkielman, D.E. Huber, L. Kavanagh and N. Schwarz, 'Fluency of Consistency: When Thoughts Fit Nicely and Flow Smoothly', in B. Gawronski and F. Strack (eds), *Cognitive Consistency: A Unifying Concept in Social Psychology* (New York, NY: Guilford Press, 2012), pp. 89-111.

53   B. Nyhan and J. Reifler, 'The Roles of Information Deficits and Identity Threat in the Prevalence of Misperceptions', *Journal of Elections, Public Opinion and Parties* (online 6 May 2018).

54   Lewandowsky, Ecker, Seifert, Schwarz and Cook, 'Misinformation and its Correction'; and Seifert, 'The Continued Influence of Misinformation in Memory'.

approaches to corrective messaging will reduce counter-arguing and reactance and be more persuasive than other message formats.[55]

A fourth strategy is to promote more careful judgement and *deliberation* by audiences about the information that they consume.[56] In fact, some scholars argue that vulnerability to disinformation is more a function of a lack of deliberation than wilful ignorance.[57] Thus, increasing audiences' motivation to engage in analytical thinking and increasing their scepticism about low-credible news sources reduces their susceptibility to disinformation.

A related strategy to increased deliberation is training and education for audiences to promote *news media literacy* (NML). NML is different from classical media literacy training, as it focuses on enhancing 'the knowledge, skills and beliefs needed to understand how news content is produced, how people make consumption choices, and how to evaluate the quality and veracity of news content'.[58] This approach is not limited to classroom settings, and NML should be deployed as part of public communication campaigns that are designed to educate mass audiences on how to be more deliberative, sophisticated and aware news' consumers.

Future Public Diplomacy Technology to Counter Disinformation

In sum, we have reviewed three common types of state-sponsored disinformation campaigns and the psychological mechanisms that explain their influence on target audiences. In turn, by understanding the motivated and unmotivated psychological biases that lead disinformation to be so successful, we at the same time have a better understanding of how to employ strategic communication and technology to counter it. In many cases, existing public diplomacy campaigns and efforts already include many of these suggested strategies and elements.

---

55 Dahlstrom, 'Using Narratives and Storytelling to Communicate Science with Non-Expert Audiences.'

56 R.K. Herrmann and J.K. Choi, 'From Prediction to Learning: Opening Experts' Minds to Unfolding History', *International Security*, vol. 31 (2007), pp. 132-161; Lewandowsky, Ecker, Seifert, Schwarz and Cook, 'Misinformation and its Correction'; P. Tetlock, *Expert Political Judgment: How Good Is It? How Can We Know?* (Princeton, NJ: Princeton University Press, 2005).

57 G. Pennycook and D.G. Rand, 'Susceptibility to Partisan Fake News is Explained More by a Lack of Deliberation than by Willful Ignorance', SSRN Working Paper (19 April 2018), retrieved from http://dx.doi.org/10.2139/ssrn.3165567.

58 Vraga and Boyd, 'Leveraging Institutions, Educators, and Networks to Correct Misinformation', p. 383.

THE PSYCHOLOGY OF DISINFORMATION 79

However, additional strategic thinking is required on how to leverage and align future public diplomacy campaigns to counter state-sponsored disinformation campaigns. These disparate efforts, furthermore, should be used in combination with each other. Although the disinformation campaign archetypes that we have discussed are presented as distinct strategies, in practice they are often combined to target a wide range of audiences and build off each other, such as by combining identity grievance and information gaslighting campaigns to flood the information environment with a high volume of emotionally laden disinformation. While some individuals would be motivated by anger, dislike and disgust to accept, and act upon, the disinformation, others may simply be cognitively exhausted and give up attempting to tell truth from fiction. In this situation, multiple counter-strategies should be employed — for instance, combining identity-affirming messaging with self-affirmation, or solutions-efficacy with self-efficacy, in combination with inoculation messaging, etc.

Furthermore, although technology use may contribute to disinformation campaigns, it does not preclude using our knowledge about the psychology of disinformation to inform the development of technological tools for countering disinformation. This approach of combining psychology with technology to counter disinformation is labelled 'technocognition'.[59] From a public diplomacy perspective, this aligns with calls for public diplomacy to do a better mission of incorporating digital engagement tools and the affordances they offer into educational diplomacy.[60]

For example, Kelly Garrett argues that technological developments such as social media have amplified the potential for disinformation campaigns to take advantage of affective polarization and use 'emotional extremity for strategic effect'.[61] Garrett argues that a possible solution is to promote the development of *emotional dampening* tools such as new online deliberative platforms or apps for discussing controversial topics among vulnerable audiences. Likewise, he also suggests creating tools to promote civility in online comment spaces and news media platforms and/or designing filters for people that target the emotional content of online messages.

Technology can help audiences deal with information gaslighting campaigns and navigate a flood of disinformation that makes them feel helpless.

---

59 Lewandowsky, Ecker and Cook, 'Beyond Misinformation'.
60 C. Hayden, 'Technology Platforms for Public Diplomacy: Affordances for Education', in J. Mathews-Aydinli (ed.), *International Education Exchanges and Intercultural Understanding* (New York, NY: Palgrave Macmillan, 2017).
61 Garrett, 'The "Echo Chamber" Distraction', p. 373.

Examples would be online or social-media games such as *Post-Facto, Bad News,* or *The News Hero* that teach online fact-checking skills or the basic design principles of disinformation campaigns. Playing *Bad News*, created by the Dutch group DROG, had a 'positive effect on students' ability to recognize and resist fake news and propaganda'.[62] Based on the theory of inoculation, research has shown that this strategy of exposing audiences to how disinformation works increases their ability, and importantly their active motivation, to identify and reject disinformation.[63] Likewise, technology can teach audiences news-media literacy and promote analytical thinking as a means to counter incidental exposure to disinformation. The new partnership between Factcheck.org and iCivics, an educational non-profit, is an example. They are collaborating to deploy an educational game to teach secondary school students and adults news-media literacy skills that would allow them to evaluate news sources and the information provided more critically.[64]

Beyond tools to dampen emotional online content and educational games, technology can enhance an important tool of educational pubic diplomacy: professional training and study tours. Successfully countering state-sponsored campaigns and making the public resilient to their influence requires training very large numbers of foreign independent journalists and media organizations, opinion leaders, civil-society organizations and allied diplomats on how to identify, verify and counter disinformation globally. However, even the largest state-sponsored cultural and educational exchange programmes only have a few thousand participants globally each year at best.

The public diplomacy community thus needs to rethink how best to use its scarce resources for these programmes to take advantage of online learning technology and virtual exchanges.[65] The Police Professionalization Exchange Program sponsored by the US State Department and administered by the educational exchange non-profit Global Ties US is one such example.[66]

---

62   J. Roozenbeek and S. Van der linden, 'The Fake News Game: Actively Inoculating Against the Risk of Misinformation', *Journal of Risk Research* (online 2018), retrieved from https://www.tandfonline.com/doi/full/10.1080/13669877.2018.1443491.

63   J. Cook, S. Lewandowsky and U.K.H. Ecker, 'Neutralizing Misinformation through Inoculation: Exposing Misleading Argumentation Techniques Reduces their Influence', *PLoS ONE*, vol. 12, no. 5 (2017), e0175799, http://dx.doi.org/10.1371/journal.pone.0175799; Roozenbeek and Van der linden, 'The Fake News Game'.

64   See 'APPC and iCivics Team Up on Game to Teach Media Literacy', retrieved from https://www.annenbergpublicpolicycenter.org/appc-partners-with-icivics-to-create-game-to-teach-media-literacy/.

65   Hayden, 'Technology Platforms for Public Diplomacy'.

66   See https://www.globaltiesus.org/our-work/public-diplomacy-a-international-exchange-programs/586-police-professionalization-exchange-program.

A significant component of this programme is providing dozens of hours of professional training on law-enforcement best practices for thousands of police officers. This highlights the potential for large-scale virtual 'exchanges' and online training platforms to provide a much greater reach to large numbers of foreign professionals and opinion leaders — especially those outside of capital regions and/or in local communities. In terms of disinformation, this provides an opportunity to devise online training programmes provided in native languages on countering disinformation for foreign journalists, civil-society organizations, opinion leaders and allied diplomats — professional training that is sorely needed in many countries.[67]

Conclusion

Although public diplomacy corrective message campaigns and technology development are necessary, they may not be sufficient to counter state-sponsored disinformation campaigns targeting foreign or domestic audiences. Public diplomacy also has to address the political and social conditions that allow disinformation to flourish, such as the loss of confidence in democratic institutions and the rise of anti-democratic movements in established and emerging democracies.[68] The future of public diplomacy thus needs to go beyond day-to-day efforts to counter disinformation campaigns and develop new online tools. Public diplomacy also needs to *reinvest* in public diplomacy programmes that address the root causes of audiences believing and sharing disinformation. These are the classic public diplomacy programmes that strengthen democratic institutions, further human rights, fight inequality and promote self-efficacy among audiences to make positive change. This also includes investment in more theory-driven formative and summative evaluation research that draws upon the available social–psychological and communication scholarship on misinformation and false beliefs and applies it to public diplomacy contexts. These are long-term goals and outcomes for public diplomacy, but they are equally important for effectively countering the influence of state-sponsored disinformation on foreign and domestic audiences.

---

67   IREX, 'Media Sustainability Index: The Development of Sustainable Independent Media in Europe and Eurasia' (Washington, DC: IREX, 2017), retrieved from https://www.irex.org/sites/default/files/pdf/media-sustainability-index-europe-eurasia-2017-full.pdf.

68   Bennett and Livingston, 'The Disinformation Order'; Lewandowsky, Ecker and Cook, 'Beyond Misinformation'.

Erik C. Nisbet

is Associate Professor at the Ohio State University (OSU) School of Communication and Political Science (by courtesy). He is a faculty affiliate with the OSU Mershon Center for International Security Studies, where he is Co-Director of the Eurasian Security and Governance programme. Nisbet is also a non-residential faculty fellow at the University of Southern California's Center on Public Diplomacy.

Olga Kamenchuk

is a Research Associate at the Ohio State University's Mershon Center for International Security Studies and Co-Director of Mershon's Eurasian Security and Governance programme. Kamenchuk is also Associate Professor (clinical) in the OSU School of Communication and Slavic and Eastern European Languages and Cultures (by courtesy).

Public Diplomacy in the Digital Age

Corneliu Bjola,[a] Jennifer Cassidy[b] and Ilan Manor[c]
[a]Oxford Department of International Development, Queen Elizabeth House, University of Oxford, Oxford OX1 3TB, United Kingdom
[b]St Peter's College, University of Oxford, Oxford OX1 2DL, United Kingdom
[c]St Cross College, University of Oxford, Oxford OX1 3LZ, United Kingdom
corneliu.bjola@qeh.ox.ac.uk; jennifer.cassidy@spc.ox.ac.uk; Ilan.manor@stx .ox.ac.uk

Received: 28 July 2018; revised: 30 November 2018; accepted: 22 January 2019

Summary

As data fast become the 'new oil', the opportunities for public diplomacy to grow as a field of practice are real and game-changing. Drawing on social informatics research, this article seeks to advance our understanding of how digital technologies shape the context in which public diplomacy operates by reshaping the medium of public communication, blurring the boundary between foreign and domestic affairs and empowering new actors. Despite inevitable challenges, the future of public diplomacy in the digital age remains bright, as digital technologies create tremendous opportunities for public diplomacy to build stronger, more diverse and more enduring bridges between offline and online communities.

Keywords

public diplomacy – digital age – digital diplomacy – social informatics

Introduction

By 2025, the number of data-driven interactions per day per person (that is, interactions between individuals and their digital devices) is estimated to increase twenty-fold, from an average of 298 in 2010 to the staggering amount of 4,909 connections, amounting to one digital interaction every 18 seconds.

Furthermore, real-time data usage will grow from 15 per cent of the datasphere in 2017 to nearly 30 per cent in 2025, meaning that the effectiveness of data-driven activities will increasingly depend on the availability of data with low-latency responsiveness (instant data).[1] In other words, the scope, volume and intensity of global data connectivity are expected to explode in the coming years. While most of these interactions will likely be mediated by intelligent assistants, the disruption produced by this transformation will have, by necessity, far-reaching implications for the way in which individuals, communities and societies define and conduct themselves as social and political actors, and, by extension, for the way in which public diplomacy as a practice of building bridges with foreign publics will adapt and evolve in the digital age.

Drawing on social informatics research, this article seeks to advance our understanding of how digital technologies shape the context in which public diplomacy operates by reshaping the medium of public communication, blurring the boundary between foreign and domestic affairs and empowering new actors. By offering insights into the relationship between information technologies and social contexts,[2] social informatics (SI) research moves beyond facile interrogations of how information technologies are functionally integrated by interested actors in their work and emphasizes instead their ability to embed themselves in the social and institutional context in which they emerge and proliferate. In other words, instead of exclusively focusing on the qualities of the technological artefact, social informatics takes a critical view of the ways in which people and information technologies interact[3] (arrow 1 in Figure 1) and seeks to bridge the gap between professional claims about the social values and uses of information and communication technologies and the empirical reality of such claims.[4] In this way we can gain a better sense of the dual enabling and constraining roles played by information technologies in shaping public diplomacy practices.[5]

---

1 David Reinsel, John Gantz and John Rydning, *The Digitization of the World: From Edge to Core* (Framingham, MA: International Data Corporation (IDC) and Seagate, November 2018), available online at https://www.seagate.com/files/www-content/our-story/trends/files/idc-seagate-dataage-whitepaper.pdf.

2 Rob Kling, 'What Is Social Informatics and Why Does It Matter?', *The Information Society*, vol. 23, no. 4 (2007), pp. 205-222.

3 Steve Sawyer and Howard Rosenbaum, 'Social Informatics in the Information Sciences: Current Activities and Emerging Directions', *Informing Science*, vol. 33, no. 2 (2000), pp. 89-95.

4 Ronald E. Day, '"Kling and the Critical": Social Informatics and Critical Informatics', *Journal of the American Society for Information Science and Technology*, vol. 58, no. 4 (2007), p. 575.

5 Mohammad Hossein Jarrahi and Sarah Beth Nelson, 'Agency, Sociomateriality, and Configuration Work', *The Information Society*, vol. 34, no. 4 (2018), pp. 244-260.

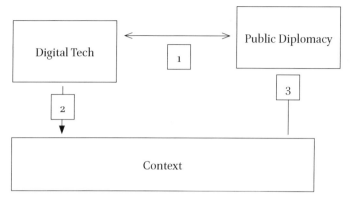

FIGURE 1   A social informatics approach to understanding the interaction between digital technologies and public diplomacy

To this end, this article will first examine how the materiality of digital technologies shapes the context in which public diplomats work (arrow 2 in Fig. 1), and, second, how the digitized context constrains and enables public diplomatic engagement (arrow 3 in Fig. 1). The analysis will be pursued in three sections, each exploring one key aspect of the evolving dynamic of public diplomacy in the digital age: the evolution of the medium of communication; the digital blurring of the foreign and the domestic; and the rise to diplomatic prominence of technological-based non-state actors. We will thus argue that despite inevitable challenges, the future of public diplomacy in the digital age remains bright, as digital technologies create tremendous opportunities for public diplomacy to build stronger, more diverse and more enduring bridges between offline and online communities.

Digital Communication: From Gutenberg to Zuckerberg

As Christer Jönsson points out, 'without communication, there is no diplomacy',[6] and rightly so, as diplomats would hardly be able to represent or negotiate their interests without the means to express them in a manner that is sufficiently intelligible to all parties. While diplomatic communication has traditionally been embedded in a textual-oriented culture[7] that has favoured

---

6   Christer Jönsson, 'Diplomacy, Communication and Signalling', in Costas M. Constantinou, Pauline Kerr and Paul Sharp (eds), *SAGE Handbook of Diplomacy* (London: SAGE, 2016), p. 79.
7   Sir Ivor Roberts, *Satow's Diplomatic Practice* (Oxford: Oxford University Press, 2016), pp. 45-60.

'constructive ambiguity' over precision, politeness over frankness, reason over passion and confidentiality over transparency, the arrival of digital technologies has infused the public sphere in which diplomacy operates with a set of new elements that have already started to reshape the way in which public engagement takes place. Some of these elements are already visible (including information overload, visual enhancement, emotional framing, algorithmic-driven engagement), others are expected to become visible soon (non-physical interaction and empathetic connectivity via augmented and virtual reality simulations), but many others are yet to reveal themselves, as the technologies to support them are still in the 'drawing board' phase (such as artificial intelligence, blockchains and 3D printing).

Take, for instance, the case of digital data, the 'bloodstream' of the digital revolution. It is expected that by 2025, the global datasphere will grow to 175 zettabytes (ZB, a trillion gigabytes), which represents ten times the 33 ZB of data generated in 2018.[8] To put things into perspective, every two days we create as much information, former Google CEO Eric Schmidt once claimed, as we had done from the dawn of civilization up until 2003, roughly five exabytes of data[9] (or 0.005 ZB). This massive process of data generation inevitably increases competition for attention in the online space and stimulates demand for new skills and the algorithmic tools that are necessary for filtering, processing and interpreting relevant data. The cognitive short cuts that online users have developed in reaction to information overload are tailored to addressing the challenge of conducting effective communication in the digital space. Visual enhancement highlights, for example, the power of images to pack a large amount of information in an easily absorbable format. Emotional framing seeks, on the other hand, to stimulate online engagement not by the quality of the information, but by the intensity of the moods and feelings conveyed about the topic under discussion, a process that has the potential to become even more intimate in the immersive context of augmented reality (AR) and virtual reality (VR) technologies.

As social informatics researchers will not hesitate to point out, the impact of these transformations on public diplomacy will much depend on how diplomats interact with the new communication features that digital technologies will make available. If these features are recognized as making useful contributions to improving the effectiveness of public diplomatic work and to

---

8   Reinsel, Gantz and Rydning, *The Digitization of the World*, p. 6.

9   M.G. Siegler, 'Eric Schmidt: Every 2 Days We Create as Much Information as We Did up to 2003', *Techcrunch*, available at https://techcrunch.com/2010/08/04/schmidt-data/.

advancing foreign policy objectives, then they are more likely to be accepted and supported by ministries of foreign affairs (MFAs), embassies, and rising non-state actors with diplomatic capacities and aspirations. If, on the other hand, these features are seen as fostering an environment in diplomatic communication that will find itself at risk of being hijacked by the 'dark side' of technology and redirected for disinformation and propaganda, then institutional resistance is likely to be much stronger. More specifically, one would expect three particular areas to influence considerations about the significance of digital technologies for the future of public diplomacy, namely whether they will prove effective in ensuring that public diplomacy messages would be better *heard, listened to* and *followed* by the relevant audiences.

Given the challenge of information overload and the growing competitiveness of the online space, machine learning will likely become an indispensable tool for studying pattern recognition and making data-driven predictions about the main issues of concern for the target audiences. As the volume of data-driven interactions continues to grow at an exponential rate, one can make oneself heard only by professionally learning how to separate 'signals' from the background 'noise' and by proactively adjusting one's message accordingly in a manner that ensures maximal visibility in the online space, in real time. Making oneself listened to would require, by extension, better understanding of the cognitive frames and emotional undertones that enable audiences to connect meaningfully with a particular message. Most importantly, the ongoing transition from a textual to a visual or audio form of communication is likely to accelerate and, consequently, public diplomacy campaigns are expected to become increasingly sophisticated in visual or audio terms. Augmented reality technology is particularly well suited to take advantage of this trend by allowing, for instance, public diplomats to use geolocation-based apps to showcase issues of interest in a tailored and interactive manner. Intelligent assistants like Amazon's Alexa or Google Home's smart speaker could also prove effective in providing tailored and engaging public diplomacy context via specially developed skill sets.

Making oneself recognized and followed as a soft-power leader would come with a particular set of challenges. First, the idea of ignoring or downplaying the significance of the digital medium is likely to turn increasingly counterproductive. 'To define yourself or be defined' has now become a critical guiding principle of digital engagement, as in fluid, overcrowded and dynamic digital contexts, diplomatic reputations, political perceptions and institutional images can be relatively easily reframed or undermined, as illustrated, for instance, by the Twitter spat between Turkey and the Netherlands when the Dutch government prevented Turkish officials from campaigning in the

Netherlands.[10] Second, digital platforms do not simply add value to pre-designed communication strategies, but they gradually usher in a new language of communication with its own grammar rules in which data, AR/VR simulations and algorithms are the new syntactic units to which various combinations of visuals, emotions and cognitive frames are attached to create semantic meaning. Third, and potentially revolutionary, the new semantic meaning to be generated by digital tools will likely be tailored not to the preferences of generic audiences, but to those of each individual, in line with his/her specific habits of news consumption and patterns of media diet that big data analytics should be able to reveal.

Moreover, the line between message and action becomes increasingly blurred, as diplomatic communication in the digital context is no longer about merely reporting or occasionally instigating action, but about performing action with diplomatic meaning and implications, especially in times of international crises. This is where the issue of *digital emotional intelligence* (DEI) — that is, the ability to read, interpret and manage emotions inhabiting the digital medium — can prove critical to the theory and practice of public diplomacy. Paying close attention to how genuinely and intensely people feel about a particular situation in their online communication can help to avoid embarrassing moments with potential disruptive implications for bilateral relations. By improving awareness of how emotions affect the thinking of digital diplomats, DEI can also help to strengthen their problem-solving capacity. Positive moods stimulate creativity, drive interest in new possibilities and foster risk-taking and ambitious planning. By contrast, negative moods tend to keep people focused on the tasks at hand, make them pay more attention to details and increase their resistance to making mistakes. Finally, DEI underscores the value of learning how to detach oneself from emotionally charged situations in the digital sphere. Managing emotional responses to powerful triggers is a difficult exercise, but with potentially strong positive implications.

To conclude, digital technologies will continue to reshape the context in which social communication takes place in a subtle but profound manner, ranging from the use of machine learning for understanding patterns of communication, the employment of intelligent assistants for message dissemination, the resetting of the 'grammar rules' of communication in support of more engaging and performative actions tailored to individual preferences and the cultivation of digital emotional intelligence to facilitate smooth digital

---

10   'Turkey–Netherlands Spat Worsens after High-Profile Twitter Accounts Hacked, Replaced with Anti-Nazi Messages', *Haaretz*, available online at https://www.haaretz.com/world -news/europe/turkish-dutch-spat-worsens-after-twitter-accounts-hijacked-1.5449073.

navigation through emotion-laden situations. On the critical side, the continued inability to process vast amounts of data in real time creates favourable conditions for the construction of 'alternative realities', in which interpretations of social reality are disconnected from evidence-based reasoning and anchored instead in deformed or falsified frames that are designed to serve the foreign policy interests of the day, as the disinformation campaigns in Europe that are attributed to the Russian government regrettably demonstrate.[11]

Domestic Digital Diplomacy: From Whitehall to Townhall

Traditionally, foreign ministries were tasked with managing relations of friendship and enmity with other states, while diplomatic communication saw interactions between diplomats and foreign constituencies.[12] Diplomats thus faced the world with their back to their nation and seldom communicated with their national citizenry. Yet globalization and digitalization have blurred the lines between the foreign and the domestic. In a globalized world, one cannot easily separate the domestic from the foreign, as local challenges such as climate change, terrorism or even employment require regional or global solutions. Digitization further blurs the distinction between domestic and foreign, as citizens' migration to digital platforms creates new opportunities for diplomats to rally domestic public support for foreign policy achievements or sway public opinion in favour of a chosen policy. From a social informatics perspective, the more that digital technologies blur the boundary between the foreign and the domestic, the more that MFAs will have to face challenges about whether they can continue to do their job effectively without also engaging in the public conversation at the domestic level.

The digital blurring of the foreign and the domestic could be best captured by the concept of domestic digital diplomacy (DDD), which refers to the use of digital platforms by governments in support of their foreign policy.[13] In 1988, Robert Putnam conceptualized diplomatic negotiations as a two-level game in

---

11   Corneliu Bjola and James Pamment, 'Digital Containment: Revisiting Containment Strategy in the Digital Age', *Global Affairs*, vol. 2, no. 2 (2016), pp. 131-142.

12   Corneliu Bjola, 'Understanding Enmity and Friendship in World Politics: The Case for a Diplomatic Approach', *The Hague Journal of Diplomacy*, vol. 8, no. 1 (2013), pp. 1-20.

13   Corneliu Bjola and Ilan Manor, 'Revisiting Putnam's Two-Level Game Theory in the Digital Age: Domestic Digital Diplomacy and the Iran Nuclear Deal', *Cambridge Review of International Affairs*, vol. 31, no. 1 (2018), pp. 3-32.

which national and international politics often collide.[14] At the national level, interest groups and constituents (such as labour unions and activist groups) pursue their interests by pressuring the government to adopt favourable policies. At the international level, governments attempt to meet the pressures of their domestic constituents, while at the same time minimizing the possible adverse impact of foreign developments. Putnam argued that 'the political complexities for the players in this two-level game are staggering', as leaders must walk the tightrope between domestic and foreign demands.

From a public diplomacy perspective, digital technologies may be used to facilitate or impede the two-level game of diplomacy. For instance, foreign policy institutions may now use digital platforms to communicate with the national citizenry to obtain public support for diplomatic treaties, which may translate into political support. In a recent paper, Corneliu Bjola and Ilan Manor explored, for instance, how the Obama White House used Twitter to engage with the American public and gather support for the Iran Nuclear Agreement, which ultimately led to Congressional endorsement of the Agreement.[15] As digitization has dramatically increased the ability of online actors to counter government communication, Bjola and Manor expect the issue of DDD to become more prominent in the coming years. MFAS will likely face a growing demand to monitor the activity of foreign opponents in the domestic public sphere, map their arguments and refute them in near-real time.

At times, the opposite may also occur, as domestic public diplomacy leads to foreign ripple effects. One classic example is a 'selfie' published by former First Lady Michelle Obama in 2014. The 'selfie' depicted the First Lady holding a sign with the hashtag 'Bring Back Our Girls', referencing the abduction of more than 270 Nigerian school girls by Boko Haram. The tweet may have been an attempt to draw US public attention to the plight of the kidnapped girls. Yet within hours of the tweet's publication, a counter campaign was launched with individuals publishing 'selfies' bearing the hashtag 'Bring Back Your Drones' and referencing the Obama administration's affinity for drone strikes. This example is not unique but rather inherent to digital communications, as online publics may accept or reject diplomatic messaging, leading to ripple effects at both the domestic and foreign levels. Overcoming this limitation requires that diplomats continue to employ digital tools towards public engagement and online conversations. Indeed, the power of digital tools lies

---

14   Robert D. Putnam, 'Diplomacy and Domestic Politics: The Logic of Two-Level Games', *International Organizations*, vol. 42, no. 3 (1988), pp. 427-460.

15   Bjola and Manor, 'Revisiting Putnam's Two-Level Game Theory in the Digital Age'.

not in their ability to disseminate messages, but to foster and nurture relationships through meaningful dialogue.

Algorithms are particularly well suited to influence diplomatic negotiations, as they enable the creation of digital content that increasingly resonates with the biases of certain populations. Big data and sentiment analysis can be used to classify conversations taking place in various digital forums. Once biased groups have been identified, digital propaganda may be disseminated among members so as to strengthen their bias and harden their political stance, thus impacting a government's ability to negotiate an agreement. During the Crimean crisis, disinformation was used to promote fake stories in Ukraine alleging that Ukrainian extremists had raped Russian women or established concentration camps in eastern Ukraine.[16] These fake stories were used in an attempt to sway public opinion against a possible agreement between Ukraine and the European Union. As algorithms grow more sophisticated, their ability to sway public opinion in a foreign country against an agreement may also grow.

Yet algorithmic technologies may also facilitate the two-level game of diplomacy. The Israeli MFA currently uses algorithms to map social-media filter bubbles that promote either positive or negative narratives about Jewish communities. Once these have been mapped, Israel's MFA attempts to engage with members of negative filter bubbles by providing factual information, countering racial stereotypes and conversing with those members who are willing to do so.[17] This, in turn, helps the MFA to build relationships with hostile online publics, which may then come to support Israel's policy stance, such as Israeli insistence that any negotiated settlement with the Palestinians include the continued military presence of Israeli forces along the border with Jordan.

Future technologies will also continue to digitally disrupt the two-level game. For instance, it is estimated that by 2025 virtual reality will provide digital publics with immersive experiences that could challenge one's notion of reality.[18] Virtual reality may be defined as an artificial environment that is experienced through sensory stimuli provided by a computer and where ones'

---

16   See 'Analysis of Russia's Information Campaign Against Ukraine' (Riga: NATO StratCom, 2015), available at https://www.stratcomcoe.org/analysis-russias-information-campaign -against-ukraine (accessed 7 July 2018).

17   Interview with the Director of Algorithmic Diplomacy at the Israeli MFA.

18   See Frost & Sullivan, 'The Global Future of Workplace Technology, Forecast to 2015: Connectivity, Convergence, Augmented Reality (AR), Artificial Intelligence (AI) and Cybersecurity to be Cornerstones of Workplace Evolution' (2 March 2016), available at http://www.frost.com/sublib/display-report.do?id=NFE7-01-00-00-00 (accessed 7 July 2018).

actions partially determine what happens in the environment. From the perspective of domestic digital diplomacy, MFAs may use virtual reality to offer citizens a virtual experience in which they are transported to the scene of a global crisis and witness first-hand the events that are unfolding on the ground. The British Foreign & Commonwealth Office (FCO) could, for instance, offer British citizens the opportunity to virtually witness the Syrian civil war. This, in turn, may enable the FCO to obtain public support for demanding that any negotiated resolution to the war include the removal of Syria's President Bashar al-Assad.

Yet virtual reality experiences may be based on fact or fiction, reality or narrative, hence the importance of the social dimension of digital technologies. The Russian MFA could also virtually transport British publics to Syria, while exposing them to a false reality in which the Assad regime is fighting Islamic terrorists rather than its own people. Subsequently, British publics may come to regard Russia's involvement in Syria as legitimate, thus harming British attempts to broker a negotiated solution to the war that sees the removal of President Assad. Importantly, digital publics may be susceptible to visual manipulation, as images play an evidentiary purpose in modern societies. They are used in courts of law and history books to prove that certain events did in fact take place. As 'seeing is believing', virtual reality could substantially disrupt the two-level game as MFAs promote false realities.

In the same vein, it is estimated that by 2025, tele-presence will replace applications such as Skype as a medium for remote communications.[19] Tele-presence is a holographic conferencing communication technology that enables people to interact with holographic images of their counterparts. Tele-presence could also substantially complicate the two-level game. As a tool for domestic digital diplomacy, holographic imagery could enable diplomats to hold townhall meetings throughout their country to raise domestic support for diplomatic treaties without ever leaving their office. As a tool for traditional public diplomacy, tele-presence may impact the diplomatic capabilities of relatively poor countries that maintain small embassies abroad. Rather than have a physical diplomat rally support for, or against, a diplomatic accord, diplomats will be able to engage holographically with foreign opinion-makers and elites, so as to facilitate or impede the domestic ratification of an international agreement.

This is not to suggest that face-to-face diplomacy will no longer hold relevance. Just as one may separate the domestic and foreign levels of diplomacy, so can one distinguish between the stage and the backstage of diplomacy.

---

19   Frost & Sullivan, 'The Global Future of Workplace Technology, Forecast to 2015'.

Tele-conferencing may especially be useful on the stage of diplomacy in which diplomats act in front of a global audience. A holographic image of a world leader may address the United Nations (UN) General Assembly, a holographic ambassador may address the UN Human Rights Council, while a holographic trade representative may give an address at a diaspora business forum. Yet the backstage of diplomacy will continue to be dominated by face-to-face interactions. For it is in the backstage that diplomats foster personal ties with stakeholders and leverage these ties to obtain national goals. Coalition-building at multilateral forums and establishing ties with diaspora leaders rest on diplomats' ability to establish a positive rapport with their counterparts. This can primarily be achieved through personal interactions.

Importantly, the blurring of the domestic and foreign realms of diplomacy is also evident when examining the impact of digital disinformation. While digital technologies may augment public diplomacy activities, one cannot ignore the fact that state and non-state actors employ digitalization towards undermining diplomatic processes. Doctored images, fake videos, bots and fictitious news sites are all used to sway public opinion, stoke emotions of fear and distrust, and erode the foundations of open societies. Thus, while some actors may use digital tools to create bridges, other use them to destroy bridges. Combating the emergence of digital disinformation has seen diplomats operate at both the domestic and foreign levels. Domestically, some MFAS now play an active role in mapping and stemming the flow of digital disinformation in their own country. The Israeli MFA and the British FCO have created digital units tasked with identifying and neutralizing foreign social-media bots and fictitious news sites. In the foreign arena, some MFAS now share their experience and expertise with their peers. The United Kingdom, for instance, is training digital units in Baltic nation MFAS so that these may also track and neutralize disinformation campaigns. Going forwards, diplomats may further contribute to their nation's digital resilience by working with other ministries on digital literacy programmes that help citizens to identify nefarious digital content. At the international level, diplomats may create coalitions with technology companies, civil-society organizations and non-governmental organizations (NGOS) so as to create a 'trusted digital environment' in which actors share the burden of mapping and neutralizing disinformation campaigns.[20]

In summary, the next wave of digital disruption will continue to blur the boundary between the domestic and the foreign and the real and the fictitious. Reaping the benefits, and contending with the limitations, of innovative

---

20   Peter F. Cowhey and Jonathan D. Aronson, *Digital DNA* (Oxford: Oxford University Press, 2017).

technologies will demand that MFAs adopt a proactive approach to digitization and begin today to acquire the skills that are necessary to practise digital domestic diplomacy as a key new component of the public diplomacy of tomorrow.

Silicon Valley Diplomacy: From State to Technology-based Representation

As digital technologies grow in their agency and impact, it seems justified to pose two pertinent questions: *who are the diplomats* and *who needs public diplomacy* in the Digital Age? In seeking to answer these questions, we can highlight two distinct future trends when it comes to evaluating the evolution of diplomatic representation and in particular its impact on public diplomacy in the digital age: the tendency to see diplomats in terms of the skills that they possess and the jobs that they do, rather than who they represent; and the ever-increasing institutionalized multilateralism aimed at a stronger international order, either by improving digital cooperation between states or transcending the need for it. From a social informatics perspective, the first tendency speaks to the digital transformation of the context in which diplomacy operates (the rise of new powerful actors with diplomatic capacity and aspirations), while the second highlights the implications that these new actors may have on new methods and forms of public diplomatic engagement.

Shining a spotlight on the latter trend first, it seems justified to state that the progressive inclusion of non-state actors in the realm of foreign policy-making is playing a seismic role in shaping the current, and undoubtedly the future, evolution of diplomatic representation, in particular the inclusion of technological giants within the borders of Silicon Valley. Indeed, this ever-intertwining relationship between these actors and a nation-state's foreign policy construction is being publicly and actively addressed by the actors themselves, signalling to the world at large that the international political order has indeed changed. The CEO of General Electric (GE) Europe, Ferdinando 'Nani' Beccalli-Falco, for example, goes as far as to call himself 'the Foreign Minister of GE' because of the nature of his work. Eric Schmidt, Google's Chairman and former CEO, has made visits to North Korea and Cuba with the public aim of meeting with state officials to promote a 'free and open internet'. Schmidt is regularly called Google's 'Ambassador to the World' for his work in representing the firm on global trips in an attempt to expand Google's operations worldwide. Thus, for the student and the practitioner of diplomacy, the trend concerning diplomatic actors and their evolving representation seems clear:

corporations are growing in their capacity to engage in public diplomacy efforts, a field that once remained almost exclusively in the domain of sovereign states.

Indeed, a host of the aforementioned actors now have resources exceeding those of some sovereign states and can bypass the formal structures of their home nation's diplomatic bureaucracy. They are also increasingly being shown to constrain the role of contemporary MFAs in setting and implementing policy, both at home and abroad. When viewed through the lens of the evolving nature of diplomatic representation, this constraint represents one of the growing challenges that has emerged within the framework of what we can now label a 'Silicon Valley foreign policy'. Non-state actors, specifically technological-based non-state actors (TBNSAs), are directly challenging our historic notions of power and influence in the realm of foreign policy-making and are shaping with considerable force the context in which MFAs now choose to conduct their public diplomacy efforts. This reshaping of the diplomatic domain by TBNSAs has been done, and it seems justified to predict that it will continue to be done, by: a) disrupting the historic structural order of diplomatic institutions (in this case, that of diplomatic representation); and b) the heightened influence and reach that these new actors now hold over the public domain — a degree of influence and reach of which MFAs could only ever dream and one that many are now rightly seeking to emulate and integrate in their future conduct of public diplomacy.

However, as with any change to the make-up of diplomatic practice, be this in regard to public diplomacy objectives or otherwise, serious challenges arise. As the Head of the UN's Independent International Commission of Inquiry on Syria, Paulo Sérgio Pinheiro, acknowledged, one serious challenge for the future of diplomacy stems 'not from the rapid increase in the number and types of international organizations, but from diplomacy's (representative actors and institutions) inability to adapt to them'.[21] As noted, TBNSAs are continuously demonstrating their capacity to take the centre stage, even when facing traditional powerful state actors. In contrast, MFAs at large are continuously demonstrating their incapability to react to the power, influence and motive of these new non-state actors. With that said, when seeking to predict and analyse the future aims and practices of public diplomacy, and how best an individual MFA can adapt the historic component of diplomatic representation to

---

21   'UN Rights Expert Deplores "Profound Failure of Diplomacy" as Syria Conflict Escalates', *United Nations News*, available at https://news.un.org/en/story/2015/06/502402-un-rights-expert-deplores-profound-failure-diplomacy-syria-conflict-escalates (accessed 4 April 2018).

meet the changing demands and needs of the new international order, we do require some sort of blueprint, a benchmark, in which to base our predictions and recommendations.

This blueprint begins first, in our view, with the case of Denmark, a nation that not only acknowledged the changing landscape of diplomatic representation, but acted upon it, and swiftly. Recognizing that the intensity of growth of international actors arose nearly exclusively from technological actors based in Silicon Valley, and that few issues today lie completely outside their purview, Denmark made the pioneering move to appoint veteran diplomat Casper Klynge as the world's first 'Tech Ambassador' to Silicon Valley. The spark, or the catalyst, for this appointment came in 2016, when Denmark noted that their national GDP for 2016 was smaller than Facebook's entire market capitalization. When publicly announcing this decision, Danish Minister for Foreign Affairs Anders Samuelsen stated: 'Companies such as Google, IBM, Apple and Microsoft are now so large that their economic strength and impact on our everyday lives exceeds that of many of the countries where we have more traditional embassies'.[22]

Furthermore, Denmark's decision, while pioneering in its initial conception, did not stand alone for long, for in November 2017, France appointed Ambassador David Martinon to Silicon Valley, thereby creating the nation's first role of 'Ambassador for Digital Affairs'. Ambassador Martinon's portfolio focuses on forming, maintaining and fostering relations between France and Silicon Valley, with his jurisdiction extending to digital issues, already present within the French MFA. This includes digital governance, international negotiations on cybersecurity, support for digital companies' export operations, intellectual property issues online, and France's participation in the Open Government Partnership in conjunction with ETAPA (the French task force for open data). These recent ambassadorial appointments signify not only the important socio-economic and political roles of technology, but also how diplomacy is evolving and adapting to the disruptive changes in our societies. These developments mark the prominence of so-called 'tech-cities' on the global scene. Nation-states are no longer the only players in international affairs; cities are also taking centre stage.

Formally creating the first ambassadorial posting to Silicon Valley undoubtedly captured the attention of people around the globe and sent a strong signal to the international community at large that the global power game was

---

22   Peter Baugh, '"Techplomacy": Denmark's Ambassador to Silicon Valley', *Politico* (20 July 2017), available at https://www.politico.eu/article/denmark-silicon-valley-tech-ambassador -casper-klynge/ (accessed 4 April 2018).

changing. This appointment demonstrated clearly what many MFAs have yet even to acknowledge: that many aspects of the historic roles and responsibilities of a nation-state's ambassador and embassy have changed, chief among them, the multitude of actors who now hold power in the international system and who thereby influence both foreign and domestic policies. As a result, MFAs are being forced to re-examine *who* represents them in the global sphere, *where* and *how*.

With that said, one should note that Ambassador Klynge's appointment did not emerge in a vacuum. Take the case of Taiwan, for example. Taiwan has increasingly and openly demonstrated its intention to deepen its relationship with Silicon Valley. The most public step came with the launch of the Asia Silicon Valley Development Plan in September 2016 by Taiwan's government. The plan is still in progress, and maintains the core aim of connecting Taiwan to global technological clusters and creating new industries for Taiwan's next generation. A number of other smaller states have followed this example and worked to create an influential presence in the region. The Republic of Ireland is one example, establishing a strong presence in northern California, with its office directing a large proportion of its attention to the technological sector, alongside other sectors including bio-pharmaceuticals and financial services. Other nations take a slightly different approach, choosing to combine private-sector expertise with the aim of bolstering and strengthening their diplomatic capacity on the ground. Priya Guha, for example, who previously held the title of the United Kingdom's consul-general to San Francisco for five years, worked extensively to convince technology start-ups to expand to Britain.

Meanwhile, it remains noteworthy that an international presence within Silicon Valley is not always easy to spot, with a number of nations preferring to engage in a more implicit manner. This style of engagement tends to reflect the motivation behind the actor in question, with indirect intervention suggesting a desire for indirect control. For example, Chinese companies frequently source failing US firms and target small enterprises making valuable technology, such as semiconductors. Chinese companies also invest heavily in dollars, and other resources, in technological firms in Europe and the United States as a way to capture innovation before it becomes 'mainstream' and loses advantage against its competitors. This is illustrated also in Sunnyvale in the heart of Silicon Valley, where US digital giants such as Microsoft, LinkedIn and Yahoo all have a presence. Next to a Google complex is a building housing the offices of Baidu, China's largest internet provider and Google's rival. Baidu opened its innovation centre, called the Institute of Deep Learning, in 2014, with a focus on a self-driving vehicle called Apollo. Other digital Chinese powerhouses, such as Alibaba, Tencent and Huawei, also have Silicon Valley research and development centres.

Regarding the direct implications for the public diplomacy efforts of the states named (and indeed unnamed, but existing in their practice), they emerge as distinct and novel when viewed in the lineage of diplomatic history. This is primarily done by leveraging the heightened influence and reach that these technological giants possess, and the increasing power that they now hold over the global public domain at large. Denmark and Ireland may be relatively small countries compared to, say, Germany, but those metrics no longer weigh up in the same way. States and the governments that they appoint have ceased to dominate people's existence in the same way that they did a century ago. Instead, it is a new era dominated by cross-national identity politics, (mis) information and data. Denmark's prioritization of 'techplomacy' is in itself a public diplomacy tool for the state. It is an area where, according to Klynge, 'we punch above our weight' among the 28 EU member states.[23] Ambassador David Martinon and Ambassador Klynge acknowledge that public diplomacy is now being conducted in a new era where material forces or wealth are not the most important trump card, but data and information instead. Technology in all its guises, Klynge states, 'will define the winners and losers of tomorrow and whether countries, including developing economies, will be able to reap the benefits of the digital age'.[24]

Another key benefit of the growing inclusion of non-state actors at the 'table of power', and the increasing power of multilateral diplomacy, has been for those MFAs that lack the resources to establish resident embassies in every country, as they can look to the virtual world as a strategic alternative. Virtual reality may give rise, for instance, to a new generation of virtual embassies. Traditionally, virtual embassies were used to overcome the limitations of traditional diplomacy such as lack of bilateral ties. America's virtual embassy to Tehran, for instance, was meant to facilitate dialogue between American diplomats and Iranian society. Studies suggest, however, that virtual embassies have failed thus far to elicit dialogue or create relationships between diplomats and foreign populations.[25] Yet that may change in the future, as virtual reality may create a more realistic and intimate experience in which diplomats meet

---

23 Nikoloay Nikolov, 'There's Now an Ambassador Representing His Country in Silicon Valley — and We Should've Had Them All Along', *Mashable*, available at https://mashable.com/2018/04/10/casper-klynge-tech-ambassador-silicon-valley-denmark/?europe=true#PhEdUhQgNaqr (accessed 15 July 2018).

24 Baugh, '"Techplomacy"'.

25 Emily Metzgar, 'Is it the Medium or the Message? Social Media, American Public Relations & Iran', *Global Media Journal*, vol. 12, no. 21 (2012), pp. 1-16.

face-to-virtual-face with foreign populations, converse with them in real time and even engage in joint cultural or sports activities. Therefore, far from being in danger of becoming an endangered activity — rendered increasingly irrelevant by technological progress — diplomatic representation in the digital age can be harnessed to increase diplomatic power and become a critical instrument in an age of complex interdependence and globalization.

Ultimately, we can see that future technologies and the actors that represent them are likely to continue to digitally disrupt diplomatic representation, first in terms of the growing incorporation of non-state entities into global affairs, which has been illustrated clearly with the proliferation and intensification of digital power houses such as Google, Facebook and Twitter, a proliferation of influence that shows no signs of slowing down, and, second, in how MFAS choose to respond (strategically or otherwise) to their increasing inclusion in the international realm at large. It is therefore more important than ever that the diplomatic arena and all those residing within it recognize this increasing evolution, and the power and influence that both entities can hold to ensure the relevance and viability of the diplomatic craft in the twenty-first century, particularly in how it can shape and push forth the aims and objectives of an MFA's public diplomacy strategy. Technological companies, too, should seek to learn the tools and apply their resources towards diplomacy to engage with countries on a national level, rather than just through global mechanisms as they currently do.

Conclusion

As digital technologies continue to reshape the context in which public diplomacy operates, it is also important to note that when used to craft and implement public diplomacy strategies, a key strategic advantage of digital platforms lies in their ability to uncover and enhance traditionally marginalized voices. The current technological climate is testament to this, as demonstrated clearly and frequently by non–state actors adopting and utilizing digital technologies to project their voices online, MFAS implementing digital campaigns in order to strengthen their interaction with minority voices online, and the creation of new diplomatic relationships between diplomatic and non-affiliated, non-official, online actors — relationships that were once deemed unconventional, or irrelevant, to the practice of public diplomacy, but that are deemed strategic today, and even necessary, for effective diplomatic practice. The stark evolution of these relationships is a direct result of new and emerging technologies, technologies that shifted the locus of power and influence within the diplomatic realm, thereby creating new opportunities for voices to be heard, to raise questions and to work towards producing a strong community online.

With that said, the direct relationship between public diplomacy and online marginalized voices can be found in a diverse range of strategies and initiatives. Indeed, prominent public diplomacy campaigns have worked to ensure that the dispossessed and the marginalized are offered the chance to find their voice. One prime example is the United Nations Educational, Scientific and Cultural Organization's (UNESCO) International Mother Language Year (2015), which sought to connect and inform all citizens about the UN's values and goals, by ensuring that any material produced was linguistically diverse and culturally relevant online material. Or the work of the Global Fund for Women (GFW), which continues to work alongside diplomatic partners worldwide to ensure access to technology, control of it, and the ability to create and shape it, as a fundamental issue of women's human rights. The GFW also works to ensure that all women can acknowledge their voice, and are given the means to express it, if they wish. Alongside diplomatic actors, the GFW holds the core aims of helping to end the gender technology gap and empowering women and girls to create innovative solutions to advance equality in their communities.

As data becomes the 'new oil', the opportunities for public diplomacy to grow as a field of practice are real and game-changing. Looking to the next five to ten years of technological transformation, we should expect the medium of public communication to be increasingly populated by machine-learning algorithms and intelligent assistants, with the fading boundary between foreign and domestic affairs making room for digital domestic diplomacy and the rise of technological-based non-state actors to challenge notions of power and influence in the realm of foreign policy-making. Despite these inevitable challenges, the future of public diplomacy in the digital age remains bright, as long as MFAs, embassies and TBNSAS continue to engage creatively and positively with digital technologies and stay committed to the mission of building bridges between offline and online communities. Digital technologies can play an influential role in how individuals, communities and societies not only interact with each other, but also how they redefine themselves as social and political actors in the digital age.

Corneliu Bjola
is Associate Professor in Diplomatic Studies at the University of Oxford and Head of the Oxford Digital Diplomacy Research Group. His research focuses on the impact of digital technology on the conduct of diplomacy, with a focus on strategic communication, digital influence and methods for countering digital propaganda. His most recent publication is the co-edited volume (with James

Pamment) on *Countering Online Propaganda and Violent Extremism: The Dark Side of Digital Diplomacy* (Abingdon: Routledge, 2018).

Jennifer Cassidy

is Stipendiary Lecturer in Politics and International Relations at St Peter's College, University of Oxford. Her primary research focuses on the themes of digital diplomacy, questioning how diplomatic agents use social media platforms during times of political crises, and to what extent their use during a conflict can be deemed effective within diplomatic crisis communication strategies. Her most recent publication is *Gender and Diplomacy* (Abingdon: Routledge, 2017).

Ilan Manor

is a D.Phil. candidate at the University of Oxford. His research focuses on diplomats' use of digital technologies during times of geopolitical crisis. His most recent publication is *The Digitalization of Public Diplomacy* (London: Palgrave Macmillan, 2019).

Digital Diplomacy: Emotion and Identity in the Public Realm

Constance Duncombe
School of Social Sciences, Menzies Building, Monash University, Clayton,
VIC 3800, Australia
constance.duncombe@monash.edu

Received: 27 June 2018; revised: 26 September 2018; accepted: 4 January 2019

Summary

Public diplomacy is increasingly facilitated through social media. Government leaders and diplomats are using social media platforms such as Twitter, Facebook and Instagram to communicate with foreign publics, changing the dynamics of interaction between broadcaster and audience. The key to understanding the power of social media in public diplomacy is the role of emotion in digital diplomacy strategies: social media statements relating to state identity can incite strong emotions that have the potential to undermine heretofore positive diplomatic relations, or provide communicative openings that move towards ameliorating crises. Examining the interaction of social media, emotion and identity provides insight into the increasing importance of digital diplomacy and the future challenges relating to digital disinformation that lie ahead.

Keywords

digital diplomacy – emotion – identity – Twitter – digital disinformation

Introduction

When Canadian Prime Minister Justin Trudeau visited India in February 2018, his first official state visit, Indian Prime Minister Narendra Modi was noticeably absent. After landing in New Delhi, Trudeau and his family were received by a junior minister for agriculture. This was very unusual, not least because Modi is well known for his penchant for personally greeting and then tweeting

EMOTION AND IDENTITY IN THE PUBLIC REALM

selfies of visiting dignitaries to his many Twitter followers. It was to be six days before the two leaders officially met, during a constructed photo opportunity at Rashtrapati Bhawan. While Trudeau spent nearly one week travelling around India and tweeting about his experiences as part of his well-established public diplomacy strategy, Modi's absence — both in real life and on social media — signalled that simmering tensions between Canada and India remained over sanctuary offered by Canada to Sikh separatists. Although this visit was 'ironically [...] meant to mend fences with India, given that India has made clear its disapproval of Trudeau's appeasement of Sikh separatists',[1] India used the visit as an opportunity to convey its dissatisfaction with the current state of affairs. A global audience was witness to this highly staged and visible diplomatic snub, which illustrates the increasing complexities of public diplomacy that will only increase over the next decade.

With the rise of social media, scholars and practitioners alike have suggested that digital diplomacy is the transformed or 'new' public diplomacy, with conventional diplomatic practices challenged or fundamentally altered by information and communications technology (ICT), as the above example demonstrates.[2] There is now a far greater focus on how political leaders and diplomats use social media as part of their public diplomacy strategies. Instead of a separate cultivated image of state identity that is broadcast to foreign publics via a one-way messaging system, social media seemingly promote interaction between these two levels of actors, potentially changing the flow of information and contributing to a better understanding of the needs and desires of both domestic and foreign publics.[3] Conventional diplomacy, too, is subject to such transformations in interaction and communication that these digital tools allow. From providing an alternative communication platform

---

1 Shivam Vij, 'Why India is Being Really Rude to Justin Trudeau', *The Washington Post* (20 February 2018), available online at https://www.washingtonpost.com/news/global-opinions/wp/2018/02/20/why-india-is-being-really-rude-to-justin-trudeau/?noredirect=on&utm_term=.ffc2d2d4662d.

2 Corneliu Bjola, 'Digital Diplomacy: The State of the Art', *Global Affairs*, vol. 2, no. 3 (2016), pp. 297-299; Corneliu Bjola and Marcus Holmes (eds), *Digital Diplomacy: Theory and Practice* (Abingdon: Routledge, 2015); Cristina Archetti, 'The Impact of New Media on Diplomatic Practice: An Evolutionary Model of Change', *The Hague Journal of Diplomacy*, vol. 7, no. 2 (2012), pp. 181-206; Brian Hocking and Jan Melissen, *Diplomacy in the Digital Age* (The Hague: Netherlands Institute of International Relations 'Clingendael', 2015).

3 Pablo Barberá and Thomas Zeitzoff, 'The New Public Address System: Why Do World Leaders Adopt Social Media?', *International Studies Quarterly*, vol. 62, no. 1 (2017), pp. 121-130; Bjola and Holmes, *Digital Diplomacy*.

when official meetings between diplomatic counterparts are difficult, managing the circulation of information across international and domestic audience levels, to facilitating transnational discourse on key policy issues between state and non-state stakeholders, a wide variety of ways exist through which digital tools are informing diplomatic practice.[4] Digital technologies can, at times, necessitate diplomacy occurring in full view of a global audience, shifting status-quo power arrangements between states broadcasting messages of persuasion and the publics receiving these messages.

Given this shift in communication dynamics, questions arise here about the power of social media. Why might Twitter, Facebook, Instagram and other social media platforms be understood as having shifted public diplomacy interaction potentially even more than technological advances such as the telegram, radio and television? I suggest that to understand the emerging changes in public diplomacy practice, we must pay greater attention to the role of emotions in facilitating these transformations. Social media platforms enable emotions that can work towards the development of trust between actors, or undermine previously stable diplomatic relationships. Why is this important? Work in psychology and journalism and communication studies demonstrates how emotional contagion — the idea that emotions can spread from one person to another, leading one to act 'in synchrony with others' — infiltrates relationships on social media, particularly Twitter networks.[5] The lack of physical contact between users is not an inhibitor to understanding emotional expression.[6] Instead, social media facilitate technologically mediated forms of emotional contagion.[7] Sharing a common social identity makes such emotional contagion online even more likely.[8] Yet research on digital diplomacy overlooks the emotional context of this phenomenon, particularly with regard to the interrelationship between emotions and identity, with some

---

4 Constance Duncombe, 'Twitter and Transformative Diplomacy: Social Media and Iran — US Relations', *International Affairs*, vol. 93, no. 3 (2017), pp. 545-562; Corneliu Bjola and Ilan Manor, 'Revisiting Putnam's Two-Level Game Theory in the Digital Age: Domestic Digital Diplomacy and the Iran Nuclear Deal', *Cambridge Review of International Affairs*, vol. 31, no. 1 (2018), pp. 3-32; Ionna Ferra and Dennis Nguyen, '#MigrantCrisis: "Tagging" the European Migration Crisis on Twitter', *Journal of Communication Management*, vol. 21 no. 4 (2017), pp. 411-426.

5 Jonathan Mercer, 'Feeling Like a State: Social Emotion and Identity', *International Theory*, vol. 6 (2014), pp. 515-535.

6 Johan Bollen *et al.*, 'Happiness is Assortative in Online Social Networks', *Artificial Life*, vol. 17 (2011), pp. 237-251 at p. 248.

7 J. Svensson, 'Power, Identity and Feelings in Late Digital Modernity', in Tova Benski and Eran Fisher (eds), *Internet and Emotions* (Cambridge: Cambridge University Press, 2013), p. 2.

8 Mercer, 'Feeling Like a State', p. 524.

studies going so far as to illustrate how Twitter use is not an appropriate strategy when nations are involved in conflict, because effective diplomacy 'needs to be more "calm"'.[9]

This article provides an initial foray into questions about public diplomacy, social media, emotion and identity. I am not offering a sustained empirical examination of the interactions of these four powerful elements; in such a short piece, it would be impossible to do so. What I seek to establish is how emotion has a role to play in digital diplomacy. We cannot fully understand digital diplomacy without considering the power of emotion in cultivating an identity that underlies public diplomacy. Greater insights into the attraction and pull of current and future disinformation campaigns — as one of the most significant challenges facing public diplomacy — can be found through this focus on emotion.

The article is structured as follows: first, it examines current approaches to emotion and identity in public diplomacy. Emotions matter in world politics, and important insights can be used to understand how this influences public diplomacy and the identity politics imbued in this practice. Second, the article illustrates how emotions are also implicated in practices relating to digital diplomacy as the 'new' public diplomacy. Social media form another key platform through which states can ascertain emotional dynamics projected by their others, and cultivate successful public diplomacy. Third, it explores how digital tools make public diplomacy both easier and harder, in light of increasing levels of digital disinformation. These are emerging yet significant problems facing public diplomacy over the next decade, which are connected to emotional dispositions that make citizens more susceptible to such campaigns.

Emotion, Identity and Public Diplomacy

The purpose of this section is to examine the literature on emotion and identity in public diplomacy, illustrating how these links provide important insights into understanding public diplomacy. While early work on public diplomacy acknowledges the important affective component of propaganda as an influencing mechanism, there nevertheless remains a need to understand how identity and emotion overlap, particularly in light of emerging digital trends in public diplomacy.

Public diplomacy is foremost about building and managing relationships. As a tool of foreign policy, it is centred on diplomatic engagement with other

---

9   Archetti, 'The Impact of New Media on Diplomatic Practice', p. 202.

publics. It is an important aspect of the development of a state's international reputation, used to persuade and influence foreign publics according to the particular agenda of that state. This creation of sympathetic relations is enacted through public diplomacy initiatives that influence foreign publics to be more attuned to, or supportive of, the interests and values held by the state in question, which are in turn defined by the identity of that state.[10] Thus, the power of public diplomacy lies not in its potential material or coercive possibilities, but in how the transmission of ideas, values and interests underpinning state identity are communicated.[11] The attraction of these ideas — what Joseph Nye has classed as 'soft power' — becomes a social mechanism though which foreign publics are persuaded to support particular policies that further enable better cooperation between two states.[12] As Nye maintains, effective soft power is the situation whereby 'one country gets other countries to want what it wants [...] in contrast with the hard or command power of ordering others to do what it wants'.[13] Thus, the legitimacy of foreign policies and the commensurate moral authority they wield correlate strongly with the 'ability to get preferred outcomes through co-optive means of agenda-setting, persuasion and attraction'.[14]

Such acts of persuasion are imbued with identity politics: states employ public diplomacy strategies not only to convince others of a particular policy agenda, but also to persuade them that the identity related to those policies has moral worth and should be recognised in their dealings with others. Public diplomacy, therefore, is a 'sub-phenomenon of foreign policy' that forms an inherent part of the constitution and performance of state identity.[15] Yet in

---

10   Bruce Gregory, 'Public Diplomacy: Sunrise of an Academic Field', *The Annals of the American Academy of Political and Social Science*, vol. 616, no.1 (2008), pp. 274-290; Erik Ringmar, 'Recognition and the Origins of International Society', *Global Discourse*, vol. 4, no. 4 (2014), pp. 446-458.

11   Sarah Ellen Graham, 'Emotion and Public Diplomacy: Dispositions in International Communications, Dialogue and Persuasion', *International Studies Review*, vol. 16, no. 4 (2014), pp. 522-539 at p. 522.

12   Graham, 'Emotion and Public Diplomacy', p. 523; Ty Solomon, 'The Affective Underpinnings of Soft Power', *European Journal of International Relations*, vol. 20, no. 3 (2014), pp. 720-741 at p. 721.

13   Joseph S. Nye Jr, 'Soft Power', *Foreign Policy*, vol. 80 (1990), pp. 153-171 at p. 166; Solomon, 'The Affective Underpinnings of Soft Power', p. 723.

14   Joseph S. Nye Jr, *The Future of Power* (New York, NY: PublicAffairs, 2011), p. 16; Solomon, 'The Affective Underpinnings of Soft Power', p. 723.

15   Rebecca Adler-Nissen and Alexei Tsinovoi, 'International Misrecognition: The Politics of Humour and National Identity in Israel's Public Diplomacy', *European Journal of International Relations*, (January 2018), DOI:1354066117745365, p. 5. See also David

comparison to foreign policy discourses of fear and 'otherness', public diplomacy has long been conceptualised within the context of propaganda, wherein convincing foreign publics of a state's identity and its connected policies follows the logic of winning the 'hearts and minds' of the other population.[16]

An important part of public diplomacy strategies is the crossover of audiences between domestic and foreign publics. While aimed at foreign publics, envisioning a complete separation from the domestic public misunderstands global interconnectedness. Public diplomacy strategies aimed at foreign publics cannot operate in isolation from the domestic constituencies that the public diplomacy seeks to sustain. Thus, public diplomacy strategies often engage with the domestic population as a way forward for building or enhancing aspects of state identity internationally.[17] Consider the Israeli public diplomacy campaign 'Presenting Israel', which used videos and associated social media platforms to mock stereotypes of Israel and Israelis, mobilising 'ordinary Israeli citizens to engage in peer-to-peer public diplomacy when travelling abroad'.[18] Rebecca Adler-Nissen and Alexei Tsinovoi demonstrate that while the campaign was highly contested both within Israel and internationally, it was nevertheless successful and provided a popular domestic focal point for Israeli discourse about state identity politics.[19]

Here we can see the important role that emotion plays not only in the implementation of public diplomacy strategies that aim to allow states to get what they want, but also in terms of identity and belonging. Scholars are increasingly recognising the importance of emotion in world politics.[20] In particular, the attractive and persuasive features of soft power that are intertwined with

---

Campbell, *Writing Security: United States Foreign Policy and the Politics of Identity* (Manchester: Manchester University Press, second edition, 1998).

16 Graham, 'Emotion and Public Diplomacy', p. 524. See also Harold Laswell, *Propaganda Technique in the World War* (Oxford: Knopf, 1927); Adler-Nissen and Tsinovoi, 'International Misrecognition', p. 8.

17 Jan Melissen, 'The New Public Diplomacy: Between Theory and Practice', in Jan Melissen (ed), *The New Public Diplomacy: Soft Power in International Relations* (London: Palgrave Macmillan, 2005), p. 13.

18 Adler-Nissen and Tsinovoi, 'International Misrecognition', p. 1.

19 Adler-Nissen and Tsinovoi, 'International Misrecognition', p. 2.

20 Emma Hutchison, *Affective Communities in World Politics* (Cambridge: Cambridge University Press, 2016); Emma Hutchison and Roland Bleiker, 'Theorizing Emotions in World Politics', *International Theory*, vol. 6 no. 4 (2014), pp. 491-514; Todd H. Hall, *Emotional Diplomacy: Official Emotion on the World Stage* (Ithaca, NY: Cornell University Press, 2015).

public diplomacy are by their very nature emotional dimensions of power.[21] For instance, Philip Seib suggests that public diplomacy is an essential resource precisely because it can reduce enmity between two actors. Although Seib is discussing the role of public diplomacy within counter-terrorism, the point regarding animosity nevertheless reflects the centrality of emotion to shaping the preferences of others and legitimising an actor's point of view.[22] In an increasingly networked world, this legitimisation is conferred by foreign publics' 'acceptance of actors' authority and participat[ion] in the diffusion of communicative power'.[23] Such approval also confers legitimacy on the desired identity that states wish to have recognised by other states and their publics. As public diplomacy is socially and politically constructed through language, we can gain insight into how a state perceives of its interests, precisely because of the interrelation between policy-making and identity.

Yet how might we best conceptualise the role of emotion in public diplomacy? Sarah Ellen Graham argues persuasively that emotion 'shapes the context of communication in global politics', and thus we must be attuned to how this is mobilised.[24] The clearest way forward is by analysing representations employed by states to signify ideational aspects that they wish to have legitimised or taken to be alluring to foreign publics. Taking Craig Hayden's cue regarding the cultivation of qualities of attraction that are communicated through mechanisms of soft power, we can understand that 'attraction is not persuasion per se, but resultant from representation acts that symbolize shared worlds'.[25] How states employ representations to communicate information, including ideas, values and the emotions connected to them, signifies which interests they want supported and the policies they desire to have legitimised.

Social media are thus party to similar representational dynamics that shape public diplomacy and legitimise, or in some cases undermine, state engagement with foreign publics. States engage in public diplomacy using social media to frame representations of identity through emotion. A question arises as to whether digital diplomacy is in fact introducing an alternative to conventional public diplomacy.

---

21 Solomon, 'The Affective Underpinnings of Soft Power', p. 723.

22 Philip Seib, 'Public Diplomacy, New Media, and Counterterrorism', *CDP Perspectives on Public Diplomacy*, vol. 2 (2011); Graham, 'Emotion and Public Diplomacy', p. 523.

23 Graham, 'Emotion and Public Diplomacy', p. 522.

24 Graham, 'Emotion and Public Diplomacy', p. 524.

25 Craig Hayden, *The Rhetoric of Soft Power: Public Diplomacy in Global Contexts* (Lanham, MD: Lexington Books, 2012), p. 45.

Digital Diplomacy and Emotion

This section examines the emerging trend of digital diplomacy, illustrating how social media form another key platform through which states can ascertain emotional dynamics projected by their 'others'. If digital diplomacy is both textual and visual, the combined aesthetics of this practice allow for powerful representations of state identity that attract and persuade foreign publics towards desired state ends. Yet the same factors that can cultivate a successful public diplomacy strategy can also be used to undermine state identity and connected interests.

Digital diplomacy is a 'strategy of managing change through digital tools and virtual collaboration'.[26] Social media platforms such as Twitter, Facebook and Instagram greatly enhance the communicative outreach of public diplomacy strategies, resulting in publics being currently much more informed about foreign policy-making through these online networks. Diplomacy now occurs within a highly mediatised environment: domestic and foreign publics alike can easily discuss policy decision-making because of this speed and diversity of social media.[27] This 'communications revolution' has also positioned public opinion as an even more significant factor for policy-making, largely because of this global audience and its corresponding never-seen-before levels of scrutiny.[28]

The power of social media as part of digital diplomacy therefore arises from the way in which this technology challenges conventional diplomatic practices. For instance, political leaders and policy-makers frequently use Twitter and Facebook alongside formal assemblies, social gatherings and unofficial meetings to broadcast policies as part of a wider attempt to convince foreign audiences about the resoluteness of such decisions. There are two unique aspects of social media that have augmented this change: the public nature of social media posts allows a global public to witness exchanges between political leaders and diplomats, and the speed of social media communication means that there is both much less time to absorb information and a need to respond equally quickly to ensure message dominance.

A curious issue arises here in terms of the scope of public diplomacy initiatives. Public diplomacy is conventionally understood as 'state-based

---

26   Marcus Holmes, 'Digital Diplomacy and International Change Management', in Bjola and Holmes (eds), *Digital Diplomacy*, pp. 23-38 at p. 24.

27   Jan Melissen, *Beyond the New Public Diplomacy*, Clingendael Paper No. 3 (The Hague: Netherlands Institute of International Relations 'Clingendael', 2011).

28   Nicholas J. Cull, 'The Long Road to Public Diplomacy 2.0: The Internet in US Public Diplomacy', *International Studies Review*, vol. 15, no. 1 (2013), pp. 123-139 at pp. 124-125.

communication aimed at influencing well-connected individuals and organizations that are capable of impacting upon a foreign government's policy choices'.[29] Yet the broadening of communication technologies has seen the development of approaches to public diplomacy that are much more inclusive of 'public expectations of openness and engagement'.[30] Public diplomacy strategies utilise social media technologies to facilitate the spread of knowledge about state identity, which in turn furthers state interest.[31] However, whereas previous public diplomacy efforts targeted specific foreign audiences, digital diplomacy strategies cannot be contained to a specific state group, by virtue of the openness of social media. Digital diplomacy allows for parallel strategies that target both foreign and domestic audiences, much in the same way that conventional public diplomacy aims to do. Yet what results is far greater amplification of public diplomacy, wherein the 'contribution of social media publics to the attention paid to a particular object (person, message, idea) by elevating other actors' (citizens, journalists, media platforms) perceptions of the object's worthiness or significance'.[32] Other actors, such as non-governmental organisations, civil-society groups and private companies are therefore more visible as public diplomacy actors than in previous years. The ongoing dispute over the Falkland Islands is a good example of the power of citizen-based public diplomacy. The Falkland Islands government and civil-society groups have harnessed social media in creative practices to command the attention of the international community — particularly the United Kingdom and Argentina — with flash rallies coordinated via Facebook and Twitter counteracting perceived misrepresentations of the Falkland Islands, and videos countermanding dominant Argentinian narratives of history, 'brought alive' and circulated to a global audience via social media platforms.[33]

The mediatisation of diplomacy is thus enabled through a hybrid media system — namely the interconnection between social media and traditional news media — that amplifies public diplomacy messages.[34] Social media

---

29   James Pamment, 'The Mediatization of Diplomacy', *The Hague Journal of Diplomacy*, vol. 9, no. 3 (2014), pp. 253-280 at p. 255.

30   Pamment, 'The Mediatization of Diplomacy', p. 256.

31   Holmes, 'Digital Diplomacy and International Change Management', p. 27.

32   Yini Zhang, Chris Wells, Song Wang and Karl Rohe, 'Attention and Amplification in the Hybrid Media System: The Composition of Donald Trump's Twitter Following during the 2016 Presidential Election', *New Media and Society* (2017), DOI:10.1177/1461444817744390, pp. 1-22 at p. 2.

33   Alasdair Pinkerton and Matt Benwell, 'Rethinking Popular Geopolitics in the Falklands/ Malvinas Sovereignty Dispute', *Political Geography*, vol. 38 (2014), pp. 12-22, p. 18.

34   Zhang *et al.*, 'Attention and Amplification in the Hybrid Media System', p. 3; Pamment, 'The Mediatization of Diplomacy'.

EMOTION AND IDENTITY IN THE PUBLIC REALM

posts, particularly those from Twitter, increasingly form the basis of current news stories. What results is a phenomenon whereby news reports about a particular tweet or Facebook post attain far wider attention, allowing the event or issue to be discussed online and offline by a global public and attract a larger audience. In doing so, this attraction has the possibility of challenging or complicating status-quo diplomatic relations, particularly in terms of representations of identity signifying a strengthening or worsening of relations between states. Even more importantly, this globalised social media–broadcast-media network is instrumental in not just the representation of state identity, but also potentially in inciting emotions related to it. This is a significant issue, as digital diplomacy practices involve a shift from conventional 'monologic' broadcast mechanisms to 'dialogic' communication emphasizing online interaction between diplomatic actors and their audiences.[35]

If text-based social media posts are imbued with emotional resonance, images employed within the digitisation of public diplomacy necessarily add an additional layer of emotional complexity to digital diplomacy. Diplomacy also relies on aesthetics, not just verbal or textual communication. The performance of diplomacy throughout history has been a deeply visual practice, which is evident in the ways in which diplomats dress, greet each other, and cultivate mementos or records of such meetings.[36] Yet the increasing digitisation of diplomacy affords greater opportunities for the use of visuals as part of successful public diplomacy strategies.[37]

One example of the intersection between aesthetics, digitisation and identity in the expansion of opportunities for public diplomacy is exemplified in the highly mediatised official greeting between New Zealand Prime Minister Jacinda Ardern and Queen Elizabeth in London as part of the Commonwealth Summit in April 2018. Ardern represented Maori culture at the highest level of government by wearing a *korowai*, a cloak of woven feathers, over her evening dress. In one of the most circulated social media images of her outfit, Ardern walks alongside her partner; the length and colours of the cloak are in full view against a background of red carpet and footmen. This image is particularly powerful for two reasons: first, for Ardern to

---

35 Ronit Kampf, Ilan Monor and Elad Segev, 'Digital Diplomacy 2.0? A Cross-National Comparison of Public Engagement in Facebook and Twitter', *The Hague Journal of Diplomacy*, vol. 10, no. 4 (2015), pp. 331-362 at p. 332.

36 Costas M. Constantinou, 'Visual Diplomacy: Reflections on Diplomatic Spectacle and Cinematic Thinking', *The Hague Journal of Diplomacy*, vol. 13, no. 1 (2018), pp. 1-23 at p. 3.

37 Constantinou, 'Visual Diplomacy', p. 3.

wear something that is so intrinsically of this place here, and for her to wear it at the event knowing that she would be photographed from every angle, [is a] real acknowledgement of her relationship with the Maori people and with New Zealand.[38]

Second, the photo was taken during the latter stages of Ardern's pregnancy, which is immediately visible in the photograph and challenges gendered expectations of women's roles in the public sphere during this time. Both elements combine to make a powerful visual statement of New Zealand identity — as a nation respectful of its indigenous heritage, while seeking greater domestic social equality — within the formal structure of the governance of empire. The hybridity of the image — a Twitter 'moment' with thousands of likes and retweets that was also circulated via online news media — represented distinct positions on both culture and gender in a very public way.

Overall, digital diplomacy is a highly emotional exercise. Texts and images shared on social media are powerful not only because of the emotions they evoke, but also because they frame representations of identity. The pervasive presence of the smartphone and the connected ease through which social media allow public statements, and photographs or memes, to be posted and shared means that individuals have an incredibly broad audience. Yet herein lies a growing concern for the future of public diplomacy: the role of digital disinformation in the targeting of foreign and domestic publics alike, which social media certainly facilitates.

The Future of Public Diplomacy

We can see how the intersubjective cultivation of emotion and identity is imbued within digital diplomacy in different ways. Yet what might this mean for the future of public diplomacy? The pervasive use of social media platforms has introduced additional complexity to public diplomacy in the form of destabilising effects caused by digital disinformation.

'Fake news' thrives within the digital sphere, and is increasingly difficult to counter. Although digital disinformation — the use of false information as a deliberate act of deception, to purposefully confuse or mislead — circulates primarily online, the wider public is nonetheless exposed to this false

---

38   Donna Campbell, cited in Andreas Illmer, 'Why Ardern's Maori Cloak, Worn to Meet the Queen, Delighted New Zealand', *BBC News* (20 April 2018), available online at http://www.bbc.com/news/world-asia-43833481.

EMOTION AND IDENTITY IN THE PUBLIC REALM

information by virtue of the hybrid media system.[39] As W. Lance Bennett and Steven Livingston have demonstrated, digital disinformation is further facilitated through the use of film that simulates a documentary format, which is easily disseminated across old and new media. This, in part, contributes to 'an "amplifier effect" for stories that would be dismissed as absurd in earlier eras of more effective press gatekeeping'.[40]

Such disinformation campaigns blur the boundaries between propaganda and 'active measures', such that we can understand them as 'digital warfare'.[41] Much like the propaganda warfare of the Cold War, the purpose of digital disinformation campaigns is to target perceived weaknesses in both political alliances and the stability of state identity. For example, citizens of Western liberal democracies are becoming increasingly mistrustful of some of the key institutions that define the social and civil structures of their states, namely the press and political institutions.[42] Russian disinformation campaigns in the United States have deliberately targeted these institutions to exploit purposefully existing political divisions in order to undermine national unity.[43] Similar strategies have been employed against various European states as part of a concerted effort to undermine European political and strategic unity.[44] In combination with these attempts to exploit weaknesses in national and regional unity, Russian digital disinformation campaigns also champion pro-Kremlin ideas and values.

Digital disinformation also relies on the omnipresence of images shared on social media. There is an important disjuncture between curated representations of reality and the idea that 'photographs are really experience captured'.[45]

---

39   Corneliu Bjola and James Pamment, 'Digital Containment: Revisiting Containment Strategy in the Digital Age', *Global Affairs*, vol. 2, no. 2 (2016), pp. 131-142; W. Lance Bennett and Steven Livingston, 'The Disinformation Order: Disruptive Communication and the Decline of Democratic Institutions', *European Journal of Communication*, vol. 33, no. 2 (2018), pp. 122-139; Yevgeniy Golovchenko, Mareike Hartmann and Rebecca Adler-Nissen, 'State, Media and Civil Society in the Information Warfare over Ukraine: Citizen Curators of Digital Disinformation', *International Affairs*, vol. 94, no. 5 (2018), pp. 975-994.

40   Bennett and Livingston, 'The Disinformation Order', p. 124.

41   Golovchenko, Hartmann and Adler-Nissen, 'State, Media and Civil Society in the Information Warfare over Ukraine', p. 976; Martin Kragh and Sebastian Åsberg, 'Russia's Strategy for Influence through Public Diplomacy and Active Measures: The Swedish Case', *Journal of Strategic Studies*, vol. 40, no. 6 (2017), pp. 773-816.

42   Bennett and Livingston, 'The Disinformation Order'; Bjola and Pamment, 'Digital Containment, p. 136.

43   Bennett and Livingston, 'The Disinformation Order'; Bjola and Pamment, 'Digital Containment, p. 136.

44   Bjola and Pamment, 'Digital Containment'.

45   Susan Sontag, *On Photography* (New York, NY: Anchor, 1977).

How the image is produced is at least as important as how it is interpreted and made meaningful by those viewing it, yet it is this interpretation that 'contains values that inevitably have as much to do with the values of the interpreter than the content of the image itself'.[46] Social media images are shared so widely and so quickly that the truthfulness of the circulated visuals is often accepted without further consideration, particularly between users sharing similar political affiliations or positions. A well-known example of disinformation using social-media images are the fake pictures of sharks in the flooded streets of New York and New Jersey following Hurricane Sandy in 2012.[47] A more recent example with far more obvious political motivations was the circulation of a doctored photograph showing Florida school-shooting survivor Emma Gonzalez tearing up the US Constitution, when the original image taken for *Teen Vogue* showed her ripping a gun-target poster in half.

What makes digital disinformation so problematic is the relationship between emotion and identity in these online spaces. Even when digital disinformation is revealed, citizens who believed the story or curated event was truthful in the first instance may still believe it when it is exposed as a falsehood. On the one hand, this is generally reflective of political homophily or 'echo-chamber' reasoning, wherein online networks largely consist of followers with similar political attitudes, identity values or beliefs, and there is a 'backfire effect' when misperceptions are corrected.[48] On the other hand, disinformation can also feel true, particularly if its purpose is to manipulate aspects of state identity and perceived weaknesses in national unity — feeling can then manifest as belief as 'people use emotion as evidence'.[49] For example, when the extent of the Russian disinformation operation and its links to the Trump campaign were revealed in early 2018, followed by the revelations of Cambridge Analytica's activities on Facebook, Trump's support base remained largely unswayed and continued to perceive him as more truthful than the established political elites.[50]

---

46   Roland Bleiker, 'Pluralist Methods for Visual Global Politics', *Millennium*, vol. 43, no. 3 (2015), pp. 872-890 at p. 875.

47   Aditi Gupta *et al.*, 'Faking Sandy: Characterizing and Identifying Fake Images on Twitter During Hurricane Sandy', *Proceedings of the 22nd International Conference on World Wide Web*, held in Rio de Janeiro, Brazil, from 13-17 May 2013 (New York, NY: Association for Computing Machinery (ACM), 2013).

48   Brendan Nyhan and Jason Reifler, 'When Corrections Fail: The Persistence of Political Misperceptions', *Political Behavior*, vol. 32, no. 2 (2010), pp. 303-330.

49   Jonathan Mercer, 'Emotional Beliefs', *International Organization*, vol. 64, no. 1 (2010), pp. 1-31 at p. 20.

50   Matt Apuzzo and Sharon LaFraniere, '13 Russians Indicted as Mueller Reveals Effort to Aid Trump Campaign', *The New York Times* (16 February 2018), available online at https://

EMOTION AND IDENTITY IN THE PUBLIC REALM

Here we can see the relevance of an important but overlooked aspect of digital disinformation: the role of the general public in enabling the spread of such false information, thereby further amplifying its effects. In examining the digital information warfare surrounding the Ukraine crisis and the shooting down of Malaysia Airlines passenger plane MH17 in 2014, Yevgeniy Golovchenko, Mareike Hartmann and Rebecca Adler-Nissen highlight how social media have allowed citizens to move from 'passive audiences to active *curators* of information'.[51] Popular examples of disinformation are often traceable to members of the public or civil-society groups inadvertently creating or sharing false information online.[52] The specific reasons why this occurs are unclear, but this study nonetheless demonstrates that states and state-sponsored groups are not the only key players in spreading disinformation online.

Digital diplomacy allows for powerful representations of state identity that attract and persuade foreign publics towards desired state ends. Yet the same factors that can cultivate a successful public diplomacy strategy can also be used to undermine state interests. Perceptions of truth rely on emotional dispositions, and strategic cultivations of disinformation online can contribute to falsehoods being understood as a true reflection of events.

Conclusion

Digital diplomacy as the 'new' public diplomacy will arguably be a permanent feature of world politics. States will continue to employ social media to pursue their national interests, albeit in full view of a global audience. An important facet of understanding the power of social media in public diplomacy is the role of emotion in digital diplomacy strategies: social media statements can incite strong reactions that have the potential to undermine heretofore positive diplomatic relations, or provide communicative openings that move towards ameliorating crises. Even more so, the spread of digital disinformation online presents political leaders and diplomats with additional complications that cannot be addressed without considering emotions and their role in cultivating state identity. Paying greater attention to the interaction of social media,

---

www.nytimes.com/2018/02/16/us/politics/russians-indicted-mueller-election-interference.html.

51   Golovchenko, Hartmann and Adler-Nissen, 'State, Media and Civil Society in the Information Warfare over Ukraine', p. 981.

52   Golovchenko, Hartmann and Adler-Nissen, 'State, Media and Civil Society in the Information Warfare over Ukraine'.

emotion and identity provides insight into the increasing importance of digital diplomacy and the future challenges that lie ahead.

Constance Duncombe
is a Lecturer in International Relations at Monash University, Australia. Her research interests lie at the intersection of critical and interdisciplinary approaches to global politics. She has published on these themes in the *European Journal of International Relations, International Affairs*, and *Global Change, Peace and Security*. Her book, *Representation, Recognition and Respect in World Politics*, is published by Manchester University Press.

Culture, Cultural Diversity and Humanity-centred Diplomacies

R.S. Zaharna
Global Media Program, School of Communication, American University,
Washington, DC 20016-8017, United States
zaharna@american.edu

Received: 28 June 2018; revised: 26 November 2018; accepted: 18 January 2019

Summary

In contemporary public diplomacy, the idea of culture and nation-state are so intertwined that notions such as 'national culture' that fuel populism or culture as a soft-power resource often go unquestioned. This article critically revisits assumptions of state-centric diplomacy that tie culture to the state. Culture as a domain of the state, which helped carve up the world in the nineteenth and twentieth centuries, has become limiting in a twenty-first-century milieu that is both culturally diverse and interconnected. The article probes the communication dynamics that are untethering culture from the state and giving prominence to forces of increased separation as well as global collaboration, including the phenomenon of humanity-centred diplomacies. Humanity-centred diplomacies' distinguishing features — global consciousness, holistic perspective, cultural diversity and process-orientation — suggest advantages over state-centric diplomacy for leveraging cultural diversity and tackling complex global problems.

Keywords

public diplomacy – culture – state-centric – humanity-centred – cultural diversity

Culture and Public Diplomacy[1]

Is culture destined to be the demon that divides? Samuel Huntington's 'Clash of Civilizations' theory tapped into the widely held assumption that distinct, identifiable cultures not only exist but are inevitably antagonistic. Today, population shifts from the Global South into Europe inspire uncertainty and conflict. Populism rallies around cultural markers to divide 'us' from 'them'. Indeed, real or imagined cultural distinctions bring to the surface questions of identity.

Public diplomacy, as both an instrument of advocacy and relationship-building, would appear to be ideally suited to help mediate cultural divisions. But is it? Despite calls for greater collaboration, is it possible that public diplomacy inadvertently fuels competition?

Consider that still larger problems threaten not just individual states, but the survival of humankind and the planet as a whole. Climate change is but one shared global problem, alongside water scarcity and global pandemics. These issues reflect the growing challenge of complexity in an interconnected world. They have been called 'wickedly complex' as the very act of trying to solve one aspect of the problem creates new problems.[2]

Ironically, the cultural diversity that is fuelling friction may also be the precise antidote for tackling wicked problems. While diversity is often cited as the main source of friction in working groups, as Scott Page wrote in *The Difference*, it is also the well-spring of innovative thinking and creative problem-solving.[3] Among the greatest sources of cognitive diversity — that is, different perspectives, modes of thinking and approaches to problem-solving — is cultural diversity. Tapping into the wealth of cultural diversity is key to unravelling the complexity of wicked problems. The critical challenge, however, as Page noted, was learning how to 'leverage diversity'.

Yet how effective is public diplomacy at leveraging cultural diversity for creative problem-solving? Learning to do so must become a primary goal of public diplomacy as the frequency and intensity of wicked problems grow. Ultimately, the question that faces public diplomacy is this: How do we square

---

1   The author thanks the editors of the vol. 14, nos. 1-2 (2019) special issue of *The Hague Journal of Diplomacy*, Jan Melissen, Jay Wang and Marcus Holmes, as well as Volker Stanzel, Michael Schneider, Natalia Grincheva, Amelia Arsenault, Brian Hughes and Diya Basu, and the anonymous reviewers, for their constructive and encouraging feedback.

2   Horst W.J. Rittel and Melvin Webber, 'Dilemmas in a General Theory of Planning', *Policy Sciences*, vol. 4, no. 2 (June 1973), pp. 155-169.

3   Scott E. Page, *The Difference: How the Power of Diversity Creates Better Groups, Firms, Schools, and Societies* (Princeton, NJ: Princeton University Press, 2008).

the circle and transform culture from a seemingly divisive demon to leveraging cultural diversity to solve complex problems?

Addressing that question is the central goal of this article. Some might argue that such a shift is not possible or even realistic, given what appears to be a stronger trend of resurgent nationalism. I would argue that not only is it possible, but that such a transformation is already well under way in the form of humanity-centred diplomacies. In contrast to state-centric diplomacy, which rests on the projection of a singular 'national culture' in the 'inter-national' system, humanity-centred diplomacies assume cultural diversity to be an inherent feature of humankind and draw upon that diversity to address pressing issues of humankind.

This article critically revisits the underlying assumptions of state-centric public diplomacy that tether culture to the state. As natural as the link between culture and 'national identity' may seem today, that link was forged during the process of state-building only in the nineteenth and twentieth centuries. While the idea of a distinct, separate cultural entity within bounded territory may have been ideally suited for the highly competitive and carved-up world at the time, it has become limiting for public diplomacy in a twenty-first-century milieu that is simultaneously both culturally diverse *and* interconnected.

To explore these ideas, we begin by critically examining how culture became linked to the state, and its role and limitations in state-centric public diplomacy. We then turn to the emerging communication dynamics that are untethering culture from the state and giving prominence to cultural diversity and the distinctive features of humanity-centred diplomacies. The article concludes with thoughts on the trajectory of humanity-centred diplomacies.

Culture and State-centric Diplomacy

In contemporary public diplomacy, the idea of culture and nation-state are so intertwined that notions such as 'national culture' or culture as a soft-power resource often go unquestioned. However, history reveals that such a link was not always so. While the tradition of cultural exchanges in diplomacy among political rulers or dynasties dates back millennia, the idea of linking people to states using culture emerged at a unique juncture in Western history during the eighteenth and nineteenth centuries.

Claiming Culture; Creating Nation-States
If one reflects on the expanse of human history, cultural diversity and cultural exchange were long the norm. Since times of antiquity, cross-fertilisation of

cultural artefacts has led to the enrichment and rejuvenation of societies. And diplomacy, along with trade and religion, played a boundary-spanning role in this cultural transmission. Ancient kings loaded their envoys with cultural treasures, from ivory combs to wild animals to the most precious of gifts, royal brides, as a means of building relations.[4]

While the link between ruling polity, culture and diplomacy enjoys a long and rich tradition, the public was not necessarily part of that mix. Often a ruling dynasty represented the dominant ethnic group, but governed or had protective arrangements over a diverse array of ethnicities. European dynasties in the eighteenth century, for example, were described by Benedict Anderson as 'elephantiasis' for their diversity:

> Romanovs ruled over Tatars and Letts, Germans and Armenians, Russians and Finns. Habsburgs were perched high over Magyars and Croats, Slovaks and Italians, Ukrainians and Austro-Germans. Hanoverians presided over Bengalis and Quebecois, as well as Scots and Irish, English and Welsh.[5]

This mix of religious and ethnic diversity was a distinctive feature of other empires at the time. The Ottoman Empire, for example, spanned from the Balkans in Europe to central Asia, and back across North Africa to the Atlantic. Identities were local and distinct from loyalties to the rulers. Cultural diversity was a given.

We see a series of shifts from the assumption of cultural diversity to cultural unification with the demise of absolute monarchs and the rise of the nation-state and nationalism. Buried in this shift from diplomatic actors working on behalf of absolute monarchs to the nation-state comes implicit ties of culture to state-centric diplomacy.

The Treaty of Westphalia of 1648 laid the foundation for the system of nation-states, each as a separate entity and defined by effective control over a territory and its people. Culture was pivotal in defining this entity and extending its control. Geoffrey Pigman highlights Louis XIV (1643-1715), who reigned during the dawn of the Westphalian era, as a monarch who played a key role in centralizing state power for France.[6] The king sought to embody state

---

4 Amanda H. Podany, *Brotherhood of Kings: How International Relations Shaped the Ancient Near East* (Oxford: Oxford University Press, 2012).

5 Benedict Anderson, *Imagined Communities: Reflections on the Origin and Spread of Nationalism* (London: Verso Books, 2006), p. 83.

6 Geoffrey Pigman, *Contemporary Diplomacy* (Oxford: Polity, 2010), p. 19.

sovereignty, proclaiming *L'Etat, c'est moi* (I am the State). The monarch set the diplomatic course for using culture to define the state:

> The driving force of early diplomacy and conquest by the Kings of France was to establish as *'natural'* and defensible frontiers for France, to create the 'hexagon' within which there could be linguistic, ethnic and political unity. As a result, the linguistic and cultural boundaries of contemporary France very nearly coincide with the political [italics added].[7]

Language played a powerful role 'in the process of cultural unification within the territory of France', according to Dennis Ager.[8] The *Alliance Française* (AF), which is today best recognized for establishing the model of contemporary cultural diplomacy aimed at foreign publics, originally had provincial AF chapters located throughout France's countryside for French-language instruction.[9]

Between 1750 and 1918, historians note a major shift, as traditional empires based on absolute monarchs were dissolving and the lines of modern states were being drawn. We see the rise of nationalism as a powerful force, as the elephantiasis of empires gave way to the need for national unity. Here, diplomacy becomes decidedly state-centric, as representation transfers from the person of the monarch to the sovereignty of the state.

Nationalism, which emerged in Europe and North America during the late eighteenth century, 'was premised on the belief in a world of exclusive nations', according to Anthony Smith. As he relates, 'The basic goals of nationalists everywhere were identical: they sought to unify the nation, to endow it with a distinctive individuality, and make it free and autonomous'.[10]

In the three pillars of nationalism identified by Hutchinson and Smith — 'unity, identity and autonomy' — we see the reinforcing aspect of culture in both defining the identity of the nation and distinguishing it from others: 'The people must be united; they must dissolve all internal divisions; they must be gathered together in a single historic territory [...] and *share a single public culture*' [italics added].[11]

---

7   Dennis Ager, *Francophonie in the 1990s: Problems and Opportunities* (Clevedon: Multilingual Matters, 1996), p. 7.

8   Ager, *Francophonie in the 1990s*, p. 8.

9   Jonathan Gosnell, 'The *Alliance Française*, Empire and America', *French Cultural Studies*, vol. 19, no. 2 (2008), pp. 227-243.

10   Anthony D. Smith, 'National Identity and the Idea of European Unity', *International Affairs*, vol. 68, no. 1 (January 1992), p. 61, available online at https://doi.org/10.2307/2620461.

11   John Hutchinson and Anthony D. Smith, 'Introduction', in John Hutchinson and Anthony D. Smith (eds), *Nationalism* (Oxford: Oxford University Press, 1994), pp. 4-5.

Dissolving internal divisions and creating a single public culture, as many have noted, relied on the creation of national symbols, myths and memories.[12] Despite obvious differences in appearances, 'governments assiduously promoted myths of shared ancestry'.[13] In the forging of a national identity, we see also the subjective sense of a growing 'consciousness of nation' — a 'self-awareness of sameness and commonality [...] and interwoven destinies'.[14]

Nationalism in the Western (Westphalian) context is distinct in that a sense of national identity preceded the formal establishment of state structures of political authority.[15] As a result, nation (identity) and state (political sovereignty) appear to have become conflated in the literature ('nation-state') as well as in public sentiment.[16] Politicians and lay people alike ask, 'Who are we as a nation?'.

Not coincidentally, perhaps, the term 'culture' emerged after the idea of a distinctive national character began to take root. The term culture was introduced in 1871 by the British anthropologist Edward B. Tylor. Tylor equated culture with civilization: 'Culture or civilization is a complex whole which includes knowledge, beliefs, arts, morals, laws, customs, and any other capabilities and habits acquired by [a human] as a member of society'.[17]

Like national borders, this definition of culture suggested something identifiable and static. Despite the reality of constant changes within a society — in almost every aspect of life, from clothes to food to norms — culture 'as a way of life' suggests an entity frozen in time. Such an entity must be preserved, promoted and, if need be, defended.

Public Diplomacy and Culturing State-centric Power

In 1918, as the tumultuous transition period from absolute monarchs to modern states came to a close in Europe, states were poised to take their place in a new era of relations among nations. If culture was politicized to help create the modern nation-state, it was further instrumentalised to project and promote

---

12   Alisher Faizullaev, 'Diplomacy and Symbolism', *The Hague Journal of Diplomacy*, vol. 8, no. 2 (2013), pp. 91-114.

13   Walker Connor, 'When Is a Nation?', in Hutchinson and Smith (eds), *Nationalism*, p. 156.

14   Walker Connor, 'A Nation Is a Nation, Is a State, Is an Ethnic Group, Is A ...', in Hutchinson and Smith (eds), *Nationalism*, p. 329.

15   Mostafa Rejai and Cynthia H. Enloe, 'Nation-States and State-Nations', *International Studies Quarterly*, vol. 13, no. 2 (1969), pp. 140-158.

16   Alisher Faizullaev, 'Diplomacy and Symbolism', *The Hague Journal of Diplomacy*, vol. 8, no. 2 (2013), pp. 91-114; and Jonathan Mercer, 'Feeling like a State: Social Emotion and Identity', *International Theory*, vol. 6, no. 3 (November 2014), pp. 515-535.

17   Edward B. Tylor, *Primitive Culture: Researches into the Development of Mythology, Philosophy, Religion, Art, and Custom* (London: John Murray, 1871), p. 1.

CULTURE, CULTURAL DIVERSITY AND HUMANITY-CENTRED DIPLOMACIES   123

state power in the 'inter-national' system. In all areas of public diplomacy, culture played a pivotal role.

The link between culture and state was foundational to the emergence of cultural diplomacy as a practice by governments of planning cultural programmes in line with broader national interests.[18] France was the first to establish the model for overseas cultural and language training with the *Alliance Française* in 1883. For many colonial powers, establishing cultural institutes was critical to assimilating the populace of colonized territories. As early as the Second World War, countries learned that cultural diplomacy was a valuable tool not only in enhancing their image, but also in wooing people's affection through music and art.[19]

International broadcasting, another early and prominent form of public diplomacy, also drew upon the idea of a national identity by quite literally projecting its voice onto the world stage. The early features and limitations of the twentieth-century mass media ideally reinforced the linking of culture and state. First radio and then television helped to create a 'national' audience, who shared national experiences together and, in the process, further solidified the idea of a shared national identity. The dominant media, or 'mainstream media', as many have noted, both produced and reflected dominant cultural values. The limited geographic reach of these media technologies further reinforced the notion of 'domestic' and 'foreign' audiences of state-sponsored communication.

Not surprisingly, perhaps, when public diplomacy gained prominence in the aftermath of the 9/11 attacks, the link between state and culture was an implicit assumption. Joseph Nye included culture as one of three 'soft power resources' that states can wield as a source of attraction. As Nye explains, 'the soft power of *a country* rests primarily on three resources: *its* culture (in places where it is attractive to others); its political values; and its foreign policies' [italics added].[20] Note the assumption of possession: '*its* culture'. Culture had become the unquestioned domain of the state.

Finally, culture was not just a critical ingredient in *nation-building*; it remains a pivotal component of *nation-branding*. Culture is a key ingredient of

---

18   Richard T. Arndt, *The First Resort of Kings: American Cultural Diplomacy in the Twentieth Century* (Dulles, VA: Potomac Books, new edition 2007).

19   Marina Perez de Acros, 'Intelligence and Cultural Diplomacy at War: The British Council in Spain, 1940-1941', International Studies Association convention, San Francisco (4-7 April 2018).

20   Joseph Nye, *Soft Power: The Means to Success in World Politics* (New York, NY: PublicAffairs, 2008), p. 11.

Simon Anholt's notion of 'competitive identity' among states.[21] Nations highlight distinctive aspects of their culture — such as heritage sites, food, traditions, or even 'our people' — in an effort to distinguish themselves from others.

While the idea of culture as a soft-power resource is appealing, the notion that culture is linked to a defined geopolitical entity, or is something that a state possesses, is worth revisiting.

Limitations of Bounded State-centric Culture

It is in some ways surprising how few have questioned the idea of culture as a domain or power resource of the state. Yet even as states claim culture as their own, culture appears flagrantly oblivious to national boundaries. Where might one draw the boundaries of Arab culture? Or Spanish culture?

If cultures observed physical boundaries, they might more readily resemble the curved silhouettes of human migration and settlement. Or perhaps cultural boundaries would take the shape of the mandala political formations of South and East Asia, where entities were defined by human loyalties to a charismatic ruler at the centre, rather than external boundaries.[22]

The limitations of affixing culture to states may account for some of the paradoxes of contemporary public diplomacy. Despite the professed goals of promoting mutual understanding and enhancing relations, culture in public diplomacy appears to be fuelling inter-state competition. The competition among cultural institutes that emerged during the Second World War has continued, and even intensified,[23] as countries have tried to broaden their reach and impact through networking and creative outreach strategies. From the early days of international broadcasting, countries have competed for listeners, viewers and credibility. That competition has now taken to the digital realm.

The idea of culture as a static, fixed thing fit well *in theory* (if not in reality) with the emerging state-centric, carved-up view of the world at the time. What was designed to appear as 'natural' in the nineteenth or twentieth century has become a liability in the highly interconnected global world of the twenty-first century. The view of culture as something static and tethered to a territory,

---

21 Simon Anholt, *Competitive Identity: The New Brand Management for Nations, Cities and Regions* (Basingstoke: Palgrave Macmillan, 2007).

22 Rosita Dellios, 'Mandala: From Sacred Origins to Sovereign Affairs in Traditional Southeast Asia', Research Paper no. 10, (Robina, QLD: Centre for East-West Cultural and Eco-nomic Studies, Bond University, 2003), available online at http://www.international-relations.com/rp/WBrp10.html.

23 David Carter, 'Living with Instrumentalism: The Academic Commitment to Cultural Diplomacy', *International Journal of Cultural Policy*, vol. 21, no. 4 (8 August 2015), pp. 478-493.

CULTURE, CULTURAL DIVERSITY AND HUMANITY-CENTRED DIPLOMACIES   125

rather than a human dynamic, will grow increasingly anachronistic with the interconnective (as opposed to international) forces of globalization and digital technologies. If culture resists boundaries, it is because people and goods, as carriers of culture, tend to resist boundaries.

Perhaps most disconcerting of all: the limitations inherent in tethering culture to state-centric public diplomacy leave it ill-equipped to address wicked complex problems. Rather than being able to leverage diversity, public diplomacy's state-centric focus may usurp culture for national use. The incentive for cooperating with those who are not like-minded may be perceived as too great a challenge or threatening to national interests. And yet it is precisely this collaboration, the ability to leverage diversity, that is most needed.

Cultural Diversity and Humanity-centred Diplomacies

If culture and people (the carriers of culture) appear oblivious to state boundaries, the open, borderless internet and digital technologies are almost irreverent. Digital technologies, which accord direct interaction among peoples, are untethering both culture and communication as domains that were once largely controlled by the state.

Digital technologies have helped to create a different conceptualization of communication that is based not on separate, individual actors, but on the combined dynamics of interconnectivity and the interactions of a multiplicity of actors. Here we see a qualitative shift from individual state actors, which have for so long dominated the study of diplomacy as statecraft. It is the shift from an individual to a more holistic perspective of an expansive and encompassing communication environment. Because of the global reach of digital technologies, cultural diversity is an inherent part of that communication universe.

This interconnectivity extends beyond state and non-state actors to the general public on social-media platforms. Social media represent new diplomatic spaces, or to use Iver B. Neumann's term, 'diplomatic sites', for public engagement.[24] The more interconnected people become, the greater the potential for direct interaction of diverse cultural perspectives, and the stronger the force towards needed adaptation and realignment. This is not always a welcome turn of events for states or publics. States may resist intrusions, erecting firewalls or even border walls. The public may also respond with resistance to

---

24   Iver B. Neumann, *Diplomatic Sites: A Critical Enquiry* (New York, NY: Oxford University Press, 2013).

diversity and instead seek out like-minded others. The rise of populism and nationalism are symptomatic of such resistance.

If division and polarization are one side of the interconnectivity coin, on the other side we find those who leverage the interactivity and interconnectivity for a more expansive global perspective. Here we see a rise of social entrepreneurs, online petitions and social-media campaigns to increase public awareness and involvement. Alongside networks of outrage, Manuel Castells also observed networks of hope.[25] Akira Iriye documented the steady growth of international collaboration in *Global Community*. As he observed, 'underneath the geopolitical realities defined by sovereign states, the (twentieth) century witnessed a steady growth of another reality — the global (and globalizing) activities by international organizations'.[26] These organizations have grown in number, variety and diversity. Their growth is part of another direction that communication technologies are leading diplomacy. Concurrent with efforts to maintain national separation and cultural divisions, we see growing global collaboration.

Humanity-centred Diplomacies

As different actors interact in the public political arena, we see the growing prominence of what might be called a 'humanity-centred diplomacy'. Humanity-centred diplomacy focuses on the larger goals of humanity and draws upon cultural diversity as the means for pursuing these goals. This phenomenon is not new, but has recently been gaining currency. Several works have used various terms to try and capture this idea of humanity-centred diplomacy — indeed, diplomacies.[27]

---

25   Manuel Castells, *Networks of Outrage and Hope: Social Movements in the Internet Age* (New York, NY: Policy Press, 2012).

26   Akira Iriye, *Global Community: The Role of International Organizations in the Making of the Contemporary World* (Berkeley, CA: University of California Press, 2002), p. 202.

27   Given the global nature of diplomacy, some of the terms used below might not easily translate to capture the meaning or intent. For example, upon reflection all diplomacy is inherently human, at least in the political arena. Sustainability has become associated with corporate social responsibility and environmentalism. Cosmopolitan, while extensively used in the literature, can carry connotations of elitism and, curiously, city diplomacy. The term 'public' can translate into 'people' or 'general', a vagueness that has plagued the concept of 'public diplomacy'. 'Public-centric diplomacy' might also easily cast the public as yet another non-state actor.

CULTURE, CULTURAL DIVERSITY AND HUMANITY-CENTRED DIPLOMACIES   127

Costas Constantinou proposed the idea of 'human diplomacy' and the transformative aspects of diplomacy to humanize the Other.[28] He distinguished between a 'hetero-diplomacy' that differentiates, and 'homo-diplomacy' that searches for commonalities. Writing later with James Der Derian, Constantinou and Der Derian advanced the idea of 'sustainability diplomacy' as a shift in attention from narrow strategic calculations of state power and national interests, which can have disastrous effects on the ground, to a larger view of diplomacy focused on regional or global interest. Constantinou and Der Derian describe sustainability diplomacy as 'peace-preserving and peace-making though not necessarily pacifist'.[29] Cosmopolitan diplomacy, based on values such as tolerance, friendship and respect, similarly resonates with humanity-centred diplomacy.[30]

Public diplomacy scholars are also raising the call for a more humanity-centred public diplomacy. Manuel Castells emphasized that public diplomacy ought to be 'the diplomacy of the public', contrasting private, self-defined interests and values against a shared public interest.[31] Juyan Zhang and Brecken Chinn Swartz suggested the idea of 'public diplomacy for Global Public Goods (GPG)', in order to capture a growing need to address the common goods of humankind.[32] Similarly, Kathy Fitzpatrick proposed 'public diplomacy in the public interest', in response to public diplomacy that is becoming 'more socially-conscious with increased focus on global issues, problem-solving, and shared goals'.[33]

---

28   Costas M. Constantinou, 'Human Diplomacy and Spirituality', Discussion Papers in Diplomacy (The Hague: Netherlands Institute of International Relations 'Clingendael', 2006).

29   Costas M. Constantinou and James Der Derian, 'Introduction: Sustaining Global Hope: Sovereignty, Power and the Transformation of Diplomacy', in Costas M. Constantinou and James Der Derian (eds), *Sustainable Diplomacies*, Studies in Diplomacy and International Relations (London: Palgrave Macmillan, 2010).

30   César Villanueva Rivas, 'Cosmopolitan Constructivism: Mapping a Road to the Future of Cultural and Public Diplomacy', *Public Diplomacy Magazine*, no. 3 (winter 2010), pp. 45-56.

31   Manuel Castells, 'The New Public Sphere: Global Civil Society, Communication Networks, and Global Governance', *The ANNALS of the American Academy of Political and Social Science*, vol. 616, no. 1 (March 2008), pp. 78-93, available online at https://doi .org/10.1177/0002716207311877.

32   Juyan Zhang and Brecken Chinn Swartz, 'Public Diplomacy to Promote Global Public Goods (GPG): Conceptual Expansion, Ethical Grounds, and Rhetoric', *Public Relations Review*, vol. 35, no. 4 (November 2009), pp. 382-387, available online at https://doi.org/16/j. pubrev.2009.08.001.

33   Kathy R. Fitzpatrick, 'Public Diplomacy in the Public Interest', *Journal of Public Interest Communication*, vol. 1, no. 1 (2017), p. 79.

At first glance, structural or tactical differences may appear as the immediate distinction between state-centric and humanity-centred diplomacies. State-centric diplomacy is concerned with individual states within the inter-state system. Humanity-centred diplomacies are focused on humanity, or the global expanse of humankind in its totality. Peering below this surface, however, we find aspects of humanity-centred diplomacies that are distinctive from state-centric diplomacy and which suggest decided advantages for navigating cultural diversity and engaging in complex problem-solving.

First, central to humanity-centred diplomacies is the awareness of being connected to others and feeling part of the larger family of humankind. Akira Iriye called it 'a greater global consciousness [...] that individuals and groups, no matter where they are, share certain interests and concerns'.[34] He pointed to this consciousness as the primary impetus in the steady growth of international organizations working together on shared problems. Costas Constantinou spoke of diplomacy's transformative aspect to find 'the Self in the Other, and the Other in the Self'.[35] This shared human consciousness, not surprisingly, is a concept found across cultural heritages. The feeling of shared humanity underlies the African concept of *ubuntu*: 'one is human through others'. Polynesians express the humanity in family that extends not only to fellow humans but natural elements. Fellow feeling and connection to others is core to Confucius philosophy and the concept of *ren* in guiding relations. Even the origin of the English word 'humanity' echoes a relational affinity: 'humanity' is from the Latin *humanitas* for human nature and kindness. This feeling of emotional connection and global consciousness distinguishes humanity-centred diplomacies from the diplomatic premise of 'national self-awareness' and traditional statecraft that has traditionally privileged rational interests and strategic action.

Second, humanity-centred diplomacies assume a holistic perspective of human and diplomatic relations. Humanity — that is, the totality of humankind together — is 'the fundamental survival unit' and core to diplomatic vision and practice.[36] We see this holistic assumption in Seçkin Barış Gülmez's definition of cosmopolitan diplomacy as going 'beyond national interests and provides the foreign policy-maker with a global geographical focus and an appeal to humanity as a whole'.[37] The holistic perspective assumes complete in-

---

34 Iriye, *Global Community*, p. 8.
35 Constantinou, 'Human Diplomacy and Spirituality'.
36 Rivas, 'Cosmopolitan Constructivism', p. 47.
37 Seçkin Barış Gülmez, 'Cosmopolitan Diplomacy', in Gerard Delanty (ed.), *Routledge International Handbook of Cosmopolitanism Studies* (New York, NY: Routledge, 2018), p. 431.

CULTURE, CULTURAL DIVERSITY AND HUMANITY-CENTRED DIPLOMACIES   129

terconnectivity; no one state can be viewed in isolation from other states or publics. All are part of an interwoven thread of interconnected relations, and the actions of one can ultimately affect all. By contrast, state-centric diplomacy represents an individual-level focus on individual political actors, including their attributes (such as power and interests, etc.) and actions (strategies and approaches, etc.). However, whereas relations may represent a strategic *choice* for states engaged in bilateral or multilateral state-centric diplomacy, relations are an unconditional *given* in humanity-centred diplomacies.

Third, the holistic perspective of humanity-centred diplomacies, by extension, also assumes cultural diversity as a core feature and dynamic of diplomatic vision and practice. Because the relational universe includes all of humanity, by definition, it encompasses the cultural and social perspectives, orientations and traditions of humankind. It is this assumption of diversity that suggests an array of 'diplomacies' rather than one 'diplomacy' that can be compared against others.[38]

Cultural diversity is not just an inherent feature of the relational universe; it is a central dynamic as well. Cultural diversity is key to the synergistic quality often found in humanity-centred diplomacies. Why? Because, given the assumed conditions of interconnectivity and cultural diversity, diplomatic actors must continually adapt and re-adapt to different others (and even different selves). On the negative side, that adaption can result in friction between differing assumptions, experiences or perspectives. Asymmetries of power may prompt efforts to control or dominate competing perspectives. On the positive side, however, the friction of direct interaction can spark an intensive need to learn about — and from — the other in order to reduce tensions. This friction point, where exchanging and engaging in different perspectives, is when leveraging diversity can actually begin to occur.

Fourth, in humanity-centred diplomacies, collaboration and process-orientation necessarily supersede the goal-orientation of state-centric diplomacy. The individual, atomized perspective of state-centric diplomacy makes it possible to assume a goal-orientated posture: the state views itself as a sole actor that singularly defines, pursues and achieves its goal. Humanity-centred diplomacies, on the other hand, because of assumed cultural diversity, recognize that the goals of one actor might not be those of another — or may even be contradictory. Yet because of interconnectivity, the need for collaboration replaces the futility of atomization. As Ali Fisher noted, 'The start and end

---

38   Constantinou and Der Derian (eds), *Sustainable Diplomacies*; and Noé Cornago, *Plural Diplomacies: Normative Predicaments and Functional Imperatives* (Leiden: Martinus Nijhoff, 2013).

point for strategic collaborative public diplomacy is working with, not controlling or even necessarily leading, others'.[39] This point is echoed by Manuel Castells, who speaks of creating a communication space: 'The aim is not to convince but to communicate, not to declare but to listen'.[40] We might also add perspective-taking and empathetic communication, which are inherently part of the process, if they are not yet in the research literature.

Within this process-orientation of humanity-centred diplomacies, two immediate areas appear most pressing. One area, which is related to the need to address wicked global problems such as climate change, is problem-solving. A second area, related to hurdles in problem-solving, is identity mediation. Identity mediation is foundational to the transformative capacity of diplomacy to accommodate perceived differences and to locate commonalities, as Costas Constantinou highlighted.[41]

In an environment that is both interconnected *and* diverse, these features of humanity-centred diplomacies suggest distinctive advantages over state-centric diplomacy in tackling wicked problems.

The distinctive advantages are evident in the different approaches and outcomes of the 2009 and 2016 climate talks. The 2009 climate talks in Copenhagen reflected a dynamic of state-centric diplomacy, played out by atomized competing states (albeit in a multilateral context). Prior to arriving at the summit, actors had separately articulated their positions and goals. The intense negotiations that followed were characterized by Donna Marie Oglesby as a 'competition of ideas' among state and non-state actors.[42] Subsequent efforts to stem unproductive competition entailed compromise and coordination, not collaboration. Oglesby described the failed summit, which resulted in no new treaty, technology, or emissions reductions, as a 'spectacle' of public diplomacy on parade.

By contrast, the Paris climate accord of December 2015 reflected the holistic perspective and global consciousness of humanity-centred diplomacies. The initiative was built upon a foundation of diversity and grew in diversity.[43] A

---

39   Ali Fisher, *Collaborative Public Diplomacy: How Transnational Networks Influenced American Studies in Europe* (New York, NY: Palgrave Macmillan, 2013), p. 202.

40   Castells, 'The New Public Sphere', p. 92.

41   Constantinou, 'Human Diplomacy and Spirituality'.

42   Donna Marie Oglesby, *Spectacle in Copenhagen: Public Diplomacy on Parade* (Los Angeles, CA: Figueroa Press, 2010).

43   Anna Naupa, 'Indo-Pacific Diplomacy: A View from the Pacific Islands', *Politics & Policy*, vol. 45, no. 5 (1 October 2017), pp. 902-917, available at https://doi.org/10.1111/polp.12226; and Timothée Ourbak and Alexandre K. Magnan, 'The Paris Agreement and Climate Change Negotiations: Small Islands, Big Players', *Regional Environmental Change* (15 November 2017), available at https://doi.org/10.1007/s10113-017-1247-9.

CULTURE, CULTURAL DIVERSITY AND HUMANITY-CENTRED DIPLOMACIES   131

coalition of Small Island and Developing States (SIDS), from the Polynesian islands in the Pacific to those in the Caribbean, spearheaded an active initiative to secure the support of larger states. Noteworthy, these areas have traditions reflecting a holistic relational view of the universe. They were aided by civil-society organizations and other public interest groups. They enlisted the support of private corporations and business executives such as Richard Branson, able to supply financial resources and media platforms larger than their own governments. That combination of diversity, sustained interaction, interconnectivity and process-orientation resulted in an accord, adopted by the consensus of 195 parties, to work to limit global warming to well below 2 degrees Celsius.

While our discussion here has contrasted state-centric and humanity-centred diplomacies, it is important to note that one does not necessarily replace the other. Even with the shift from an 'inter-national' system based on separateness to a global arena of interconnectivity, states and state-centric diplomacy will continue to play major roles. As Kathy Fitzpatrick suggested, it may be more advantageous and accurate to see such changes as an expanded perspective of diplomacy.[44] Indeed, that expansion is holistic and global.

Conclusion

In looking ahead, we may speculate on the trajectory of humanity-centred diplomacies. At the moment, the prospects might not look so promising.

As globalization deepens and technological advancements leapfrog, every aspect of people's lives, from communication to finances to education to politics, becomes more interconnected. An accelerated pace of change invites intensified resistance. This is the paradox of 'populism on steroids': the more integrated and interconnected people become, the more vehemently they may resist integration and seek to erect barriers. We might expect such reactions to intensify so long as publics perceive the need to maintain a sense of separate, bounded and singular identity in the face of greater interconnectivity and diversity.

While state-centric and even actor-centric diplomacy may dominate the immediate term, the long-term trajectory favours humanity-centred diplomacies. Humanity-centred diplomacies reflect and align with the trends of a more interconnective, interactive and culturally diverse global political arena. Humanity-centred diplomacies also align with ongoing megatrends in

---

44   Fitzpatrick, 'Public Diplomacy in the Public Interest'.

twenty-first-century communication dynamics that assume interconnectivity *and* diversity. Humanity-centred diplomacies are inherently network-based and collaborative. These characteristics run parallel to social-media platforms and emergent media and thus are likely to have an added advantage.

As globalization intensifies, two main functions of humanity-centred diplomacies are likely to become in higher demand. Greater interconnectivity and interactivity will call on diplomacy's capacity to mediate between identities, finding commonalities among differences. And, as the severity of wicked problems such as climate change increases, collaborative approaches that are inherent in humanity-centred diplomacies will become a pragmatic imperative rather than an idealistic luxury.

If humanity-centred diplomacies appear idealistic or even simplistic, it may be because communication strategies that recognize our complex relational universe are under studied. Holistic and relational approaches are largely viewed through the dominant individualistic lens of communication and appear more altruistic than globally strategic or advantageous. What is desperately needed is more research from a holistic perspective.

Here it is possible to return to our original question: How do we square the circle and transform culture from a seemingly divisive demon to leveraging cultural diversity to solve complex problems? The answer: by expanding the perspective and mission of public diplomacy. Over the past two decades, there has been intensive study of state-centric and actor-centric public diplomacy — how to advance state interests, accrue soft power, enhance images, or differentiate national brands. The same, if not more, intensive study is now needed to explore humanity-centred diplomacies, particularly in the areas of the two vital functions of identity mediation and problem-solving. This article is a call for such research.

Finally, this article is also a call for globalizing public diplomacy. The realization that the link between state and culture was a politically constructed reality raises the possibility of deconstructing that nineteenth-century legacy and cultivating a new, more holistic vision for the twenty-first century. We need to globalize our understanding of diplomacy from a limited, state-centric perspective that focuses on separate, definable and bounded entities, to a global, holistic vision that encompasses humanity at large. This is not about replacing, but expanding our vision. Culture and cultural diversity can play a pivotal role in shifting this perspective, offering a more expansive, global vision of diplomacy, and even diplomacies in the plural. Squaring the circle of culture-as-demon to cultural-diversity-as-saviour is the promise of humanity-centred diplomacies, and for globalizing the field of public diplomacy.

R.S. Zaharna

is Professor of Public Communication and Director of the Global Media Program at the School of Communication, American University, in Washington, DC, as well as a Faculty Fellow with the Center on Public Diplomacy at the University of Southern California. She received the 2018 Distinguished Scholar Award in International Communication from the International Studies Association. Her books include: *Battles to Bridges: US Strategic Communication and Public Diplomacy after 9/11* (New York, NY: Palgrave Macmillan, 2010); *The Cultural Awakening in Public Diplomacy* (Los Angeles, CA: Figueroa Press, 2012); (co-edited with Amelia Arsenault and Ali Fisher) *The Connective Mindshift: Relational, Networked and Collaborative Approaches to Public Diplomacy* (London: Routledge, 2013); and *Globalizing Public Diplomacy* (Oxford: Oxford University Press, forthcoming).

Public Diplomacy and Hostile Nations

Geoffrey Wiseman
Asia–Pacific College of Diplomacy, Australian National University, Acton,
ACT 2601, Australia
geoffrey.wiseman@anu.edu.au

Received: 28 June 2018; revised: 24 October 2018; accepted: 12 December 2018

Summary

This article considers public diplomacy's future through the prism of public diplomacy between hostile nations. It first sketches democracies' past and present use of public diplomacy in hostile relations with non-democracies. It then discusses five particular challenges for democracies in their future thinking about the public diplomacy–hostile nations' nexus. These challenges are: accounting for public diplomacy's theoretical significance in hostile relations; deciding between isolating or engaging adversaries; avoiding the stigma of propaganda; managing democratic expectations; and settling on an appropriate role for governments. Democratic countries' responses to these challenges will impact public diplomacy's future, notably regarding its effectiveness in relation to hostile nations. The article concludes that public diplomacy is not a panacea for easing hostile bilateral relations. However, it is one of many elements that a judicious government can use — drawing on four ideal-type variants of public diplomacy — in order to improve relations with an adversarial state.

Keywords

public diplomacy – definitions of public diplomacy – hostile relations – hostile nations – adversarial states – engagement – polylateralism – omnilateralism

© KONINKLIJKE BRILL NV, LEIDEN, 2019 | DOI:10.1163/9789004410824_011

Introduction[1]

The purpose of this article is to consider public diplomacy's future, as seen through the prism of public diplomacy between hostile nations. The focus is on democratic states in hostile, or adversarial, relations with non-democratic states. In such adversarial diplomatic relationships, democracies have essentially two strategic policy choices: whether to isolate or engage the adversary. Accepting that binary choice for analytical purposes, the article first sketches democracies' past and present use of public diplomacy in hostile relations with non-democracies. The article then speculates on the future of public diplomacy between hostile states, identifying and discussing five particular challenges that democracies will need to address concerning their public diplomacy approach towards non-democratic adversaries. These challenges are: (1) evaluating public diplomacy's wider theoretical, or strategic, relevance; (2) mitigating the isolate-or-engage dilemma; (3) avoiding the stigma of propaganda; (4) managing rising democratic expectations; and (5) settling on a role for governments in public diplomacy.

In the context of growing scholarly and policy interest in public diplomacy and its associated concepts,[2] I offer several working hypotheses about democracies' use of public diplomacy towards states with which they are in hostile, or adversarial, relations:

– That diplomatic engagement is generally more effective than isolation.
– That good public diplomacy cannot compensate for bad foreign policy.
– That a democracy's image or brand must closely resemble reality.
– That democracies' public diplomacy towards adversaries, even the more odious ones, should not be seen as a one-way monologue, but as a mutual, long-term dialogue of some kind.

---

1   This was the central theme of Geoffrey Wiseman (ed.), *Isolate or Engage: Adversarial States, US Foreign Policy and Public Diplomacy* (Stanford, CA: Stanford University Press, 2015). I draw on this book below. See also Mel Gurtov, *Engaging Adversaries: Peacemaking and Diplomacy in the Human Interest* (Lanham, MD: Rowman & Littlefield, 2018); Jeffrey R. Fields, 'Engaging Adversaries: Myths and Realities in American Foreign Policy', *Diplomacy & Statecraft*, vol. 26, no. 2 (June 2015), pp. 294-321; Miroslav Nincic, *Renegade Regimes: Confronting Deviant Behavior in World Politics* (New York, NY: Columbia University Press, 2005).

2   Jan Melissen, 'Public Diplomacy', in Pauline Kerr and Geoffrey Wiseman (eds), *Diplomacy in a Globalizing World: Theories and Practices* (New York, NY: Oxford University Press, 2nd edition 2018), pp. 200-202.

- That four ideal-type variants, or definitions, of public diplomacy can be identified, each offering varying utility in dealing with hostile relations: (1) a narrow *traditional foreign ministry to foreign public* approach; (2) a *whole-of-government* approach; (3) a *new public diplomacy* approach; and (4) a *people-to-people* (P2P) approach.[3]

These working hypotheses about the public diplomacy–hostile nations' nexus underpin the analysis that follows. While I draw on my previous work on the United States' (US) public diplomacy towards adversarial states, I also refer here to non-US examples. For manageability, I focus, first, on bilateral, or dyadic/binary, relationships, steering clear of other hostile configurations such as 'deadly triangles'.[4] Second, as already noted, my analysis and case selection is based on the public diplomacy of democratic states in hostile relations with non-democratic states, an approach that arguably fits theoretically within democratic peace theory. And, third, I am considering the use of public diplomacy in the sense that a democratic actor is seeking to influence foreign publics in a hostile state with the strategic objective of *regime behaviour change* (incentivizing an adversarial government to engage more cooperatively) and not with the strategic objective of *regime change* (ousting an adversarial government from power).

Democracies' Use of Public Diplomacy in Hostile Relations: Past and Present

Public diplomacy — traditionally seen as the purposive efforts of states to influence foreign publics — is only one instrument that democratic states can use to influence publics in non-democratic states that they view as hostile, or adversarial. Other instruments include coercive measures short of war, such as economic sanctions, assertive military exercises, deception, covert action and espionage.[5] As discussed further below, public diplomacy — which on most accounts in democracies implies open-source, fact-based efforts to influence foreign publics — should eschew such 'dark arts', aiming instead to engage foreign publics openly and transparently. So how have democratic

---

3   This framework is advanced in Wiseman, *Isolate or Engage*, see pp. 12-13 and 298-299.

4   Michael A. Allen, Sam R. Bell and K. Chad Clay, 'Deadly Triangles: The Implications of Regional Competition on Interactions in Asymmetric Dyads', *Foreign Policy Analysis*, vol. 14, no. 2 (April 2018), pp. 169-190.

5   Jennifer Sims, 'Diplomacy and Intelligence', in Kerr and Wiseman, *Diplomacy in a Globalizing World*, pp. 244-261.

nations attempted to influence and engage with publics in non-democratic adversarial states?

An important consideration for public diplomacy is whether or not the two adversaries (one democratic, the other not) exchange reciprocal diplomatic relations, usually manifested in the form of diplomatic missions — typically embassies in each other's capital city and consulates in non-capital cities. Where embassies are not present, public diplomacy efforts have until fairly recently been limited to, for example, international broadcasting. Where embassies are present in respective hostile-state capitals, there is clearly an institutional basis from which to operationalize public diplomacy programmes. Assessments are mixed about the effectiveness of public diplomacy activities at diplomatic missions in an adversary's capital. Historically, evidence from memoirs shows that some ambassadors and senior diplomats who are resident in a hostile capital intuitively recognize their public diplomacy roles and do what they can under tight constraints. Most famously and consequentially, in the early post-Second World War Soviet Union, George Kennan, as *chargé d'affaires* at the United States' Moscow Embassy, was able to base his 'Long Telegram' on a distinction he made between the 'paranoid' *leaders* of the Soviet Union and the *Russian people*, a distinction he could likely not have made had he been reporting from outside the country. Similarly, in the waning years of the Cold War, the US Ambassador to Russia, the 'peripatetic' Jack Matlock, engaged effectively with both influential and ordinary Soviet citizens, which informed his reporting to Washington about the Soviet decline.[6] In the past, creative ambassadors such as Jack Matlock thus used *themselves* as public diplomacy instruments.

In 2012, US Ambassador to Libya Christopher Stevens adopted a similar approach, with tragic consequences, leading to his death at the hands of militants in the Libyan city of Benghazi, an event that captured worldwide attention and pointed to an emerging reality: that diplomats trained and socialized to conduct traditional official-to-official diplomacy are likely to be called upon — increasingly, at some risk — to venture out from behind the embassy walls and to engage face to face with non-official interlocutors, rather than leaving public outreach functions to their specialist public-diplomacy colleagues. Today, most (effective) ambassadors and diplomats of all ranks and streams see themselves in this light. Increasingly, public diplomacy is less and less seen as a specialized

---

6   Robert English, 'Soviet Union/Russia: US Diplomacy with the Russian "Adversary"', in Wiseman, *Isolate or Engage*, pp. 35, 43; see also Jack F. Matlock Jr, *Autopsy on an Empire: The American Ambassador's Account of the Collapse of the Soviet Union* (New York, NY: Random House, 1995).

category of diplomatic practice (as remains the case formally in the US Foreign Service). As Bruce Gregory has argued persuasively, public diplomacy's future emerges as an integral, almost taken-for-granted dimension of diplomacy as a whole.[7] This view conceptualizes Jan Melissen's earlier observation that public diplomacy has progressively become 'woven into the fabric of mainstream diplomatic activity'.[8]

When hostile states are in — or moving towards — diplomatic relations, educational, scientific, cultural and sports exchanges are often used as front-line public-diplomacy instruments. The American Fulbright scholarship programme has acquired worldwide respectability.[9] During the latter years of the Cold War, Pugwash conferences brought nuclear scientists together from the former Soviet Union and the United States, producing ideas that helped to bring the Cold War to an end.[10] Ping-pong diplomacy famously enabled the United States' opening with China in the early 1970s. And baseball greased the wheels of normalization of diplomatic relations between the United States and Cuba in the final years of the Obama administration.[11]

While such lower-level contacts can form a web of relationships enabling normalization of relations between hostile nations, high-level visits, such as President Nixon's to China in 1972 and Deng Xiaoping's US tour in 1979, can lead to high-profile, high-stakes opportunities for public diplomacy. A high-level visit often gives a leader an opportunity to communicate with the adversarial state's public, either directly or through symbolic activities (such as attending sporting or cultural events to show respect for the other country's culture). These visits can lead to the forming of friendships between leaders

---

7 Bruce Gregory, 'Mapping Boundaries in Diplomacy's Public Dimension', *The Hague Journal of Diplomacy*, vol. 11, no. 1 (2016), pp. 1-25.

8 Jan Melissen, 'The New Public Diplomacy: Between Theory and Practice', in Jan Melissen, *The New Public Diplomacy: Soft Power in International Relations* (Basingstoke: Palgrave Macmillan, 2005), p. 11. For even more recent evidence that the public diplomacy examples set by Kennan and Matlock are now the rule, see Michael McFaul, *From Cold War to Hot Peace: An American Ambassador to Putin's Russia* (Boston, MA: Houghton Mifflin Harcourt, 2018).

9 Nancy Snow, 'International Exchanges and the US Image' in Geoffrey Cowan and Nicholas J. Cull (eds), *Public Diplomacy in a Changing World*, special issue of *The Annals of the American Academy of Political and Social Science,* vol. 616 (March 2008), pp. 198-222.

10 Geoffrey Wiseman, *Concepts of Non-Provocative Defence: Ideas and Practices in International Security* (Basingstoke: Palgrave Macmillan, 2002), pp. 93-94. On the soft-power and public-diplomacy value of military exchanges, see Carol Atkinson, *Military Soft Power: Public Diplomacy through Military Education Exchanges* (Lanham, MD: Rowman & Littlefield, 2014).

11 Peter C. Bjarkman, 'Stalled US–Cuba Détente and the Uncertain Future of Cuba's National Pastime', *Public Diplomacy Magazine*, vol. 17 (winter/spring 2017), pp. 37-43.

PUBLIC DIPLOMACY AND HOSTILE NATIONS

that can aid diplomacy, as mentioned above, and may go some way in 'de-demonizing' leaders, a good example being Deng's visit. But summits can also go wrong, embarrassing the host, as when Soviet leader Mikhail Gorbachev arrived for his May 1989 summit with Deng Xiaoping just as tens of thousands of protesters assembled in Tiananmen Square in support of Gorbachev's liberal reforms in the USSR.[12]

Libya's Muammar Gaddafi was adept at global grandstanding, while Cuba's Fidel Castro made brash use of the United Nations General Assembly to reach international audiences. Hugo Chávez of Venezuela was an effective, if petulant, master of this personalized form of public diplomacy, by seizing the world stage for short periods, and not always with favourable results for his country. Still, the general lesson here is that charismatic, authoritarian leaders in adversarial relations with democracies, from Castro to Chavez, have cleverly pitched their public diplomacy in ways that seek to influence not only publics in countries that they consider hostile to them, but to global opinion as well.

In a 2016 article about the public-diplomacy dimension of summitry between adversaries, Zohar Kampf suggests that world leaders are increasingly bypassing their own national diplomatic systems and appealing directly to foreign audiences, as a complement to direct dialogue with their foreign-leader counterpart — with the aim of influencing the adversary's public. Kampf describes such moves as a 'rhetorical bypass'.[13] For Kampf, political leaders seek to 'warm the hearts' of, or 'instil fear' in, the foreign audience. A good example of the former was Egyptian President Anwar Sadat's visit to Jerusalem in 1977, when he aimed to undercut Israel's enemy narrative by directly engaging with the Israeli people in a speech filled with hope to Israel's Knesset that was broadcast live.[14] In contrast, Kampf argues, Israeli Prime Minister Benjamin Netanyahu has publicly disputed Iranian President Hassan Rouhani's diplomatic efforts to negotiate the 2015 Iran nuclear deal, appealing to the American public to reconsider the true intentions behind Rouhani's 'charm offensive', and warning that faith in the Iranian leader's efforts will inevitably lead to the construction of weapons used against them. Volatile personal Twitter exchanges between US President Trump and North Korea's leader Kim Jong-un in 2018 underscored the risks involved in rhetorical by-passing. Yet subsequent Twitter

---

12   David Hastings Dunn and Richard Lock-Pullan, 'Diplomatic Summitry', in Costas M. Constantinou, Pauline Kerr and Paul Sharp (eds), *The Sage Handbook on Diplomacy* (Los Angeles, CA: SAGE, 2016), p. 236.

13   Zohar Kampf, 'Rhetorical Bypasses: Connecting with the Hearts and Minds of People on the Opponent's Side', *Journal of Multicultural Discourses*, vol. 11, no. 2 (2016), p. 151.

14   Kampf, 'Rhetorical Bypasses', p. 158.

comments by Trump praising Kim point to the potential benefits of rhetorical by-passing. Either way, new technologies portend a likely future involving elite one-on-one public-diplomacy exchanges between leaders of states in an adversarial relationship: the antithesis of a grass roots, people-to-people (P2P) approach.[15]

Track-two initiatives — that is, informal interactions involving non-officials and/or officials acting in a personal capacity — provide an avenue of contact with adversarial states, while keeping some distance in order to float new ideas. These initiatives have the advantage over strictly non-governmental-based public diplomacy in that they involve participants close to governments on both sides of a hostile relationship. They have been used with varying degrees of success in the US–China and the US–Iran cases. In the hard cases, such as US–North Korea relations, track-two efforts have met with only limited success.[16]

Beyond government supported track-one and track-two initiatives, non-governmental organizations (NGOs) have been and remain an important means of contact with hostile or inhospitable foreign publics. The North Korea case illustrates how difficult it is for NGOs to engage with publics, even on a limited basis, in closed societies. Russia's attempts to rein in American foundations and think tanks operating in Russia under Vladimir Putin underscore the limits on non-governmental actors' ability to mitigate public hostility in an adversary state. Clearly, any future shift towards a more NGO-based public diplomacy should avoid romanticizing NGOs and their ability to affect other

---

15   Matt Stevens, 'Trump and Kim Jong-un, and the Names They've Called Each Other', *The New York Times* (9 March 2018), available online at https://www.nytimes.com/2018/03/09/world/asia/trump-kim-jong-un.html (accessed 5 June 2018).

16   Scott Snyder, 'North Korea: Engaging a Hermit Adversarial State', in Wiseman, *Isolate or Engage*, pp. 85-109. Selig S. Harrison, a journalist who covered Asian affairs for *The Washington Post* and later worked as a think-tank scholar and advocate of engagement with North Korea, made eleven trips over four decades as a rare guest of the country's regime; see Emily Langer, 'Selig Harrison, Reporter and Scholar Who Covered — and Shaped — Asian Affairs, Dies at 89', *The Washington Post* (6 January 2017), available online at https://www.washingtonpost.com/national/selig-harrison-reporter-and-scholar-who-covered--and-shaped--asian-affairs-dies-at-89/2017/01/06/5d6b45f6-d425-11e6-9cb0-54ab630851e8_story.html (accessed 5 June 2018). Highly publicized visits to Pyongyang by former American professional basketball star Dennis Rodman were not generally seen as serious public diplomacy, but arguably they humanized Kim Jong-un to some extent and were an expression, if idiosyncratic, of US soft power; see Caitlin McDevitt, 'Rodman: Kim Jong Un is "a Good Dad"', *Politico* (9 September 2013), available online at https://www.politico.com/blogs/click/2013/09/rodman-kim-jong-un-is-a-good-dad-172118 (accessed 5 June 2018).

PUBLIC DIPLOMACY AND HOSTILE NATIONS

states' governments or publics.[17] Tourism and business contacts can be an indirect avenue for public diplomacy with hostile nations. In the case of Cuba, US tourism to the island arguably helped to spread American values and culture. In the case of Hugo Chavez's Venezuela, US oil workers arguably created personal relationships between the two countries, despite strained relations between the two governments.[18]

Scholars have also influenced public-diplomacy efforts in hostile nations. They can provide information back home about an adversarial state, and their work sometimes feeds back to the adversarial state, potentially influencing events there. In the Soviet case, Robert Tucker's insights on Stalin (written at Princeton University) played a role in glasnost-era reconsiderations of the Soviet past.[19]

Cultural exchanges — books, television, music, art, theatre, fashion and movies — are widely thought by public-diplomacy practitioners and scholars to play a positive role in how democratic countries are perceived by an adversarial state's public. In the US case, it often (but not always) helps that American culture has been pervasive worldwide, even in states that are hostile to the United States.[20] Yet, as argued below, culture can only take matters so far in the absence of formal diplomatic relations. As Suzanne Maloney has observed in the US–Iran case, public diplomacy can support efforts to overcome decades of mutual animosity, but 'it cannot supplant the vital role of formal diplomatic engagement between governments for handling crises and thorny security dilemmas'.[21]

While a case can be made that public diplomacy's impact must be assessed within a broader and ever-expanding spectrum of cultural — or soft-power — interaction, even where direct, official contacts remain constrained or even non-existent, some scholars are not convinced that such programmes are consequential. For example, Robert M. Entman advocates 'mediated public

---

17   Samy Cohen, *The Resilience of the State: Democracy and the Challenges of Globalization*. Translated by Jonathan Derrick (Boulder, CO: Lynne Rienner, 2006). See also Sidney Tarrow, *The New Transnational Activism* (Cambridge: Cambridge University Press, 2005).

18   William M. LeoGrande, 'Cuba: Public Diplomacy as a Battle of Ideas', in Wiseman, *Isolate or Engage*, pp. 231-258; and Michael Shifter, 'Venezuela: The United States and Venezuela: Managing a Schizophrenic Relationship', in Wiseman, *Isolate or Engage*, pp. 259-279. See also Michael J. Bustamante and Julia E. Sweig, 'Buena Vista Solidarity and the Axis of Aid: Cuban and Venezuelan Public Diplomacy', in Cowan and Cull (eds), *Public Diplomacy in a Changing World*, pp. 223-256.

19   English, 'Soviet Union/Russia', in Wiseman (ed.), *Isolate or Engage*, p. 37 and pp. 44-45.

20   Simon Anholt, *Brand America* (London: Marshall Cavendish, 2010).

21   Suzanne Maloney, 'Iran: Public Diplomacy in a Vacuum', in Wiseman (ed.), *Isolate or Engage*, p. 200.

diplomacy', an approach that places less emphasis on citizen-to-citizen activities and more on actions designed to shape elite opinion.[22] Guy J. Golan's mediated public-diplomacy approach builds on his view that 'America's rivals actively use their broadcasting channels to frame and interpret American culture, political values and policy according to their own political interests' and that the United States is being 'defined by others'.[23] As with Entman, Golan is more sceptical of social media's potential to influence unfriendly foreign publics. Rather, he sees international broadcasting as a more effective tool. Thus, democratic states with sufficient resources can use (revamped) traditional mass communication methods to influence public opinion in adversarial states.[24] Others argue that Voice of America has in fact successfully reinvented itself as a multi-media broadcasting organization with a variety of streaming audio, video and social media platforms in languages such as Mandarin. Still others stress how Russia has poured resources into its Russia Today (RT) network and China into the Xinhua News Agency.[25] Yet most international broadcasters now self-identify as global media organizations and avoid the term *broadcasting*. Golan and Entman's scepticism about the potential of social media as a tool to influence unfriendly publics may have merit, but their apparent bright-line distinction between social media and international broadcasting seems increasingly problematic.[26]

Overall, many ambassadors, public-diplomacy practitioners and scholars have generally embraced internet-based platforms such as Twitter and Facebook as new frontline tools in their public diplomacy arsenal. However, their effectiveness in hostile-nation contexts remains contested, as argued by the mediated public-diplomacy advocates. Much depends on how well the adversarial government is able to limit its citizens' access to the internet

---

22   Robert M. Entman, 'Theorizing Mediated Public Diplomacy: The US Case', *Press/Politics*, vol. 13, no. 2 (April 2008), p. 89.

23   Guy J. Golan, 'The Case for Mediated Public Diplomacy', *Diplomatic Courier* (19 July 2013), available at https://www.diplomaticourier.com/2013/07/19/the-case-for-mediated-public-diplomacy-2 (accessed 29 May 2018).

24   For a compelling argument about how inadequate government funding for international broadcasting limits one democracy's soft power–public diplomacy efforts, including how to compete *inter alia* with Chinese activities in South-East Asia and the South Pacific, see Graeme Dobell, Geoff Heriot and Jemima Garrett, *Hard News and Free Media as the Sharp Edge of Australian Soft Power*, Strategy Paper (Barton, ACT: Australian Strategic Policy Institute (ASPI), September 2018).

25   See, for example, Zhuqing Cheng, Guy J. Golan and Spiro Kiousis, 'The Second-Level Agenda-Building Function of the Xinhua News Agency', *Journalism Practice*, vol. 10, no. 6 (2016), pp. 744-762.

26   I am grateful to a reviewer for this insight.

PUBLIC DIPLOMACY AND HOSTILE NATIONS   143

and those who take advantage of such access may be singled out as dissidents and punished.[27] If the past has been characterized by a generally optimistic public-diplomacy view about social media's potential for democratic change in authoritarian states, the future could well see the pendulum swing in a pessimistic direction — given mounting revelations about business malpractice by social-media giant Facebook and others, such as the disgraced political data firm Cambridge Analytica, and in view of widespread manipulation of social media by individuals and governments.[28]

The Future of Public Diplomacy between Hostile Nations

Building on the above account of the past and present, what challenges can we expect to impact public diplomacy's future in democracies? Generally, the forces of globalization, the shifting balance of power between major states and between states and non-state actors, and revolutionary advances in communications technology will shape that future.[29] In particular, I see five challenges for democratic public diplomacy in relation to their non-democratic adversaries.

The Theory Challenge

In the landmark 2008 special issue of *The Annals* on public diplomacy, Bruce Gregory enquired whether public diplomacy was an academic field.[30] Contemporaneously, Robert Entman argued that 'the field of public diplomacy has lacked frameworks to guide research and practice'.[31] In the years since, scholarly literature on public diplomacy has proliferated impressively. Does considered thinking about the public diplomacy–hostile nations nexus help resolve such theoretical challenges as those raised by Gregory and by Entman?

My two contentions about public diplomacy's theory challenge are: (a) that public diplomacy is not currently a theory (and therefore not an academic

---

27   Alec Ross, 'Digital Diplomacy and US Foreign Policy', in Paul Sharp and Geoffrey Wiseman (eds), *American Diplomacy* (Leiden: Martinus Nijhoff, 2012), pp. 217-221.

28   For an account of how an authoritarian government manipulates Twitter, see Katie Benner, Mark Mazzetti, Ben Hubbard and Mike Isaac, 'Saudis' Image-Makers: A Troll Army and a Twitter Insider', *The New York Times* (20 October 2018).

29   For an account of these trends, see Philip Seib, *The Future of Diplomacy* (Cambridge: Polity, 2016).

30   Bruce Gregory, 'Public Diplomacy: Sunrise of an Academic Field', in Cowan and Cull (eds), *Public Diplomacy in a Changing World*, pp. 223-256.

31   Entman, 'Theorizing Mediated Public Diplomacy', p. 87.

field), but rather a practice; and (b) that public diplomacy is a key instrument of soft power. The first contention — that public diplomacy is not a theory — begs the question whether diplomacy more broadly is a theory? I think it is on the general grounds that the systematic study of diplomacy helps us describe, explain and predict a great deal about how world politics function. Moreover, in terms of normative theory, diplomacy is clearly prescriptive in the sense that it provides rules of the road for how international conflict can be managed.[32]

Even if seen as a practice rather than a theory, public diplomacy scholarship — multi-disciplinary and practice-based — contributes to theorizing in many ways. For example, public diplomacy speaks directly to theories of influence.[33] A strong theoretical trend in the literature is that public diplomacy should be seen less in *monologic* (one-sided) terms and more in *dialogic* (two-sided) terms.[34] Applying this to dyadic adversarial relationships, both sides are attempting to influence the other's public. As discussed further below, democracy-based programmes fall prey to the belief that democracy is a one-way street: 'we' influence 'them' to be more democratic. In contrast, in post-modernist theorizing, democracies define their own identity, the national 'self', in relation to the adversarial, foreign 'other,' rather than in relation to international friends and allies. This 'self-imaging' was most dramatically on display throughout the Cold War, when the democratic United States pitted itself against the totalitarian Soviet Union in a process that can be called 'other-imaging'. This self–other identity formation can be detected today, for example, *vis-à-vis* China, Iran, Syria, Cuba and North Korea.[35] In constructivist theory, what this means is that official diplomats and programmes do not simply represent a set of fixed national interests and a fixed, say, American national identity to its adversaries. Rather, diplomats reproduce and reconstitute an American identity and culture that is dynamic and ever changing. Thus, every act of diplomacy in general and public diplomacy specifically is not simply an act of representation, but also one of identity formation. Accordingly,

---

32   For a persuasive argument on how diplomacy and diplomats contribute to a theory of international relations, see Paul Sharp, *Diplomatic Theory of International Relations* (Cambridge: Cambridge University Press, 2009).

33   For a useful recent analysis of power, see Darren J. Lim and Victor A. Ferguson, 'Power in Australian Foreign Policy', *Australian Journal of International Affairs,* vol. 72, no. 4 (2018), pp. 306-313.

34   Geoffrey Cowan and Amelia Arsenault, 'Moving from Monologue to Dialogue to Collaboration: The Three Layers of Public Diplomacy', in Cowan and Cull (eds), *Public Diplomacy in a Changing World,* pp. 10-30.

35   Rebecca Adler-Nissen, 'Stigma Management in International Relations: Transgressive Identities, Norms, and Order in International Society', *International Organization,* vol. 68 (winter 2014), pp. 143-176.

democratic public-diplomacy practices directed at adversarial states are not solely representations of, say, the United States; they are also identity formations of the United States in which the very opposition with the 'other' has an effect back on the 'self'. In other words, public diplomacy must be seen to promote the interests of the democratic state concerned *and* the adversarial state or it will fail. Public diplomacy is conducted with the adversary rather than against it.[36] Thus, a democracy's public diplomacy must be seen to promote the interests of the adversarial state — and especially its citizens — as well. The 'practice turn' in International Relations adds further support to this argument.[37]

My second contention — that public diplomacy is an instrument of soft power — risks implying that public diplomacy is an instrument of soft power only. Soft power itself is not a theory — in the sense noted above, that it cannot describe, explain and predict — but it is more than a strategic policy concept, such as containment and détente. Perhaps it is best characterized as an analytical category of power. Governments and other governance actors certainly do wield soft power through public diplomacy. Moreover, public diplomacy is also an instrument of hard power. It can be a force multiplier of hard power; for example, by generating support for military alliances, encouraging states to remain neutral in wartime, or leveraging public support for military exchanges and economic assistance.

In sum, theorizing about public diplomacy — without insisting that it is a separate field that acknowledges diplomacy as the 'master institution' (to borrow Martin Wight's famous phrase),[38] that draws on emerging practice theory, and that builds on current identity and relational research — can gain real purchase by focusing more than it has in the past on public diplomacy between hostile nations.[39]

---

36 This argument resonates with earlier international-security concepts, such as the 'security dilemma' and 'common security', both of which dealt with how leaders need to take account of the adversary's security interests; see Geoffrey Wiseman, *Concepts of Non-Provocative Defence: Ideas and Practices in International Security* (Basingstoke: Palgrave Macmillan, 2002), pp. 52-53 and 88.

37 Ole Jacob Sending, Vincent Pouliot and Iver B. Neumann (eds), *Diplomacy: The Making of World Politics* (Cambridge: Cambridge University Press, 2015); see also Geoffrey Wiseman, 'Diplomatic Practices at the United Nations', *Cooperation and Conflict*, vol. 50, no. 3 (2015), pp. 316-333.

38 Martin Wight, *Power Politics* (Harmondsworth: Penguin, 1986), p. 113.

39 R.S. Zaharna, Amelia Arsenault and Ali Fisher (eds), *Relational, Networked, and Collaborative Approaches to Public Diplomacy: The Connective Mindshift* (New York, NY: Routledge, 2013); Linwan Wu, 'Relationship Building in Nation Branding: The Central

The Diplomatic-Representation Challenge

Democratic governments have to decide whether to isolate or engage their non-democratic, adversarial rivals. In such hostile bilateral relationships, are democratic-country public-diplomacy efforts — designed to improve relations rather than dislodge a regime — helped when both rivals have diplomatic representation in each other's capitals? As noted above, the historical evidence is mixed. On the one hand, relations between the United States and China and between the United States and Russia have waxed and waned even with the presence of American embassies in Moscow and Beijing.

On the other hand, the more diplomatically isolated an adversarial state (consider China under Mao, North Korea since the 1950s and Iran since 1979), the harder it is to conduct almost any form of public diplomacy, since contact, which is essential to public diplomacy, is severely limited. The European view has been that on-the-ground public diplomacy is more likely to be effective than over-the-horizon radio, television and new-media programming. Cutting diplomatic ties with an adversary for extended periods (the American view) leads to a lack of communication and information, which can produce and exacerbate stereotypes and biases that distort a relationship, as well as lead to increased hostility. Moreover, the absence of diplomatic representation forces both sides to signal their views via public media (as with the Trump–Kim Twitter exchanges described above), but this is risky and is arguably more about sending messages to adversarial governments than to adversarial publics. The hostile Turkey–Armenia relationship lingers at least in part because of the lack of formal diplomatic relations.[40] And US–Vietnam relations seem to have improved since the establishment of full diplomatic relations in the mid-1990s and the arrival of Pete Peterson, a former Vietnam War prisoner of war, as the United States' first ambassador.

The Propaganda Challenge

For democracies, the propaganda challenge is how they overcome the lingering suspicion that, in Geoffrey Berridge's sharp observation, public diplomacy 'is simply propaganda rebranded'.[41] Ever since Edmund Gullion coined public diplomacy as a useful euphemism in 1965, Berridge argues that '"[P]ublic diplomacy" is what we call our propaganda; "propaganda" is what the other side

---

Role of Nation Brand Commitment', *Place Branding and Public Diplomacy*, vol. 13, no. 1 (February 2017), pp. 65-80.

40 Mehmet Sinan Birdal, 'The Closing of the Opening: The AKP's Armenian Policy', *Public Diplomacy Magazine*, vol. 17 (winter/spring 2017), pp. 51-56.

41 Geoffrey Berridge, *Diplomacy: Theory and Practice* (Basingstoke: Palgrave Macmillan, 5th edition 2015), p. 200.

PUBLIC DIPLOMACY AND HOSTILE NATIONS 147

does'. For Berridge, 'Makers of propaganda have traditionally distinguished between white propaganda — the former admitting, but the latter concealing, its source. "Public diplomacy" is the modern name for white propaganda directed chiefly at foreign publics'.[42] Moreover, as I have argued elsewhere, democratic foreign ministries and related public-diplomacy partners fail to see how their adversaries can see their own benign public-diplomacy efforts as propaganda.[43] Thus, authoritarian states such as Russia, China, Iran, Cuba and Venezuela see US public diplomacy as malignant and offensive and their own activities as benign or defensive. There is something to Berridge's complaint. In the past fifteen years, public diplomacy scholarship and practice in democracies has generally separated itself conceptually from the penumbra of propaganda, with conceptual assists from concepts such as soft power and nation branding. In their enthusiasm to promote public diplomacy, some advocates have let non-democratic countries such as China off the propaganda hook by allowing assertive public diplomacy, branding and soft power to be described in relatively benign terms. On this view, many public-diplomacy advocates have unwittingly provided conceptual cover for China to present its rise as merely an expression of soft power and deft public diplomacy rather than realpolitik or geopolitics.[44] The emergence of the 'sharp power' concept — just as China moves more assertive internationally, for example with its aggressive efforts to militarize the South China Sea — may prove to be a much-needed corrective.[45]

As coined by Christopher Walker and Jessica Ludwig, sharp power is the idea that countries such as Russia and China manipulate open political and digital-information environments in democracies. They contrast sharp-power techniques of distraction and manipulation with soft-power techniques of attraction and persuasion, urging more assertive responses by democracies.[46] In response, Joseph Nye warns against overreaction to sharp power, arguing that while Russian and Chinese 'information warfare' is real, sharp power is in fact a form of hard power. Nye warns that democracies should not imitate such

---

42   Berridge, *Diplomacy*, pp. 208 and 198.

43   Wiseman, *Isolate or Engage*, pp. 287, 288 and 294.

44   Robert Ross, 'China: American Public Diplomacy and US–China Relations, 1949-2012', in Wiseman, *Isolate or Engage*, pp. 59-84.

45   Falk Hartig, 'How China Understands Public Diplomacy: The Importance of National Image for National Interests', *International Studies Review*, vol. 18, no. 4 (December 2016), pp. 655-680.

46   Christopher Walker and Jessica Ludwig, 'The Meaning of Sharp Power: How Authoritarian States Project Influence', *Foreign Affairs* (16 November 2017), available online at https://www.foreignaffairs.com/articles/china/2017-11-16/meaning-sharp-power (accessed 29 May 2018).

methods, as that would undercut the advantages that arise from soft power.[47] Sharp power's implications should not be under-estimated, as alleged Russian interference in the Brexit campaign and in the 2016 US presidential elections suggest and as public concerns grow about Chinese interference in other democracies, such as Australia. Democracies need to respond to misinformation and to misrepresentations of their policies by non-democracies, while prudently heeding Nye's warning. It is worth considering whether Nye's reduction of 'sharp power' to a form of hard power is too restrictive and whether it might better be understood as a form of hard power combined with soft power? Moreover, it remains to be seen whether 'sharp power' will usefully be added to the power lexicon as an analytically distinct subset of hard power, or an unnecessary addition to his 'hard', 'soft' and 'smart'-power categories.[48]

These qualifications notwithstanding, current concerns about sharp power imply that future intellectual and policy interest in public diplomacy is best encapsulated under soft power as the best strategic-policy framework for how countries can better seek to influence publics in hostile states.[49] The challenge, and my concluding point, is that debates about the future of public diplomacy will need to revisit — critically — the concept's moorings in propaganda and to devote considerable reflection on definitions and concepts of power that swirl around diplomacy and soft power.[50]

The Rising-Expectations' Challenge

Related, and in some tension with the propaganda challenge, is a widely held assumption in many democracies that public-diplomacy practices will help to bring about a future world order with democracies ascendant. Part of the reason for these rising expectations is that citizens in democracies in general and Americans in particular — especially since the end of the Cold War, the demise of the communist governments in Eastern Europe and the 2011-2012 'Arab

---

47   Joseph Nye, 'How Sharp Power Threatens Soft Power: The Right and Wrong Ways to Respond to Authoritarian Influence', *Foreign Affairs* (24 January 2018), available online at https://www.foreignaffairs.com/articles/china/2018-01-24/how-sharp-power-threatens-soft-power (accessed 29 May 2018).

48   I am indebted to a reviewer for these points.

49   In Australia, for example, the renaming of the Department of Foreign Affairs and Trade's Public Diplomacy, Communications and Scholarships Division to the Soft Power, Communications and Scholarships Division — thus widening the Division's scope so that soft power is now seen as the wider concept that includes public diplomacy — reflects this trend. On the soft power–public diplomacy nexus, see, for example, Caitlin Byrne, 'Introduction to the Special Issue: Recasting Soft Power for the Indo-Pacific', *Politics & Policy*, vol. 45, no. 5 (October 2017), pp. 685-704.

50   Discussion in this paragraph owes much to insightful queries from a reviewer.

Uprising' — put great faith in the power of popular demonstrations against totalitarian and authoritarian governments. When this faith is added to the belief that the internet is making communication easier and control of information more difficult, the result can be a perception that public diplomacy and the spread of democratic values are unstoppable. However, reliance on public diplomacy as a central instrument — for example, of US policy for influencing Iran, North Korea, Cuba, or other relatively closed, adversarial states — fails to consider what is a serious disconnect between (strategic) objectives and (instrumental) capabilities. Overcoming decades of animosity and resolving profound differences on urgent security issues, such as the nuclear ambitions of Iran and North Korea and sharp ideological differences with Cuba, require a much broader mobilization of diplomatic instruments and resources than public diplomacy has to offer. Nonetheless, public diplomacy can support such efforts in various ways, but their impact should not be over-stated. For example, the P5+1[51] nuclear agreement with Iran in 2015 demonstrated strong evidence of US whole-of-government diplomacy, in which teams led by the US Secretaries of State and Energy negotiated an agreement in partnership with other countries that combined hard and soft-power tools, secret bargaining and some public diplomacy. The United States' opening to Cuba late in President Obama's second term resulted from more than a year of secret negotiations by a White House national security staffer and a US Foreign Service officer working with Holy See diplomats.[52] As for US–North Korea negotiations over North Korea's nuclear programme begun under President Trump, they reveal little public diplomacy — and little spread of democratic values. As argued above, public leader-to-leader interactions can change quickly, especially when unpredictable individuals are involved, and again without much of a role for traditional public diplomacy. Moreover, as also argued above, high-level contact must be buttressed in the long term by formal diplomatic engagement between the two governments.

The Role of Governments' Challenge

A fifth challenge for public diplomacy's future between hostile nations is determining whether a democratic government's links to public diplomacy activities is an advantage or disadvantage.

---

51   P5+1 refers to the United Nations Security Council's permanent five members (China, France, Russia, the United Kingdom and the United States) plus Germany.

52   William M. LeoGrande and Peter Kornbluh, *Back Channel to Cuba* (Chapel Hill, NC: University of North Carolina Press, 2015), epilogue at pp. 418-453.

As foreshadowed above, democratic governments in adversarial relations will need minimally to balance judiciously four public diplomacy variants: (1) a narrow 'traditional government to foreign public' approach, which focuses on a country's foreign ministry and embassies; (2) a 'whole of government to foreign public approach', which involves many government departments and agencies; (3) a 'new public diplomacy' approach, conducted by both governmental and non-governmental actors; and (4) a 'people-to-people' (P2P), 'citizens diplomacy' or 'whole-of-society' approach, in which publics engage directly with other publics.[53] This is, of course, an ideal-type analytical framework, and the four approaches are not mutually exclusive. But the framework allows us to consider better the options and their likely consequences. The key is to recognize when each approach — or combination of them — will be most effective in engaging with a hostile adversary's public.

The traditional, foreign-ministry-based variant (1) and the increasingly accepted whole-of-government variant (2) still fall under the 'mediated public diplomacy' rubric (generally state-based and shorter term).

The state–non-state, multi-actor variant (3) is more 'unmediated' (less statist and longer term) than the ministry of foreign affairs and whole-of-government variants. Building on state-centric notions of *bilateral* and *multilateral* diplomacy, I have promoted the idea of *polylateral* diplomacy as diplomacy's third dimension — a term that characterizes relations between state and non-state actors.[54] Among many issues for future research and discussion is the extent to which non-governmental actors participate as independent diplomatic actors (arguably some now do) or as partners, collaborators, or co-opted agents with governmental actors.[55]

Category (4) in my ideal-type framework, the P2P-based approach, is more 'unmediated' than the other three variants, the most non-state based and the longest term. However, this category seems highly problematic as a public diplomacy category. Thus, as Bruce Gregory has argued, the P2P variety sits more easily with cross-cultural internationalism — the sweeping flow of cross-border connections that exist apart from diplomacy. Unless there is some connection with governments, however direct or indirect, this P2P approach puts the analyst on a slippery slope to the view that all cross-border connections

---

53 A well-known exposition of this view is Manuel Castells, 'The New Public Sphere: Global Civil Society, Communications Networks, and Global Governance', in Cowan and Cull (eds), *Public Diplomacy in a Changing World*, pp. 78-93.

54 Geoffrey Wiseman, '"Polylateralism": Diplomacy's Third Dimension', *Public Diplomacy Magazine* (summer 2010), pp. 24-39.

55 For earlier work, see Shamima Ahmed and David M. Potter, *NGOs in International Politics* (Bloomfield, CT: Kumarian Press, 2006), pp. 57-74.

between people are public diplomacy.[56] This conceptual conundrum notwithstanding, the silver lining is that it is now possible to consider diplomacy's future as having a fully developed fourth, 'omnilateral' dimension — which, building on my third-dimension definition, I would define as *the conduct of relations between at least two non-state entities, with a modicum of international standing, in which there is a reasonable expectation of systematic relationships, involving some form of reporting, communication, negotiation and representation, but not involving mutual recognition as sovereign, equivalent entities.*[57]

While there is some way to go to elaborate diplomacy's omnilateral dimension, the best short-term conceptual future for public diplomacy is conveyed in Gregory's idea that the 'public diplomacy' concept should be replaced in favour of 'diplomacy's public dimension'.[58] Gregory wisely puts the diplomacy horse before the public diplomacy cart.[59] Accordingly, all diplomats have a public role, not only those who are assigned to the public diplomacy division in the ministry at home and to the relevant section at a diplomatic mission abroad. In this view, traditional diplomats still play a role. US diplomats in China point to how they facilitate engagement of US private-sector and civil-society actors — US city mayors, state governors, business executives and others — seeking access in China. And Chinese officials often turn to US embassies and consulates for advice on possible partners in the United States. Public diplomacy is indeed woven into the fabric of mainstream diplomatic activity, and this trend is likely to continue.[60]

The challenge for democratic governments seeking to influence foreign publics in adversarial states, then, is to find ways to reconcile the need for government strategies and programmes, on the one hand, with the view that non-governmental, arms-length strategies are the most effective. The

---

56 Gregory, 'Mapping Boundaries in Diplomacy's Public Dimension', pp. 20-23. Gregory argues that scholars and practitioners benefit from mapping boundaries, however porous, between category domains. See also Wiseman, *Isolate or Engage*, pp. 298-299.

57 My thinking here owes much to the ground-breaking work of Costas Constantinou; see, for example, Costas M. Constantinou, 'Between Statecraft and Humanism: Diplomacy and its Forms of Knowledge', *International Studies Review*, vol. 15 (2013), pp. 141-162. Immanuel Kant used the term 'omnilateral' in a broad sense to refer to the will of all individuals. In diplomacy, Adam Watson used it more narrowly to describe 'quasi-parliamentary conferences', such as the UN General Assembly; see Adam Watson, *The Dialogue between States* (New York, NY: Routledge, 2004), p. 151.

58 Gregory, 'Mapping Boundaries in Diplomacy's Public Dimension'.

59 For a contrary view that public diplomacy should be treated as a separate field of study, see Kadir Jun Ayhan, 'The Boundaries of Public Diplomacy and Non-State Actors: A Taxonomy of Perspectives', *International Studies Perspectives* (2018), pp. 1-21.

60 With thanks to a reviewer for clarifying this point.

soft power–public diplomacy nexus points to a possible reconciliation. Soft power — in its indirect *affective* rather than its direct *normative* forms — is creatively ambiguous and could be seen as having P2P connotations, while public diplomacy programmes are more directly seen to be connected to governments. Given a general preference for P2P approaches with little or no governmental involvement, the dilemma for public diplomacy advocates is that they may need to relinquish the term 'public diplomacy' to describe their favoured option, or move to the view that diplomacy at large has a fourth, people-to-people, dimension.

Conclusion

This analysis suggests a useful, if constrained, role for public diplomacy in resolving hostile relations between adversarial states in the years ahead. While the record is mixed, on balance, mutual diplomatic relations lessen these constraints, which in turn increases the prospect of relations improving between bitter rivals. However, any expectation that public diplomacy can change an adversarial state's behaviour in the short term is bound to be disappointed; it is only over the long term that public diplomacy can greatly aid the normalization of state-to-state relations and state–society relations. This long-term condition underscores the difficulty of evaluating public diplomacy's influence, a notoriously difficult task even under 'normal' diplomatic circumstances.[61] Under 'adversarial' circumstances, evaluating public diplomacy becomes considerably more difficult.

Public diplomacy is not a panacea for easing hostile bilateral relations. However, it is one of many elements that a judicious democratic government can use — or better yet, as I have suggested, allow to occur — in order to improve relations with an adversarial state. Ideally, I foresee a more people-based, rather than a more state-based, future for public diplomacy, in which governments enable exchange-like programmes and then step back and let their citizens do the rest over the long term.[62] In other words, there are grounds for reversing the order of my four ideal-types so that the new order of priority would be: (1) people-to-people; (2) new public diplomacy; (3) whole-of-government; and (4) traditional foreign-ministry public diplomacy.

---

61   Pierre C. Pahlavi, 'Evaluating Public Diplomacy Programmes', *The Hague Journal of Diplomacy*, vol. 2, no. 3 (2007), pp. 255-281.

62   A good example is the Australian international student mobility New Colombo Plan.

Notwithstanding the considerable literature that is critical of soft power as a concept and analytical tool,[63] I see the balance of academic and policy interest shifting towards wider acceptance of soft power as a compromise, strategic-policy concept and public diplomacy as a key governmental instrument along with others. Smart power is arguably facile as a synthesis of hard and soft power, but it has intuitive appeal. Still other questions remain as to where public diplomacy fits as a multiplier of hard power. Sharp power poses genuine intellectual and policy challenges. I suspect that the sharp-power challenge in particular will shift the policy and scholarly debate from a generally optimistic view of soft power and public diplomacy's potential to a more pessimistic view of the genuine threats emanating from hostile, authoritarian adversaries. In that future context, I concur with Joseph Nye that democracies should avoid the temptation to employ sharp power of their own, as such an approach would undermine a democracy's massive normative soft-power advantage.

In sum, public diplomacy will enjoy a brighter future to the extent that those who think about it and those who practise it embrace the idea of diplomacy's public dimension, resisting the epistemic temptation to consolidate public diplomacy as a separate field and set of practices and situating their valuable work under broader conceptions of diplomacy.[64]

Geoffrey Wiseman

is Professor and Director of the Asia–Pacific College of Diplomacy at the Australian National University. He has worked at the Ford Foundation, the University of Southern California and in the Strategic Planning Unit of the Executive Office of the United Nations Secretary-General. He is a former Australian foreign service officer, serving in three diplomatic postings (Stockholm, Hanoi and Brussels) and as private secretary to the Australian foreign minister. With Pauline Kerr, he co-edited *Diplomacy in a Globalizing World: Theories and Practices* (Oxford: Oxford University Press, 2018).

---

63 See, for example, Craig Hayden, *The Rhetoric of Soft Power: Public Diplomacy in Global Contexts* (Lanham, MD: Lexington Press, 2012), especially chapter 2 on 'Evaluating Soft Power'.

64 Acknowledgements: I am indebted to the editors of this special issue for their adroit guidance and also to the anonymous reviewers for excellent, detailed comments on a draft. I also wish to thank Lachlan King for his research assistance.

US Public Diplomacy and the Terrorism Challenge

Philip Seib
School for Communication and Journalism, USC Annenberg, Los Angeles,
CA 90089-0281, United States
seib@usc.edu

Received: 27 June 2018; revised: 9 September 2018; accepted: 31 October 2018

Summary

Public diplomacy can be one element of multifaceted counter-terrorism strategy, but to be successful it must be used in timely fashion as a preventive tool. One key to reducing the threat posed by terrorism is to turn off terror groups' recruiting faucets, and public diplomacy can play an important role in doing this. This article explores the vulnerability of certain populations and how they might be reached and strengthened in ways that undercut terrorist recruitment. This includes recognizing the importance of religion in terrorist recruiting and how it may be addressed constructively. Further, traditional pubic diplomacy programmes such as educational and cultural exchanges have been underestimated as a mean of counteracting the 'othering' that increases vulnerable populations' susceptibility to terrorist recruitment.

Keywords

public diplomacy – terrorism – counter-terrorism – Islam – economic development – social media

Introduction

During the past decade, the most noted defeats inflicted on terrorist organizations have been through conventional military action, with some other (less acclaimed) successes by law enforcement agencies and the intelligence community. The 2011 US Special Operations' attack in Abbottabad, Pakistan, which killed Osama bin Laden, and the lengthy 2016-2017 siege of Mosul, Iraq, which deprived (the self-proclaimed) Islamic State of one of its strongholds were different in scale but similar in being *post facto* responses to terrorist acts.

© KONINKLIJKE BRILL NV, LEIDEN, 2019 | DOI:10.1163/9789004410824_012

US PUBLIC DIPLOMACY AND THE TERRORISM CHALLENGE   155

Preventive measures to disrupt terrorist operations have fared less well, in part because no government has yet designed a comprehensive counter-terrorism strategy that consistently prevents, rather than retaliates for, extremist violence. After five years of fighting in Iraq, the US military recognized that its counter-insurgency strategy needed to be adjusted. The new doctrine, as articulated by General David Petraeus, included points that could be useful in 'soft' counter-terrorism measures. Petraeus wrote:

> We cannot kill our way out of this endeavour. [...] Realize that we are in a struggle for legitimacy that will be won or lost in the perception of the Iraqi people. [...] Develop and sustain a narrative that works, and continually drive the themes home through all forms of media.[1]

When the point is reached at which conventional military force must be relied upon as the principal counter-terrorism strategy, efforts to contain terrorist recruitment and activity will already have failed. This is in large part because of policy-makers' reflexive embrace of traditional military action when faced with a dangerous enemy, which makes sense when an enemy commits itself to conventional battleground tactics, but such terrorist behaviour is an aberration. Most terrorist organizations' leaders understand that they will be fatally overmatched when following such a course. They know that to survive requires two basic measures: minimize exposure to kinetic counter-terrorism operations; and recruit followers in large enough numbers to replace losses and expand influence.

Addressing the former measure is largely the business of the military, intelligence and law enforcement communities. For the latter, public diplomacy can play a useful, albeit not exclusive, role. Responding to terrorism requires comprehensiveness and diverse tactics. Just as an Iraqi battlefield may be the site of part of this response, so too may a London school classroom be an appropriate venue for efforts to undercut the appeal of extremism. (Note that the latter approach draws its share of criticism, particularly from those who consider such efforts as easily slipping into fostering ethnic or religious profiling.)[2]

---

1   David H. Petraeus, 'Multi-National Force–Iraq Commanders' Counterinsurgency Guidance', *Military Review* (September-October 2008), pp. 2 and 4.
2   Kimiko de Freytas-Tamura, 'British Efforts to Identify Potential Radicals Spurs Debate Over Profiling', *The New York Times* (9 February 2016).

Is terrorism prevention an appropriate public diplomacy task? Can public diplomacy be an effective part of larger counter-terrorism strategy? If not, why not? Assuming that public diplomacy is defined as advancing national interests through outreach to foreign publics, this would seem to be a perfectly acceptable assignment. In this instance, the national interest is clear — preventing terrorism. Foreign publics, with assistance, may become more effective in adjusting their socio-political environments in ways that make them less hospitable to extremism.

As for these efforts needing to be strategic rather than merely tactical, counter-terrorism is not a boxing match, so more must be involved than punch and counter-punch. Messaging should be based on a carefully considered set of premises that involve more than preventive persuasion, but rather are built upon a commitment to strengthen civil-society institutions that by their existence will help create an environment in which violent extremism would have difficulty in gaining a foothold.

This strategy is related to the larger issue of redefining and expanding the role of public diplomacy within the spectrum of foreign affairs. Before the early years of this century, most people around the world had only a tenuous grasp of global affairs, because information flows were narrow in scope and limited in diversity of viewpoints. Diplomacy was the domain of an elite corps of professional diplomats, such as Britain's Harold Nicolson, who soon after the end of the Second World War wrote:

> There was a feeling that foreign affairs were a specialized and esoteric study, the secrets of which lay beyond the scope of the ordinary layman's experience or judgment. [...] In the days of the old diplomacy, it would have been regarded as an act of unthinkable vulgarity to appeal to the common people upon any issue of international policy.[3]

Today, such an observation is quaintly unrealistic because 'the common people' — now more politely referred to as 'the public' — may choose from among an almost unlimited array of information resources that are accessible on one's mobile phone with a tap and glance. Given that global publics can, in many cases, now become as engaged with the larger world as they choose to be, appealing to them has become not an 'act of unthinkable vulgarity', but rather a political necessity.

Necessary it may be, but appealing to global publics is today a highly competitive matter. Being heard above the cacophony of countless media venues

---

3   Harold Nicolson, *Diplomacy* (London: Oxford University Press, second edition 1950), pp. 10, 168.

and then, once heard, being convincing is a far more complex task that it was during the days of more hegemonic international communication. Hence, if the expanded relevance of public diplomacy is recognized, it is logical that public-diplomacy tools and tactics be used widely by governments' foreign-policy agencies, including those that are tasked with counter-terrorism.

Targeting Terrorist Recruitment

Daniel Byman noted that:

> There is no consistent path to radicalization. Some recruits are motivated by the killing of Muslims in wars, while others recoil at discrimination. Some are socially alienated, while others simply seek the thrill of blowing stuff up and killing people.[4]

Terrorist organizations such as the Islamic State recruit in various ways. Family connections have proved successful, such as cousin recruiting cousin; so have face-to-face contacts, in home and diasporic communities. Perhaps the most secure and broadest recruitment efforts have been through social media venues, although this approach most likely inspires activism by 'recruiting' independent operators rather than enlisting active participants in a terrorist group's core organization. As J.M. Berger, Mia Bloom and others have noted, Islamic State operatives have devoted considerable effort to courting prospective recruits one-on-one online.[5] Again, public diplomacy's role in countering such ventures is to help make the recruiting grounds inhospitable for extremist recruiters.

Terrorist Messaging

How to go about this? For a start, take ideas from the extremists' playbook; mimic their messaging formats to deliver the flipside of their content. When terrorist sites show 'infidels' murdered in purported *jihad,* the counter-message should present photographic evidence of the Muslims killed in terror attacks

---

4 Daniel Byman, *Al Qaeda, the Islamic State, and the Global Jihadist Movement* (New York, NY: Oxford University Press, 2015), p. 219.

5 J.M. Berger, 'Tailored Online Interventions: The Islamic State's Recruitment Strategy', *Combating Terrorism Center Sentinel,* vol. 8, no. 10 (October 2015), available online at https://ctc.usma.edu/tailored-online-interventions-the-islamic-states-recruitment-strategy/; Mia Bloom, 'Constructing Expertise: Terrorist Recruitment and "Talent-Spotting" in the PIRA, Al Qaeda, and ISIS', *Studies in Conflict and Terrorism,* vol. 40, no. 7 (2017), available online at https://www.tandfonline.com/doi/abs/10.1080/1057610X.2016.1237219.

and the impact of these deaths on the victims' families, and so on. Designing such content must be done with care — many in this audience are wary about outside intervention — and it must be delivered promptly, forcefully and consistently. The communicators of Islamic State, Al Qaeda, Al Shabaab and other such groups are skilful opportunists. They must be outmanoeuvred at their own game.

In this context, the terrorist paradigm (for the moment) is Islamic State (IS). Despite its significant defeats in Mosul, Raqqa and elsewhere, Islamic State's media versatility between 2014 and 2017 was impressive. IS techies proved themselves to be energetic, creating an array of new media baubles: smartphone apps; multilingual videos; a radio station (*Al Bayan*); *jihadist* chants (*nasheeds*); an online magazine (*Dabiq*); and even video games. It also has its own news agency, *Amaq*, which it uses to send news releases with headings such as 'Breaking News' and 'Exclusive', often first doing so in English when seeking broad international coverage.[6]

The diverse IS media repertoire is evidence of the rapidly growing sophistication of terrorist media capabilities. Just a decade before the explosive presence of IS was recognized, Al Qaeda was content to make videotapes through its *As Sahab* production facility and send them to television channels such as Al Jazeera in hopes that edited versions would be broadcast. Al Qaeda also worked online, producing an online magazine, *Voice of Jihad* (*Sawt al-Jihadi*) and training manuals such as *Technical Mujahid Magazine*, which emphasized cybersecurity as well as calling on 'Muslim internet professionals to spread and disseminate news and information about the *Jihad* through e-mail lists, discussion groups, and their own websites'.[7]

International broadcasting has long been one of the core elements of public diplomacy, featuring the likes of Voice of America and Radio Free Asia. Today, such broadcasting enterprises remain important, but they account for a considerably smaller portion of the global communication universe.

Socio-economic Issues

It is important to understand these and similar terrorist communication capabilities in order to counter them effectively. It is also necessary to recognize conditions that may contribute to young people's susceptibility to terrorist recruitment. After the 2011 Arab uprisings, Tunisia was touted as the country most likely to build on its nascent democratic reforms, but Tunisia sent more

---

6   Philip Seib, *As Terrorism Evolves* (New York, NY: Cambridge University Press, 2017), p. 119.

7   Gabriel Weimann, *Terror on the Internet* (Washington, DC: United States Institute of Peace, 2006), pp. 65 and 67.

foreign fighters to Islamic State than any other country, which indicates the depth of frustration among its people. Writing in *The New Yorker,* George Packer observed that the 2011 uprisings gave young Tunisians 'the freedom to act on their unhappiness. By raising and then frustrating expectations, the revolution created conditions for radicalization to thrive'. Education, even higher education, is not in itself the answer, because, as Packer found, 'educated Tunisians are twice as likely to be unemployed as uneducated ones because the economy creates so few professional jobs'. One IS supporter told Packer: 'If you want to stop terrorism, then bring good schools, bring transportation — because the roads are terrible — and bring jobs for young people'.[8]

Along similar lines, Kartika Bhatia and Hafez Ghanem wrote:

> Our analysis shows that while it seems to be true that unemployment on its own does not impact radicalization, unemployment among the educated leads to a greater probability of radicalization. Hence, our work provides empirical support to the view that relative deprivation is an important driver of support for violent extremism. Individuals whose expectations for economic improvement and social mobility are frustrated are at a greater risk of radicalization.[9]

That makes sense. If someone has a job and is working to support their family, they may be less likely to be lured away by appeals based on political or religious issues, while if they are despairing about making ends meet and finding themselves in a hopeless financial situation, they might be more susceptible to extremist recruitment. Yet the backgrounds of the hijackers in the 9/11 attacks on the United States make clear that such criteria are not necessarily determinative. Mohamed Atta, the leader of the hijacking team, had a degree in architectural engineering from Cairo University. Other members of the 'Hamburg contingent' involved in the 9/11 attacks had studied at German universities. These men's radicalization had pronounced religious components, but there was no evidence that financial factors were behind their suicidal terrorism.[10]

Nevertheless, the idle young man in a Jordanian refugee camp or a young woman in a poverty-ridden Paris *banlieue* might be less susceptible to extremist

---

8   George Packer, 'Exporting Jihad', *The New Yorker* (28 March 2016).
9   Kartika Bhatia and Hafez Ghanem, *How Do Education and Unemployment Affect Support for Violent Extremism,* Brookings Institution Global Economy and Development Working Paper no. 102 (March 2017), available online at https://www.brookings.edu/wp-content/uploads/2017/03/global_20170322_violent-extremism.pdf.
10 National Commission on Terrorist Attacks upon the United States, *The 9/11 Commission Report* (New York: Norton, 2004), pp. 160-165.

overtures if their lives included more hope and less despair. If that is so, a case can be made for public diplomacy efforts that offer alternatives to the status quo. The distinction between public diplomacy and development assistance may be artificial, based more on protecting bureaucratic turf than on effectively reaching targeted publics. In many parts of the world, contacts from the United States are viewed with scepticism, if not hostility, and the most likely way to overcome that may be to provide a satisfactory answer to 'How will this help me?'

As described by the University of Southern California's Center on Public Diplomacy, public diplomacy is 'a key mechanism through which nations foster mutual trust and productive relationships and has become crucial to building a secure global environment'.[11] On a more pragmatic level, the fundamental mission of public diplomacy is to advance the national interests of the sponsoring state. If this is the case, and if counter-terrorism (or 'countering violent extremism') is deemed to be in the national interest in terms of 'building a secure global environment', then public diplomacy strategies and tactics might be adjusted to more directly address this.

To use the United States government as an example, the 'Joint Strategic Plan FY 2018-2022' issued by the Department of State and the US Agency for International Development (USAID) stated one of its goals as:

> [...] to degrade global terrorism threats so local governments and security forces can contain them and restore stability. We will work to consolidate military gains against ISIS [Islamic State in Iraq and Syria], AQ [Al Qaeda], and other terrorist organizations and stabilize liberated areas by supporting local partners that can re-establish the rule of law, manage conflict, and restore basic services. *We believe that diplomatic engagement and targeted development assistance to stabilize affected areas will help prevent new recruitment, reduce levels of violence, promote legitimate governance structures that strengthen inclusion, and reduce policies that marginalize communities* [emphasis added].[12]

This sounds good, but it leaves unclear which persons within which agencies are to be responsible for doing this work. How much of the effort would fall to the State Department's public diplomacy professionals? Delegating this responsibility and providing the necessary funding to public diplomacy offices would be logical if policy-makers are sincere about using public diplomacy in efforts to undermine terrorist recruitment and operations.

---

11   See https://uscpublicdiplomacy.org/page/what-pdf.

12   See https://www.state.gov/documents/organization/277156.pdf (February 2018), p. 26.

Religion

Religious studies scholar Huston Smith observed, 'The surest way to the heart of a people is through their faith'.[13] That would seem to place religion at the heart of public diplomacy, but religion's role in diplomacy varies greatly around the world. Its broad effect on culture and on public opinion is often little understood. Barry Rubin noted, 'In modern times, religion has increasingly been seen in the West as a theological set of issues rather than a profoundly political influence in public life'.[14] Depending on the nature of the state and the culture, separation between the theological and the political may be a fundamental premise, or this division may be non-existent. Along similar lines, former US Secretary of State Madeleine Albright noted 'the immense power of religion to influence how people, think, feel, and act'. She wrote: 'Religion at its best can reinforce the core values necessary for people from different cultures to live in some degree of harmony; we should make the most of that possibility'.[15]

Terrorist organizations such as Al Qaeda and Islamic State define their mission and shape their appeal in religious terms. They claim that their bloody actions are conducted in the name of religion as they defend fellow Muslims. This defames Islam and should be forcefully challenged by public diplomacy efforts. Many policy-makers, however, are wary about adding a religion component to public diplomacy. For the United States, this is partly rooted in the Constitutional mandate for separation of church and state, even though this is applicable only to domestic governance, not foreign affairs. The concept, however, seems to be a strand of the American diplomatic DNA. As a result, diplomats contemplating outreach may decide that foreign religious sensitivities are so volatile that attempts at engagement related to religion would be unwise.

Such timidity means passing up a potentially valuable connection with a targeted public. Some diplomats recognize this: Albright is among those who have proposed that US embassies' staffs should include a religion attaché.[16] Another former US State Department official, Haroon Ullah, endorsed a straightforward approach that is of particular relevance to counter-terrorism: 'In the area of public diplomacy [...] we should be directly challenging the idea

---

13   Huston Smith, *The Illustrated World's Religions* (San Francisco, CA: HarperCollins, 1994), p. 13.

14   Barry Rubin, 'Religion and International Affairs', in Dennis R. Hoover and Douglas M. Johnston (eds), *Religion and Foreign Affairs* (Waco, TX: Baylor University Press, 2012), p. 521; see also Philip Seib, *The Future of Diplomacy* (Cambridge: Polity, 2016), pp. 96-99.

15   Madeleine Albright, *The Mighty and the Almighty* (New York, NY: Harper Perennial, 2007), pp. 67, 78.

16   Albright, *The Mighty and the Almighty*, p. 76.

that the West is absolutely opposed to Islam'.[17] Given that terrorist organizations such as Islamic State and Al Qaeda put their version of Islam at the centre of their recruitment efforts, it is self-defeating not to address this in counter-terrorism and through public diplomacy programmes more generally.

Among the religion-oriented initiatives that could be part of public diplomacy efforts is outreach to Islamic education. Many Islamic schools (*madrasas*) emphasize rote learning of the Qur'an and other religious texts to the exclusion of teaching critical thinking. This eases the way for radicalization of the students. Broadening curricula and pedagogy can be done, even in the presumably inhospitable environment of places such as western Pakistan. A US-based non-governmental organization (NGO), the International Center for Religion and Diplomacy (ICRD), has found success in its work there with more than 5,000 *madrasas,* encouraging the teaching of religious tolerance, human rights and other such topics. Working in western Pakistan since 2004, the ICRD has recently passed supervision of the projects to local control, while successfully encouraging Pakistani universities to begin training programmes for *madrasa* teachers and developing resources for teaching peace-building and conflict resolution, based on Islamic principles.[18] In the Arab world, the ICRD has supplemented its emphasis on education with programmes to strengthen civil society in Saudi Arabia, Morocco, Tunisia, Yemen and Syria.

If an NGO can accomplish so much, it stands to reason that governments' public diplomacy efforts could follow similar paths and perhaps achieve similar success. Doing so, whether the emphasis is on education or other facets of civil society, would require an enlightened recognition of the synergy between religion and diplomacy.

Creating Narratives

Narratives are the heart of public diplomacy. They are the stories crafted to appeal to the publics that a government wants to influence. Narratives emphasize attributes that these publics are thought to admire and perhaps would want to emulate. Soft power, built on the preference for attraction rather than coercion, relies heavily on narratives.

That might sound like an idealized approach to global affairs, but narratives are also useful for those who are intent on creating conflict and spreading terror. Modern terrorist organizations such as Al Qaeda and Islamic State have shown themselves skilled at developing and sustaining narratives. A 2018 RAND report prepared for the US Army noted that Islamic State's narrative 'is

---

17   Haroon Ullah, *Digital World War* (New Haven, CT: Yale University Press, 2017), p. 239.

18   See https://icrd.org/programs/asia/pakistan/#program-565.

US PUBLIC DIPLOMACY AND THE TERRORISM CHALLENGE 163

incredibly effective, for both unifying the group's operations and messages and providing a compelling frame to supporters and potential supporters'.[19]

Alister Miskimmon, Ben O'Loughlin and Laura Roselle wrote that 'Al Qaeda's narrative sought to convince Muslim audiences to understand the on-going conflict as part of a wider historical global attack on Islam by a belligerent Zionist–Crusader alliance'. This was a straightforward formulation that, according to Miskimmon, O'Loughlin and Roselle, 'offered great certainty for those confused or disappointed by world events'.[20] Al Qaeda's leader, Osama bin Laden, recognized the advantage of having an often-repeated, easily comprehensible theme around which to rally his supporters.

Islamic State communicators were even more adroit at this. They constructed a narrative about Islam being under siege and a caliphate being constructed as a secure homeland — not merely a battleground — for Muslims. One of the principal arguments advanced by Islamic State has been that Muslims are widely vilified and, as noted by Jad Melki and May Jabado, 'the caliphate is an alternative world where the Muslim is desired and successful, rather than being alienated and considered a nuisance, a message perpetuated by many right-wing Western politicians'.[21] Islamic State bolstered its case with recruiting videos showing not only fighters in action, but also doctors working in an Islamic State hospital and men with their sons at an Islamic State playground. The narrative was that Islamic State was not a collection of psychopaths, but rather a community dedicated to building a safe and thriving home for devout Muslims.

Given the bloody histories of Al Qaeda and Islamic State, one would think that effective counter-narratives could have been designed and constructed quickly. But that did not happen. The US government's response after the 2001 terror attacks was largely ineffective. The State Department's public diplomacy office created products such as a series of short videos showing Muslim Americans embracing life in the United States. This 'Shared Values' campaign, which cost US\$ 15 million (and was derided by some as the 'Happy Muslims' videos), never gained traction. In some Muslim countries, television stations

---

19   Christopher Paul, Colin P. Clarke, Michael Schwille, Jakub P. Hlavka, Michael A. Brown, Steven S. Davenport, Isaac R. Porche III and Joel Harding, *Lessons from Others for Future US Army Operations in and through the Information Environment* (Santa Monica, CA: RAND, 2018), p. 16.

20   Alister Miskimmon, Ben O'Loughlin and Laura Roselle, *Strategic Narratives* (New York, NY: Routledge, 2013), p. 42.

21   Jad Melki and May Jabado, 'Mediated Public Diplomacy of the Islamic State in Iraq and Syria: The Synergistic Use of Terrorism, Social Media, and Branding', *Media and Communication,* vol. 4, no. 2 (2016), p. 100.

found the spots so insipid that they refused to air them. From there, the State Department tried various approaches, including sarcasm directed at excerpts from Islamic State's own videos. These efforts were identified as US government products, which presumably did not enhance their credibility. Nothing the US State Department tried seemed to resonate with the young Muslims at whom the messaging was directed.[22]

That changed when the State Department made a fresh start by creating a Global Engagement Center (GEC) led by Michael Lumpkin, a former US Department of Defense official. Using Facebook profile data to identify young people who appeared interested in extremist causes, the GEC sponsored advertisements that appeared on these young persons' cell phones and computer screens. The content was forcefully anti-jihadist, always in the language of the audience. During the six months beginning in September 2016, the advertisements were seen more than 14 million times. The GEC also placed their advertisements on YouTube; any YouTube user searching for Islamic State videos would see the GEC spots.[23] The number of viewings does not necessarily equate with effectiveness, but at least the US effort was technologically innovative.

In Britain, the Home Office's Research, Information and Communication Unit (RICU) reported that Al Qaeda's narrative 'combines fact, fiction, emotion and religion and manipulates discontent about local and international issues. The narrative is simple, flexible and infinitely accommodating'. The RICU report recommended that such extremist narratives be challenged, and it noted that such an effort's objective 'is not to dismiss "grievances" but undermine Al Qaeda's position as their champion and violent extremism as their solution'.[24]

Furthermore, to counter extremist messaging, Joseph Nye wrote that 'democratic leaders must use soft or attractive power to disseminate a positive narrative about globalization and the prospects for a better future that attracts moderates and counters the poisonous jihadist narratives on the Web'.[25]

As with any public diplomacy effort, counter-terrorism requires understanding the targeted publics, especially how they perceive their place in the global community. H.L. Goodall, Jr., Angela Trethewey and Kelly McDonald wrote that when engaging in strategic communication, 'Do not seek to control a message's

---

22   Greg Miller and Scott Higham, 'In a Propaganda War against ISIS, the US Tried to Play by the Enemy's Rules', *The Washington Post* (8 May 2015).

23   Joby Warrick, 'How a US Team Uses Facebook, Guerrilla Marketing to Peel off Potential ISIS Recruits', *The Washington Post* (6 February 2017).

24   Alan Travis, 'Battle Against Al Qaeda Brand Highlighted in Secret Papers', *The Guardian* (26 August 2008).

25   Joseph Nye, 'How to Counter Terrorism's Online Generation', *The Financial Times* (13 October 2005).

meaning in cultures we do not fully understand. Control over preferred interpretations is a false goal in a diverse mediated communication environment'.[26] Therefore it may make sense to outsource message development to those who know the audience better — in this case, Arab media producers. The US State Department finally did this, encouraging Arab media corporations such as the Saudi-owned Middle East Broadcasting Center to develop entertainment content. One example is 'Black Crows', a television series that aired during Ramadan in 2017 and depicted Islamic State with unrestrained harshness, particularly in illustrating how Islamic State has treated women.[27] How successful this series was in stirring anti-IS sentiment is debatable, but the concept of encouraging Arabs to speak to Arabs in counter-terrorism efforts makes sense.

This programme was more sophisticated in its approach than anything the US government had produced, but its impact was difficult to measure. At least it provided a new, widely discussed element in regional debate about Islamic State. This case illustrates both the potential and the limits of public diplomacy efforts: potential in terms of using media products to affect public discourse; and limits in the sense that even a country that is committed to using public diplomacy might not always understand the publics that it wants to reach.

Possible Changes

In the struggle against terrorism, public diplomacy has had a reputation in some circles as being not particularly useful — inherently too 'nice' to be effective when dealing with terrorists — and therefore marginalized within the larger government bureaucracy. There is some truth to this, and thus to become more relevant, public diplomacy must adapt to changes in the environment in which it must work.

The successes of the Global Engagement Center that are noted above are exceptions, not the rule. Late in US President Obama's administration, its mission was altered to place prime emphasis on counteracting Russian information warfare, but during Secretary of State Rex Tillerson's subsequent tenure (which ended in March 2018), the GEC was given little direction or money, and

---

26 H.L. Goodall, Jr, Angela Trethewey and Kelly McDonald, 'Strategic Ambiguity, Communication, and Public Diplomacy in an Uncertain World', in Steven R. Corman, Angela Trethewey and H.L. Goodall, Jr, *Weapons of Mass Persuasion: Strategic Communication to Combat Violent Extremism* (New York, NY: Peter Land, 2008), p. 35.

27 Ben Hubbard, 'Arab TV Series Dramatizes Life under ISIS', *The New York Times* (16 May 2017).

for a time it did not have a single Russian speaker on its staff to carry out its new tasks.

Making public diplomacy more relevant in the future in facing counter-terrorism and other contemporary challenges will require honing a hard edge on soft power. This does not mean that conventional public diplomacy programmes such as educational and cultural exchanges should be jettisoned. In fact, they will remain of great value in suggesting alternative life goals to young people who otherwise might be susceptible to extremists' appeals. These are long-term ventures and their results might not become apparent for years. Also, they must be supplemented by projects designed to meet the specific demands of fighting smart, resilient terrorist enemies.

This means, for example, that information programmes — broadcast, on-line and other — must be as innovative and persistent as those produced by extremists. They must be created by the best possible sources, even if this means setting aside pride of authorship in favour of relying on a greater amount of outsourcing, particularly when seeking to reach the young people targeted by extremist recruiters. A 2016 Chatham House report cited alienation growing out of feelings of disempowerment and stressed the need for 'provision of platforms for young people to express their views'.[28]

This relates to the ways in which the rise of new media affects public diplomacy. Connectivity, especially provided by social media, empowers publics in unprecedented ways, or at least creates aspirations of empowerment. These publics, individually and collectively, expect to be listened to and to participate in conversations that were formerly dominated by corporate information providers and governments. Instead of being a passive 'audience' receiving information through one-way communication, individuals can respond to the sources of information. They can also build their own online communities of interest within which ideas — positive and negative — can be exchanged. In some circumstances, this can be used to stimulate political mobilization, which also may be positive or negative. If social media venues are filled with young voices complaining about being discriminated against and being unable to find jobs or access social services, the task of extremist recruiters becomes much easier. If, on the other hand, social media conversations focus

---

28   Claire Spencer and Saad Aldouri, 'Young Arab Voices: Moving Youth Policy from Debate into Action', Chatham House Research Paper (May 2016), p. 2, available online at https://www.chathamhouse.org/sites/files/chathamhouse/publications/research/2016-05-13-young-arab-voices-spencer-aldouri.pdf.

on programmes offering opportunity, then violence and martyrdom will more likely seem pointless.[29]

This points to a larger issue. In the United States and other countries, public diplomacy has been used in spotty ways as a second-tier supplement to civil and military strategies, and too often it is reactive rather than proactive. Many public diplomacy programmes — ranging from the British Council's English-language training to the American creation of the TechGirls exchange programme[30] — offer young people positive options. But they tend to be isolated, rather than parts of a coherent policy.

If public diplomacy is to be of maximum value in counter-terrorism, it needs to become more prominent as governments shapes their foreign policy, especially in programmes that help countries build or strengthen civil society. Former Egyptian Foreign Minister Nabil Fahmy observed that 'terrorism in the Middle East is a direct derivative of the breakdown of the social contract and the absence of effective state institutions'.[31] A 2016 US State Department report echoed this: 'In many environments where the risk of violent extremism is high, development has failed to take root, governance is weak, access to education and training is limited, economic opportunities are few, and unemployment is high'.[32]

These are fundamental issues that, for various reasons, have remained inadequately addressed by many nations' policy-makers. A holistic approach to public diplomacy, giving it a more central role in foreign policy, will not be a panacea, but among the publics it reaches it may help to create a future of more solid resistance to the allure of extremism.

Philip Seib

is Professor of Journalism and Public Diplomacy and Professor of International Relations at the University of Southern California (USC). He served as Director of the USC's Center on Public Diplomacy from 2009-2013, and as Vice Dean

---

29   Seib, *As Terrorism Evolves*, p. 170.

30   TechGirls is an exchange programme that in 2016 brought 27 teenage girls from Algeria, Egypt, Jordan, Morocco, Palestine and Tunisia to the United States to participate in three weeks of training in the STEM fields (science, technology, engineering and mathematics). In addition to classroom training, they received mentoring from tech industry leaders. Admittedly, 27 is not a large number, but there are now more than 100 alumnae of the programme and they have trained more than 2,300 other teenage girls in their home countries.

31   Nabil Fahmy, 'A Call for Arab Diplomacy', *Cairo Review of Global Affairs*, no. 21 (spring 2016), p. 81.

32   'Department of State and USAID Joint Strategy on Countering Violent Extremism' (May 2016), available online at https://www.state.gov/documents/organization/257913.pdf.

of the USC's Annenberg School for Communication and Journalism from 2015-2016. He is the author or editor of numerous books, including *Headline Diplomacy* (New York: Praeger, 1996); *New Media and the New Middle East* (New York: Palgrave Macmillan, 2007); *The Al Jazeera Effect* (Washington, DC: Potomac Books, 2008); *Toward A New Public Diplomacy* (New York: Palgrave Macmillan, 2009); (with Dana Janbek) *Global Terrorism and New Media* (New York: Routledge, 2010); *Al Jazeera English* (New York: Palgrave Macmillan, 2012); *Real-Time Diplomacy* (New York: Palgrave Macmillan, 2012); and *The Future of Diplomacy* (Cambridge: Polity, 2016). His latest book is *As Terrorism Evolves: Media, Religion, and Governance* (Cambridge: Cambridge University Press, 2017). He is editor of an academic book series on international political communication, co-editor of a series on global public diplomacy, and was a founding co-editor of the journal *Media, War & Conflict.*

The China Model of Public Diplomacy and Its Future

Kejin Zhao
Department of International Relations, Tsinghua University, Beijing 100084, People's Republic of China
kejinzhao@mail.tsinghua.edu.cn

Received: 30 July 2018; revised: 16 January 2019; accepted: 27 February 2019

Summary

Since 2012, China's top leadership has argued that China's public diplomacy should integrate with the 'New Model of Major-Country Diplomacy with Chinese Characteristics'. Among this series of initiatives, China formulates a public diplomacy model that is different from those of other countries. China's model of public diplomacy falls under the unified leadership of the Communist Party of China (CPC), but coordinates various public diplomacy players culturally rather than institutionally. The current trends of China's public diplomacy include to evolve from listening to telling, and to be more confident, positive and active. Based on empirical studies, this article concludes that China's public diplomacy since 2012 has created a unique model that emphasises cultural and other informal norms under the CPC's leadership. Moreover, public diplomacy will be regarded as a necessary wisdom to understand how China has integrated with the world harmoniously.

Keywords

China Model – public diplomacy – party diplomacy

Public Diplomacy and the China Model

Public diplomacy has been an increasingly hot topic since the early twenty-first century, because of the 9/11 attacks in 2001 and the United States' public

© KONINKLIJKE BRILL NV, LEIDEN, 2019 | DOI:10.1163/9789004410824_013

diplomacy response. Although the Communist Party of China (CPC) has always conducted such activities as 'civil diplomacy [*minjian waijiao*]' and 'external communication [*duiwai xuan chuan*]', there is a significant difference between the public diplomacy of Western countries and these activities, the main reason being that there is literally no equivalent of 'public [*Gong gong*]' in Chinese. In Chinese culture, the term 'public' often refers to governmental affairs instead of social or private affairs as it does in English. Influenced by Chinese culture, Japan, South Korea, Vietnam and other neighbouring countries of China also do not adopt the concept of 'public' as it is in English, and the so-called 'public diplomacy' in these countries is mostly quasi-public diplomacy, or even just official diplomacy in civil society.

With its different understanding of 'public diplomacy', China's public diplomacy has been greatly influenced by the United States from the very beginning, focusing on 'public relations' and 'media campaign', rather than on 'cultural diplomacy' and 'new public diplomacy'[1] as in the European countries. The SARS virus that ravaged China in 2003 triggered a global tide of negative judgement towards China, including various kinds of 'China threat' criticisms, which in turn directed the Chinese leadership's attention towards public diplomacy. However, since China has been facing 'structural weakness'[2] in the global opinion market, the media offensive in China's public diplomacy quickly encountered difficulties, making China seek to strengthen cultural exchanges using its inherent 5,000 years of cultural resources. Under the guidance of Liu Yandong, then Vice-Premier of the State Council, a larger scale of cultural exchange mechanisms between China and foreign countries has been launched since 2009, serving as one main pillar of China's public diplomacy. The Confucius Institutes and abundant public diplomacy projects have attracted worldwide attention to China's public diplomacy.[3]

China's public diplomacy has apparently undergone a process of the passive learning curve, because of growing pressure from the global debate regarding political legitimacy. In order to narrow the legitimacy gap effectively, Chinese

---

1   Jan Melissen (ed.), *The New Public Diplomacy: Soft Power in International Relations* (Basingstoke: Palgrave Macmillan, 2007).

2   Zhang Zhizhou, 'Huayu zhiliang: tisheng guoji huayuquan de guanjian' [The Quality of Discourse: The Key to Advance China's International Discursive Power], *Hongqi Wengao* [*The Red Flag Review*], no. 14 (2010).

3   Yang Jiechi, 'Nuli kaichuang zhongguo tese gonggong waijiao xin jumian' [Strive to Initiate the New Horizons of Public Diplomacy with Chinese Characteristics], *Qiushi*, no. 4 (2011), pp. 43-46.

THE CHINA MODEL OF PUBLIC DIPLOMACY AND ITS FUTURE 171

leaders then resorted to public diplomacy.[4] However, China's practice of public diplomacy is not merely a replication of the European and American public diplomacy theories and models. The CPC's leadership, together with China's profound civilisation, have endowed China's public diplomacy with Chinese elements in practice. Public diplomacy in China has achieved innovation, transformation and localisation, developing into the so-called 'China Model' of public diplomacy. To date, however, well-known scholars such as Ingrid d'Hooghe, Jay Wang, Falk Hartig and Kingsley Edney have studied Chinese public diplomacy as external observers, mainly focusing on the approaches, methods and specific skills of Chinese public diplomacy, instead of taking Chinese public diplomacy as a whole and studying its special model and systematic changes as internal observers. In this case, further study of the China Model will be helpful in understanding the basic logic of Chinese public diplomacy in the long term, as well as foreseeing the future trends of Chinese public diplomacy in practice.

China Model or Chinese Characteristics?

People are always interested in the so-called China Model. Nevertheless, there is little discussion on whether China's public diplomacy is really a particular model. Many scholars have studied the models of public diplomacy. One example would be Eytan Gilboa, who presented three models of public diplomacy: the Cold War Model; the Non-state Model; and the Domestic Public Relations Model[5] — these are simple, clear and of significant operability. However, since one country may employ three models of public diplomacy simultaneously, such classification may face the problem of overlapping categories.

This article classifies public diplomacy models by the following two variables: power structure; and level of institutionalisation. The former variable — power structure — indicates whether the power of public diplomacy is centralised in the hands of governments or spreads out to various social actors. In this case, public diplomacy could be classified into traditional public diplomacy or new public diplomacy. The second variable — the level of institutionalisation — refers to whether there are public laws and formal institutions governing public diplomacy, according to which public diplomacy could be classified

---

4   Kejin Zhao, 'The Motivation behind China's Public Diplomacy', *Chinese Journal of International Politics*, vol. 8, no. 2 (2015), pp. 167-196.

5   Eytan Gilboa, 'Mass Communication and Diplomacy: A Theoretical Framework', *Communication Theory*, vol. 10, no. 3 (2000), pp. 275-309.

into institutionalised public diplomacy with systematic laws and formal rules, or politicised public diplomacy with few laws and formal rules. Based on this taxonomy, we can examine the characteristics of China's public diplomacy model by assessing its power structure and level of institutionalisation. In general, China's public diplomacy is fundamentally a type of 'party diplomacy' with cultural coordination and informal norms.

Power Structure: No Trivial Things in Foreign Affairs

Distinct from those of Western countries, China's public diplomacy is led by the CPC, a system referred to as the 'Whole-Nation System [*Ju guo Ti zhi*]', under which the power structure is undeniably centralised to a large extent. According to the Amendments to the Constitution of the People's Republic of China adopted at the First Session of the 13th National People's Congress on 11 March 2018, Chapter I Article 1, 'The leadership of the Communist Party of China is the defining feature of socialism with Chinese characteristics'. Meanwhile, the Constitution of the CPC stipulates that the fundamental organizational principle of the Party is 'democratic centralism'. At the 19th National Congress of the CPC in 2018, General Secretary Xi Jinping emphasised that 'the Party exercises overall leadership over all areas of endeavour in every part of the country'.[6] The policy operation model is 'determined by the centre and implemented by different organs [*zhong yang jue ding, ge fang qu ban*]'. The central leadership makes major policy decisions, while the specific execution is left to relevant political agencies, including the People's Congresses, central and local governments, political consultative conferences, public organisations and so on. This can be regarded as the uniqueness of the Chinese public diplomacy model.

The power structure of Chinese public diplomacy is highly centralised in the CPC Central Committee. Moreover, the structure can also be summarised as a unique system of 'party-led diplomacy' as well as 'centralized management [*guikou guanli*]'.[7] The decision-making organ of the Chinese centralised public diplomacy model is the CPC's Central Foreign Affairs Leading (Small) Group, which is responsible for coordinating diplomatic matters. In March 2018, the Group was redesignated to the Central Foreign Affairs Commission as

---

6 Xi Jinping: 'Secure a Decisive Victory in Building a Moderately Prosperous Society in All Respects and Strive for the Great Success of Socialism with Chinese Characteristics for a New Era', report delivered at the 19th National Congress of the Communist Party, available online at http://www.xinhuanet.com/politics/2017-10/27/c_1121867529.htm (accessed 14 May 2018).

7 Kejin Zhao, *Dangdai zhongguo waijiao zhidu de zhuanxing yu dingwei* [*The Transition and Position of Chinese Diplomatic System in Contemporary China*] (Beijing: Current Affairs Press, 2013).

a consultative and coordinating agency in foreign affairs. Therefore, the power structure of China's public diplomacy is not found within the central government, but in the CPC's Central Foreign Affairs Commission. In terms of execution, Chinese public diplomacy follows the principles of 'No Trivial Things in Foreign Affairs' and 'centralized management', which means that as long as foreign affairs are concerned, traditional or non-traditional, they must adhere to the party leadership.

Level of Institutionalisation: Cultural Coordination, Not Institutional Coordination

In terms of the level of institutionalisation of its public diplomacy, China is also different from other countries. Various kinds of actors have engaged in Chinese public diplomacy, including official agencies such as China's Ministry of Foreign Affairs, Ministry of Commerce, Ministry of Education, Ministry of Culture and the International Department of the CPC's Central Committee, as well as public groups such as trade unions, the Communist Youth League, the Women's Federation, the Federation of Industry and Commerce, the Federation of Returned Overseas Chinese and the Council for the Promotion of International Trade (to name a few). Almost all of these actors are proactive about engaging in public diplomacy, while none have sufficient legal basis to act as the 'specialized agency of public diplomacy'. So far, China has not enacted any laws specifically governing public diplomacy. The institutions, personnel and budgets are unstable, with current institutions thus not completely institutionalised. In fact, although many organisations are competing to gain a slice of public diplomacy in the CPC's foreign affairs management system, not all of the actors have the qualifications and opportunities to engage in public diplomacy.

Given the phenomena above, China's public diplomacy attaches much significance to a complex informal cultural coordination mechanism. In response to the international criticisms, the CPC's leadership of public diplomacy is not in charge of all matters, whether pivotal or trivial, but is a political and ideological directing. In recent years, the CPC's Central Committee has launched a series of people-to-people exchanges as well as cross-cultural events to promote public diplomacy. Through the combination of 'Go Global' and 'Bring In' strategies, together with the 'Let China Know the World' and 'Let the World Know China' approaches, a multi-level (central, local and grassroots), multi-channel (government, enterprises, media and society, etc.) and all-round (public communication, friendly exchange and people's livelihood cooperation) public diplomacy mechanism has been gradually established, which not only enhances the world's understanding of China, but also expands China's political influence and gives China a greater say in the international arena. As a result, despite the relatively low level of institutionalisation, under the guidance of the CPC's informal arrangements, China's public diplomacy has become a 'loudspeaker' in a series of norms and practices, gradually switching from the listening side featuring 'listening to the world', to the 'telling' side of highlighting 'telling the Chinese story well, spreading China's voice well'.[8]

Trends of China's Public Diplomacy: From Listening to Telling

In recent years, as China has become the world's second-largest economy, the international community has become increasingly concerned with China's rise and its implications for the world. 'China threat', 'China collapse', 'Why China is capable', 'Why the CPC is capable' and other kinds of complex arguments linger continuously. The aim of China's public diplomacy is thus to spread the China Dream presented by President Xi to the international community.

In the long run, China's public diplomacy is highly likely to develop along the following four trends:

First, more emphasis will be laid on Chinese characteristics. At the Central Foreign Affairs Meeting held from 28-29 November 2014, Xi Jinping emphasised that China must have a new model of major country diplomacy with Chinese characteristics:

> On the basis of summing up practical experience, we must enrich and develop the ideas of foreign affairs so that our country's foreign service will have distinctive Chinese characteristics, Chinese style and Chinese spirit'.[9]

'Whether it is government diplomacy or public diplomacy, we must highlight "Chinese characteristics" and we must strive for worldwide understanding and support for the China Dream'.[10] The key is to explain the meaning of 'Chinese

---

8   'Xi Jinping Attending Central Working Meeting on Foreign Affairs and Making Important Remarks' (29 November 2014), available online at http://news.xinhuanet.com/ttgg/2014-11/29/c_1113457723.htm.

9   *Xinhua Agency*, 'Xi Jinping Attends the Central Working Conference on Foreign Affairs and Delivers an Important Speech' (29 November 2014), available online at http://www.xinhuanet.com/politics/2014-11/29/c_1113457723.htm (accessed 14 May 2018).

10   Qizheng Zhao, 'China Enters a New Phase of Public Diplomacy', *CPChNews* (11 April 2018), available online at http://theory.people.com.cn/n1/2018/0411/c40531-29918421.html (accessed 14 May 2018).

characteristics' to the world. However, the connotation of 'Chinese characteristics' has not been interpreted clearly enough.

Actually, the substantial aim of emphasising Chinese characteristics is to
attach a great deal of weight to ensuring a firm grasp of ideological leadership and the right to speak up internationally, as evidenced by Xi's speech on
19 August 2013, that 'ideological work is an extremely important task of the
party'. Xi has repeatedly emphasised that 'among the public and ideological
works under the condition of an overall opening-up, an important task is to
guide general populations to get a more comprehensive and objective understanding of contemporary China and the world'.[11] Another piece of evidence
would be the high-profile conference held by the CPC's Central Committee on
4 May 2018, to commemorate the 200th anniversary of the birth of Carl Marx,
during which Xi declared the CPC's firm belief in the scientific correctness of
Marxism. Clearly, the growing emphasis on Chinese characteristics implies that
China must highlight Marxism's key role in guiding its public diplomacy. The
deeper motive comes from the need to distinguish itself from the European
and American capitalist ideologies and to further consolidate Xi Jinping's political legitimacy — 'Thought on Socialism with Chinese Characteristics for a
New Era' is acknowledged by the CPC as the Marxist theory of the twenty-first
century. Evidently, the demand to consolidate the political legitimacy of the Xi
Theory as the guiding ideas for the CPC is what characterises China's current
public diplomacy.

Second, more attention will be attached to cultural self-confidence. In addition to the growing emphasis on Chinese characteristics, China's public diplomacy also attaches more significance to cultural self-confidence [*wen hua zi
xin*]. Chinese government leaders no longer use the Western concept of 'public diplomacy' in public disclosures, but instead turn to other relatively local
concepts, such as 'cultural diplomacy [*wen hua wai jiao*]', as well as 'people-
to-people exchange [*ren wen jiao liu*]', which are crucial signals implying that
China is now highlighting cultural self-confidence. China has been shedding
greater light on 'cultural self-confidence' since 2012, especially the importance
of promoting its excellent traditional culture while achieving creative transformation and innovative development. Xi commented that 'the excellent traditional Chinese culture is the spiritual lifeblood, the "root", and the "soul" of
the Chinese nation'.[12] In his opinion, if China loses its 'root' and 'soul', it would

---

11 'Xi Jinping Delivers Speech at National Conference on Propaganda and Ideological Work',
    CPChNews (21 August 2013), available online at http://cpc.people.com.cn/n/2013/0821/
    c64094-22636876.html (accessed 14 May 2018).

12 Xi Jinping, *The Governance of China* (Beijing: Foreign Language Press, 2014).

lose the foundation of its diplomacy. President Xi therefore emphasised that China would need to promote exchange among different civilisations, but at the same time would also need to strengthen China's faith and determination in itself. Certainly, Xi, like his predecessors, also emphasised that China should revitalise the positive parts of China's traditional cultural heritage to adapt to the new era and promote innovation. Accordingly, China's public diplomacy should focus on contributing China's wisdom to global governance reform. China will doubtless present more and more initiatives on global development and transnational governance based on Chinese cultural confidence in the coming decades.

As a major part of manifesting China's cultural self-confidence, public diplomacy is required to play an active role in 'explaining China to the world', strengthening China's capacity in international communication and empowering China with a greater say in the international arena. Facing great changes in relations between China and the world, Xi Jinping has emphasised the need to build stronger cultural self-confidence, tell Chinese stories and further spread Chinese voices in the world. On 25 October 2013 at the Central Working Conference on Neighbourhood Diplomacy, Xi pointed out that it was particularly necessary to strengthen China's campaign, public diplomacy, non-governmental diplomacy and people-to-people exchanges among its neighbouring countries. It was necessary for China to make friends and build friendships with its neighbours. The Chinese Dream should be associated with the wish for a better life for all the people in China's neighbouring countries, and potential regional development prospects in those countries, which is how the idea of 'a community of shared future for mankind' took root in China's neighbourhood.[13] In November 2014 at the Central Working Conference on Foreign Affairs, Xi once again proposed that China should upgrade its soft power, tell Chinese stories better, and improve its ability to tell Chinese stories internationally.[14] In recent years, China has emphasised 'explaining China to the world' and improving its ability to tell its story at the international level. It shows that the main focus of China's public diplomacy is not 'listening' but 'advocating and telling', which will also be a major trend of China's public diplomacy in the future.

---

13 'Xi Jinping Makes an Important Speech at Working Conference for Neighborhood Diplomacy', *People's Daily* (25 October 2013), available online at http://politics.people .com.cn/n/2013/1025/c1024-23332318.html (accessed 14 May 2018).

14 Xi Jinping, 'Carry Forward Traditional Friendship and Jointly Open up New Chapter of Cooperation' [*Hongyang chuantong youhao, gongpu hezuo xin pian*], *People's Daily* (18 July 2014), p. 1.

Third, more 'China Plans' will be shared with the world. When China was weak in the past, it was incapable of proposing a China Plan for global challenges. However, with the continuous accumulation of China's capabilities, China shows more enthusiasm about providing public goods for the international community, regionally and globally. China's public diplomacy now channels more efforts into proposing Chinese plans, contributing Chinese wisdom and providing more public goods.[15] This China Plan [*zhong guo fang an*] is to adhere to the path of peaceful development and to promote the construction of a new model of international relations and a community with a shared future for mankind. In recent years, China has proposed a number of international and national initiatives, such as the Asian Infrastructure Investment Bank, the New Development Bank with its fellow BRICS nations (Brazil, Russia, India, China and South Africa), the Silk Road Fund and the Belt and Road Initiative (BRI), all of which are key derivatives of this China Plan. Given the strong vigour demonstrated by the idea of 'a community of shared future for mankind' in China's contemporary international relations and diplomatic practices, this idea was written into the 19th CPC National Congress Meeting Report and the newly revised CPC constitution at the 19th CPC National Congress Meeting, escalating into one of the main guidelines of the new era.

In the eyes of Chinese leaders, the 'American Plan' has the 'Washington Consensus' as its main content, while the 'European Plan' has its main idea as promoting regional integration. The idea of 'a community of shared future for mankind' aims to surpass both of these. Different from the ideas of 'colour revolution', 'democratic output' and 'new interventionism', which are promoted through the 'Western Plans', China adopts an attitude of 'respect', 'tolerance' and 'non-discrimination' towards related countries, which paves the way for China's public diplomacy.

Fourth, more stress will be laid on cultural as well as people-to-people exchanges. Since the 18th National Congress Meeting of the CPC in 2012, in the context of global challenges such as global economic imbalances, China has proposed an initiative to promote the construction of the BRI, which aims to achieve win–win cooperation and common development. More than one hundred countries and international organisations have responded positively to this initiative. A large number of early projects have already blossomed and have been written into the resolutions of the United Nations and other international organisations. From China's perspective, the BRI is essentially a 'Friendship Circle' that facilitates win–win cooperation, and would be one of

---

15   Kejin Zhao, 'Public Diplomacy for International Global Public Goods', *Politics & Policy*, vol. 45, no. 5 (2017), pp. 706-732.

the focal points of China's public diplomacy from now to the future. In designing and promoting the Initiative, Xi Jinping highlighted the significance of people-to-people exchanges, regarding them as one of the 'Five Exchanges'[16] to promote the BRI. Xi believes that the key to a new model of international relations lies in an affinity with their people, and such an affinity largely stems from mutual understandings. He has stated several times that it is necessary for China to 'make friends and build good relationships' with the rest of the international community, and this could be achieved through the approach of 'moving people by sincerity, warming people by heart and touching people by affection'.[17] Politicians, diplomats, experts and scholars, media elites and non-governmental organisations (NGOs) dedicated to friendly non-governmental communication could all play a role in realising this vision.

As for the task of winning people's support, promoting people-to-people exchanges is the most effective vehicle and channel. President Xi believes that China must vigorously strengthen cultural exchange and reciprocal communication, while public diplomacy remains the most profound way to achieve this goal. In July 2017, the General Office of the CPC's Central Committee and the General Office of the State Council jointly issued the 'Several Opinions on Strengthening and Improving the People-to-People Exchange Work between China and Foreign Countries' to map a path for strengthening people-to-people exchanges. In November 2017, China's Ministry of Education established the Chinese–Foreign Humanities Exchange Centre. Moreover, Liu Yandong, after fulfilling her tenure as the Vice-Premier of the State Council, continues to devote herself to the promotion of people-to-people exchanges between China and foreign countries. The central goal of people-to-people exchange is to promote mutual understandings among people. From a long-term perspective, the priority of the people-to-people exchange's approach will only be increasingly enhanced, not the other way around.

---

16 The Five Exchanges were first proposed by Xi Jinping in his vision for the Belt and Road Initiative in 2013. According to Xi, the Belt and Road Initiative should be jointly constructed with policy exchange, infrastructure exchange, trade exchange, financial exchange and people-to-people exchange as a whole.

17 Xi Jinping, 'Speech at the 60th Anniversary of the Founding of the Chinese People's Association for Friendship with Foreign Countries and the China International Friendship Conference', *People's Daily* (16 May 2014), available online at http://politics.people.com.cn/n/2014/0516/c1024-25023611.html (accessed 14 May 2018).

Implications for Established Models

Most academic scholars and practitioners usually take the definition of public diplomacy for granted, as dealing with the influence of public attitudes on the formation and execution of foreign policies,[18] or as the process through which connections with the people of a country are pursued to advance the interests and extend the value of those represented.[19] In particular, Jan Melissen underlines the importance of the socially constructed network into diplomacy to coin the 'new public diplomacy'.[20] Both definitions on public diplomacy have already been established as consensus around the world. However, China's endeavours to develop public diplomacy since 2012 may create new implications for established models and even contribute an alternative model of public diplomacy.

Distinct from that of Western powers, China's model of public diplomacy is fundamentally party diplomacy led by the CPC, a system referred to as the 'Whole-Nation System'. Under such a system, China's public diplomacy has formed a party-dominated model and all the endeavours to develop public diplomacy should serve the party's preference rather than the government policy. This model is characterised by the fact that the CPC has centralised the power of public diplomacy. Government agencies and social actors under and surrounding the CPC, as well as a set of social networks, should be formed under the unified leadership of specified government departments. In this case, instead of being driven by a clear system of laws and rules as in the United States and European countries, the operation of these social networks in public diplomacy is driven more by the CPC's domestic policy agenda than foreign policy agenda.

Party diplomacy will undoubtedly play a leading role in all endeavours related to public diplomacy in China for a long time. Significantly, the CPC's Central Committee has launched a big campaign known as 'Two Upholds', which asks all Party members and agencies to maintain Xi Jinping as the core leader of the CPC and its central committee and to maintain the authority of the Central Committee and its unified central leadership over political issues. This campaign indicates that all participants and players involved in public diplomacy and foreign affairs in China would have to follow the rules

---

18 Nicholas Cull, '"Public Diplomacy" before Gullion: The Evolution of a Phrase', *CPD Blog* (Los Angeles, CA: USC Center on Public Diplomacy, 18 April 2006), available online at https://www.uscpublicdiplomacy.org/blog/public-diplomacy-gullion-evolution-phrase.
19 Melissen (ed.), *The New Public Diplomacy.*
20 Melissen (ed.), *The New Public Diplomacy.*

in the coming years. A good example is the new public law regulating international NGOs in China. As Chinese NGOs have been playing an increasingly active role in China's diplomacy since the new millennium, the CPC started to specify the responsibilities of these lower-level organisations. A case in point is the *Law of the People's Republic of China on Administration of Activities of Overseas Non-Governmental Organisations in the Mainland of China*, announced on 28 April 2016, which initiated the laws and directives governing grassroots exchanges.[21] Based on this new legislature defining the allocation of responsibilities, international NGOs in China are regulated by the Ministry of Foreign Affairs and the Ministry of Public Security, while Chinese NGOs abroad are supported and promoted by the CPC's International Department. With leadership shared among these three ministries, Chinese grassroots associations — including companies, the media, think tanks, local groups and public organisations — will establish increasingly closer ties with their international counterparts. Obviously, in the next ten years or even longer timeframe, the centralised power structure of Chinese public diplomacy is not likely to see any fundamental change. China's model of public diplomacy, to some extent, is more inclined towards party diplomacy or people-to-people diplomacy with their cultural and informal norms than public diplomacy with its public law. Institutionally, the International Department of the CPC's Central Committee will play a more substantial role in public diplomacy than China's Ministry of Foreign Affairs and other governmental agencies in the long run. In the eyes of the International Department of the CPC, public diplomacy is only one of the major pillars of China's party diplomacy as a whole, besides international party exchanges and people-to-people exchanges.

Conclusions

Although China's public diplomacy started relatively late, China has formed a practical party-driven model of public diplomacy with strong Chinese characteristics. With the deepening of relations between China and the international community, China's public diplomacy will have more Chinese characteristics and lay more emphasis on its cultural self-confidence. However, an inevitable trend is that China's public diplomacy will have to shift its focus, from the

---

21   Xi Jinping, 'Order of the President of the People's Republic of China' (28 April 2016), available online at http://www.mps.gov.cn/n2254314/n2254409/n4904353/c5548987/content .html.

listening side of 'listening to the world' to the telling side of 'telling the Chinese story well, spreading the Chinese voice well'.[22]

As a result, how to prevent China's public diplomacy from falling into 'Chinese-centrism' is also a problem that deserves more attention. As China is increasingly approaching the centre stage, other countries of the world will have to learn how to get along with China, regardless of whether they like it or not. Correspondingly, regardless of the Chinese leadership's attitudes towards the concepts and ideas of public diplomacy, the role of public diplomacy will still be strengthened, helping China to become harmoniously integrated with the international community and to build a new type of international relations.

Kejin Zhao

is tenure-track Professor and Dean of the Department of International Relations, Tsinghua University. He has a Ph.D. in International Relations from the School of International Relations and Public Affairs of Fudan University, and from 2005-2009 he worked at the Center for American Studies, Fudan University. Since 2009, he has been teaching and researching at Tsinghua University in Beijing. His research mainly focuses on US government and politics, public diplomacy and Chinese diplomacy. He has published more than 80 papers in academic journals and has written many books, including *Diplomacy beyond Foreign Ministries* (Beijing: Peking University Press, 2015) and *Public Diplomacy: Theory and Practice* (Shanghai: Fudan University Press, 2007) [both in Mandarin].

---

22 'Xi Jinping Attending Central Working Meeting on Foreign Affairs and Making Important Remarks' (29 November 2014), available online at http://news.xinhuanet.com/ttgg/2014-11/29/c_1113457723.htm.

Political Leaders and Public Diplomacy in the Contested Indo-Pacific

Caitlin Byrne
Griffith Asia Institute, Griffith University, Nathan, QLD 4111, Australia
c.byrne@griffith.edu.au

Received: 22 August 2018; revised: 2 January 2019; accepted: 24 January 2019

Summary

Public diplomacy practice is intensifying across the Indo-Pacific as global actors compete to keep pace with the emerging geopolitical realities of a contested world order. China's rise is the dominant feature. It comes as the United States retreats from global leadership, further heightening the sense of uncertainty in the region. Amid this strategic re-ordering, competition to influence narratives, set political agendas and frame the rules of a changing order is intense. The stakes for public diplomacy could not be higher and the implications for political leaders are significant. This article examines the role of Indo-Pacific political leaders through the lens of public diplomacy. While there are significant differences in approach, findings suggest that the imperative for political leaders to inform, engage and influence public audiences increasingly lies in the desire to shape the narrative and thus the nature of a regional order that will be favourable for their national interests.

Keywords

public diplomacy – political leadership – Indo-Pacific– strategic narrative – power – influence

Introduction

Political leaders have become increasingly relevant in shaping and contesting narratives of power and influence in the twenty-first century. Nowhere is this more evident than in the Indo-Pacific region.[1] China's rise is the region's dominant feature. Under President Xi Jinping's leadership, China offers the narrative of a 'New Era' of development for the region, marked by an ambitious agenda of 'absolute control at home and unprecedented influence worldwide'.[2] The very notion of the Indo-Pacific, advocated by other powers in the region, notably Japan, India and Australia, working in quartet formation with the United States, aims to counterbalance China's influence. Underpinned by values of openness, freedom and a commitment to international law, this is a narrative that has captured the discourse of strategic publics across the region. Caught in the middle of the emerging contest, South-East Asian leaders abide by their well-established preference for collective rather than unilateral leadership. Pressure is building on the Association of South-East Asian Nations (ASEAN) to cement the Indo-Pacific narrative further, although it is not yet clear whether and how ASEAN leaders will respond.

This article argues that political leaders within the Indo-Pacific are increasingly turning to strategic public diplomacy as they seek to define and shape the narrative of regional order that will be most conducive to their national interests. At first glance, there is nothing new here, as political leaders have long been viewed as instruments of public diplomacy. However, this contribution reveals the contemporary significance of political leaders as agents of public diplomacy in times of change and contest. In particular, it draws attention to leaders from across the emerging Indo-Pacific, who, unlike leaders of the West, have not typically been the subject of such study. As the pendulum of political and economic power shifts towards this vast and diverse geopolitical construct, Indo-Pacific leaders will be increasingly responsible for steering critical policy agendas, institutions and norms that hold regional and even global significance.

Three emerging leadership dynamics are visible within the currents of Indo-Pacific strategic re-ordering and provide the focus of this study. They are:

1. China's great power leadership under President Xi underpinned by the mission to 'seek happiness for the Chinese people and rejuvenation for the Chinese nation';[3]

---

1 The Indo-Pacific region was defined in Australia's 2017 *Foreign Policy White Paper* as 'stretching from the eastern Indian Ocean to the Pacific Ocean connected by Southeast Asia, including India, Northeast Asia and the United States'.

2 Rowan Callick, 'The Neighbourhood in a State', in Caitlin Byrne and Lucy West (eds), *The State of the Neighbourhood* (Brisbane: Griffith Asia Institute, 2018), p. 11.

3 Xi Jinping, 'Secure a Decisive Victory in Building a Moderately Prosperous Society in all Respects and Strive for the Great Success of Socialism with Chinese Characteristics for a

2. the complementary approaches of the leaders of Japan, India and Australia, working cooperatively to establish a 'free and open Indo-Pacific' as a counterbalance to China's great power dominance; and
3. the institutional consensus-based approach of South-East Asian leaders working through ASEAN.

Variations in approach are evident, yet findings suggest that the imperative for political leaders to inform, engage and influence public audiences increasingly lies in the desire to shape narratives in the contest for power and influence within the region. For these actors, the deeply political and strategic nature of public diplomacy is of relevance. Indeed, as Donna Oglesby observes:

> Public diplomacy actors do not lay the good intentions pavement for a universal civilization. They recognize that in a pluralistic international society, contesting ideas drive agendas, social movements, revolutions and policy choices. Their task, with varying levels of power and persuasiveness, is to influence the problem definition and therefore the political outcome of the issues under debate.[4]

A broader study of leadership across the region might consider other examples, such as the 'people-centred' model advocated by South Korea's President Moon Jae-in, the enigmatic leadership of North Korea's Supreme Leader Kim Jong-Un, the flawed leadership example set by 2001 Nobel Peace Prize laureate and now Myanmar State Counsellor Aung San Suu Kyi, or even the populist style of Philippine President Rodrigo Duterte. However significant these and other examples might be for the study of leadership and public diplomacy, they have limited bearing on the emerging strategic order of the Indo-Pacific that forms the focus of this study, and are therefore outside the scope of discussion.

Political Leaders and Public Diplomacy

Political leadership and public diplomacy go hand in hand. In today's hyperconnected world, political leaders are increasingly recognized as the physical

---

New Era', speech delivered to the 19th National Congress of the Communist Party of China (18 October 2017).

4 Donna Oglesby, 'The Political Promise of Public Diplomacy', *Perspectives*, vol. 4, no. 1 (March 2014), available online at: http://www.layalina.tv/publications/the-political-promise -of-public-diplomacy-by-donna-marie-oglesby/.

embodiment of the state that they represent: its values, policies, institutions and aspirations. They play an instrumental role in communicating and projecting the image of that state to global public audiences. Their presence, rhetoric and interactions with others, especially with other leaders, foreign media academics and diaspora, as well as their behaviour — online and in real time — can shape public perceptions towards their nation, its citizens and policies.

In international relations, it is widely accepted that 'leadership matters most at times of crisis, strategic vulnerability or when international conditions are fluid'.[5] The role that political leaders play to consolidate collective action in the global sphere, 'providing solutions to common problems [...] and mobilizing the energies of others to follow these courses of actions'[6] requires a sophisticated skill set. Arguably, leaders draw increasingly on the skills of public diplomacy, the broad aims of which are to 'understand cultures, attitudes and behaviours; build and manage relationships; and influence thoughts and mobilize actions to advance [their] interests and values'.[7]

Unlike professional diplomats, political leaders are beholden to their domestic constituencies, even when engaging on the world stage. The pressure to maintain popular support and 'face' at home holds true for leaders representing democratic and authoritarian nations alike.[8] At the same time, the ubiquitous nature of global media means that the actions and words of leaders at home can play a key role in shaping the perceptions of global publics and driving wider strategic discourse — even when this is not intended. The intersection between domestic and external audiences creates notable tensions for the political leader, but aligns to public diplomacy's Janus-faced orientation.[9] Wherever political leaders find themselves, whether at the podium of the United Nations (UN) General Assembly or on the floor of a local factory at home, as long as they are in public view, they are increasingly considered to be on the 'world stage'.

---

5   Katherine Morton, 'Political Leadership and Global Governance: Structural Power versus Custodial Leadership', *China Political Science Review*, vol. 2 (2017), p. 477.

6   Nannerl O. Keohane, *Thinking About Leadership* (Princeton, NJ: Princeton University Press, 2010), p. 19.

7   Bruce Gregory, 'American Public Diplomacy: Enduring Characteristics, Elusive Transformation', *The Hague Journal of Diplomacy*, vol. 6, nos. 3-4 (2011), p. 352.

8   Chung-in Moon and David Plott, 'A Letter from the Editors', *Global Asia*, vol. 13, no. 3 (September 2018).

9   For further discussion of public diplomacy's domestic dimension, see Ellen Huijgh and Caitlin Byrne, 'Opening the Windows on Diplomacy: A Comparison of the Domestic Dimension of Public Diplomacy in Canada and Australia', *The Hague Journal of Diplomacy*, vol. 12, no. 4 (2012), pp. 395-420.

The extent to which political leaders have embraced the public diplomacy dimension of their role is inconsistent. For some, the fit is not a natural one, but evolves over time. Others bring a personal charisma and a natural affiliation for engaging public audiences, including through social media. Regardless, the reality of today's global diplomatic environment, including an increasing emphasis on summitry — diplomacy conducted at the highest levels of political authority — means that most political leaders are unable to escape the public diplomacy dimensions of the leadership role. This is especially so for leaders across the Indo-Pacific, who are acutely aware of how their interactions 'will be read by competitors and mass publics'.[10] Indeed, despite the reservations of professional diplomats, political leaders are more regularly in the public view — communicating, negotiating and advocating national interests. The strategic significance is not to be dismissed, for many political leaders realize the 'power that comes from being able to set the agenda and determine the framework for debate'.[11] Thus they can no longer be viewed merely as *instruments* of public diplomacy. To do so is to deny the extent and potential of their diplomatic *agency* — that is, their capacity to effect change within the organizational framework of diplomatic practice[12] — and, in doing so, potentially to alter the larger power dynamics at play. The engagement of political leaders in the diplomatic process is, as Harold Nicolson pre-empted, inevitably political.

Political Leadership and Public Diplomacy: An Indo-Pacific View

The significance of political leaders as public diplomats, whether performing their duties at home or engaging through more formal diplomatic processes, is particularly critical in the Indo-Pacific, a region that is marked by deep transformation and shifting political discourse.[13] When examining political

---

10   Richard Feinberg and Stephan Haggard, 'Talking at the Top: Past, Present and Future Summit Diplomacy in Asia', *Global Asia*, vol. 13, no. 4 (December 2018), p. 16, available online at: https://www.globalasia.org/v13n04/cover/talking-at-the-top-past-present-and -future-summit-diplomacy-in-asia_richard-feinbergstephan-haggard.

11   Joseph Nye, 'Donald Trump and the Decline of US Soft Power', *The Strategist* (12 February 2018).

12   For full discussion of diplomatic agency, see Rebecca Adler-Nissen, 'Diplomatic Agency', in Costas M. Constantinou, Pauline Kerr and Paul Sharp (eds), *The SAGE Handbook of Diplomacy* (Los Angeles, CA: SAGE, 2016), pp. 92-103.

13   Moon and Plott, 'A Letter from the Editors'.

leadership in this region, the focus must first turn to China, a nation cast by some as 'the quintessential Indo-Pacific power'.[14]

Leading China's Rejuvenation

Under the leadership of President Xi Jinping, China is openly seeking to build influence within the Indo-Pacific region. Although initially slow to engage in public diplomacy practice, China has stepped up its investment in the past decade. Estimates suggest annual public diplomacy spending in excess of US$ 10 billion a year, more than the combined spending of the United States, United Kingdom, France, Germany and Japan.[15] Ingrid d'Hooghe notes that China's public diplomacy objectives are intricately tied to its rising leadership ambitions:

> [... to] help make China's economic and political rise palatable to the world; contribute to the global recognition of Chinese values and policies; increase the government's legitimacy; and that it is indispensable in the fight for China's right to speak and to co-exist with the liberal international world order with its own political model.[16]

Since taking office in 2012, President Xi has taken centre stage as producer and director of the nation's public diplomacy efforts — actively and deliberately engaging public audiences at home and abroad in his ambition to realize the 'great rejuvenation of the Chinese nation'. Recent developments — including the designation of Xi as the 'core' of the Communist Party of China (CCP), the inscription of 'Xi Jinping Thought' into the constitution and the removal of term limits for his presidency — signal that Xi will personally shape the values and institutions that will guide China's leadership within the region for some time to come. In doing so, Xi has bound his leadership authority to the CCP, having 'diligently gone about reclaiming political dominance for the CCP as the vanguard party and for himself as the party's representative'.[17] Utilizing methods akin to the one-way propaganda of the Cold War era, Xi himself has come to define the CCP and China in this 'New Era'.

---

14   Rory Medcalf, 'A Term Whose Time Has Come: The Indo-Pacific', *The Diplomat* (4 December 2012).

15   As reported in Soft Power 30, 'China's Soft Power: A Comparative Failure or Secret Success', *USC Center on Public Diplomacy Blog* (25 August 2017).

16   Ingrid d'Hooghe, 'China's Public Diplomacy Shifts Focus: From Building Hardware to Software', *China Policy Institute Analysis* (24 October 2013).

17   Julie Bowie and David Gitter, 'Abroad or at Home, China Puts Party First', *Foreign Policy* (5 December 2018).

The significance of Xi's 'great helmsman' persona at home is not to be discounted. It appears that domestic publics are targets and instruments of the public diplomacy process: to be informed and educated as uncritical supporters and advocates of Xi's policy platform. Xi has embedded himself in the lives of ordinary Chinese through multiple platforms and institutions. David Shambaugh observes that:

> Xi kitsch is to be found in shops across the country; television programs celebrate his wise leadership; multimedia tracks his every utterance and activity; and his exhortations bombard the public daily through a ramped up propaganda apparatus.[18]

Xi's influence now reaches far into China's digital and social spheres. Rowan Callick suggests that Xi is actively 'transforming the internet in the name of cyber sovereignty into a great tool of control, delivering him broader and deeper power' over the Chinese population.[19] While opportunities for dissent within the People's Republic of China have always been limited, recent moves have ensured that they have now been firmly squashed through Xi's method of 'algorithmic governance'.[20] Chinese domestic publics and diaspora have become adept at self-censorship, while propaganda messaging aimed at 'guiding' discussion, alongside increased state infiltration and the monitoring of chat sites, have become common features of China's digital space. Indeed, 'building a renewed sense of national identity that can be widely embraced with pride among a billion Chinese at home',[21] and many more living throughout the region, is central to Xi's ambitions. Moreover, for many, Xi's vision justifies tightening social controls. As Graham Allison notes, 'few in China would say that political freedoms are more important than reclaiming China's international standing and national pride'.[22]

Just as he has done at home, Xi has leveraged his leadership persona on the global stage in a bid to build China's influence and credibility as a global

---

18   David Shambaugh, 'All Xi, All the Time: Can China's President Live Up to His Own Top Billing', *Global Asia*, vol. 13, no. 3 (September 2018), p. 17.

19   Rowan Callick, Address to the Asia Pacific Council.

20   Mark Chorzempa, Paul Triolo and Samm Sacks, 'China's Social Credit System: A Mark of Progress or a Threat to Privacy', *Peterson Institute for International Economics Policy Brief* (June 2018).

21   Graham Allison, 'What Xi Jinping Wants', *The Atlantic* (31 May 2017), available online at https://www.theatlantic.com/international/archive/2017/05/what-china-wants/528561/.

22   Allison, 'What Xi Jinping Wants'.

power that contributes to global public goods. Under Xi's leadership, China has 'upped its game', making significant contributions to the UN's operating budget, global peacekeeping, overseas development assistance, and actively engaging in global policy development from public health, to disaster relief, energy and sea-lane security, counter-terrorism and anti-piracy operations.[23] Xi is prominent on the global stage. He has successfully hosted major leadership summits, including the Asia Pacific Economic Cooperation (APEC) in 2014, the Group of Twenty (G20) in 2015, the Shanghai Cooperation Organization (SCO) in 2018, as well as notable bilateral visits, including with US President Trump, Japan's Prime Minister Abe and India's Prime Minister Modi. Major projects such as the Asian Infrastructure Investment Bank (AIIB) and the Belt and Road Initiative (BRI) — both launched under Xi — speak further to his ambition to increase China's global influence and ultimately set the terms of the emerging regional agenda. Xi asserts that China 'will keep contributing Chinese wisdom and strength to global governance'.[24] While many may welcome China's contribution, when cast against China's rising military and economic influence in the region, Xi's words strike an ominous tone.

While projecting China's influence overtly on the global stage, Xi has also ramped up the controversial global influence activities of the United Front Work Department. Working through extensive diaspora, student, business and media networks abroad, the United Front aims to 'win support for China's political agenda, [and] accumulate influence overseas'.[25] However, media reports revealing the extent and frequently subversive nature of these activities have done little to improve China's positioning in the region. Instead, they signal a shift in China's public diplomacy under Xi, whereby China must not only reassure, but also 'dictate how it's perceived and that the world is biased against China'.[26] They also raise wider concerns across the region that Xi's pursuit of soft power in the region has a dangerously sharp edge.[27]

---

23   Shambaugh, 'All Xi, All the Time', p. 19.

24   Xi, 'Secure a Decisive Victory in Building a Moderately Prosperous Society in all Respects and Strive for the Great Success of Socialism with Chinese Characteristics for a New Era'.

25   James Kynge, Lucy Hornby and Jamil Anderlini, 'Inside China's Secret "Magic Weapon" for Worldwide Influence', *Financial Times* (26 October 2017).

26   Kynge *et al.*, 'Inside China's Secret "Magic Weapon" for Worldwide Influence'.

27   Joseph Nye, 'China's Soft and Sharp Power', *The Strategist* (8 January 2018); and Anne-Marie Brady, 'NZ vs China: We Could be the Next Albania', *NZ Herald* (21 February 2018). See also Anne-Marie Brady, 'Magic Weapons: China's Political Influence Activities under Xi Jinping', Wilson Centre Paper, (18 September 2017); and Nick McKenzie, 'Power and Influence: The Hard Edge of China's Soft Power', *ABC Four Corners* (5 June 2017).

Counterbalancing Narratives: 'Free and Open Indo-Pacific'

China's increasing global prominence has prompted other regional powers to consider how they might effectively counterbalance the influence of the rising great power in the region. Thus, the narrative of a 'free and open Indo-Pacific' — an idea initially spearheaded by Japan's Prime Minister Abe and now sustained by key regional democracies, India and Australia, with the support of the United States — has begun to gain traction.

Shinzō Abe, now one of the region's most experienced leaders, laid the foundations for the 'Indo-Pacific' during his first term in office. In his 2007 speech to the Indian Parliament, Abe's reference to the 'dynamic coupling of the Indian and Pacific Oceans'[28] caught the attention of strategic publics — academics, political commentators and journalists — in India, Japan, the United States and Australia. Abe later used news opinion pieces to promote the idea of the four nations working in coalition as 'Asia's democratic security diamond' to preserve and promote key values, including freedom of navigation, democracy, the rule of law and respect for human rights.[29] It was a proposal that was reinforced by plans for a Quadrilateral Security Dialogue (also known as 'the Quad'), involving the four nations. Even though the Quad failed to take shape at that time, Abe continued to engage deliberately and publicly with key leaders to advance the narrative. Those early efforts gave rise to a complex web of interwoven bilateral and trilateral links, which sustained a loose coalition of the four nations, enabling reconstitution of 'the Quad' (at least at the official level) one decade later.

India's Prime Minister Modi alongside the Australian prime minister of the day,[30] although both cautious of their respective complex relationships with China, have followed Abe's lead. For all three nations — Japan, India and Australia — the Indo-Pacific narrative reflects a new geopolitical convergence: it usefully maintains pressure for US engagement in the region at a time when US President Trump appears intent on withdrawal from other domains, while establishing a platform for values-based discourse that seeks to dilute China's influence, while encouraging China to observe the established rules-based order. The three leaders have advanced the narrative through complementary

---

28   Shinzō Abe, 'Confluence of Two Seas', address delivered to the Parliament of the Republic of India, New Delhi (22 August 2007), available online at: https://www.mofa.go.jp/region/asia-paci/pmv0708/speech-2.html.

29   Shinzō Abe, 'Asia's Democratic Security Diamond', *Project Syndicate* (27 December 2012).

30   Australian political leadership is hampered by ongoing leadership spills, which bring their own public diplomacy challenges for the nation. The most recent saw Malcolm Turnbull replaced by Scott Morrison as prime minister and leader of Australia's Liberal National Coalition government in August 2018.

public diplomacy activities, carefully targeted to draw strategic audiences into the Indo-Pacific narrative, but calibrated to avoid suggestions that they might be strategizing the containment of China.

Bilateral and multilateral summitry involving political leaders (including foreign and defence ministers) promote their regular dialogue. Bilateral leaders' meetings are now held on an annual basis for the three powers (Japan–India and Australia–Japan), with significant media coverage, while leaders of all three nations tend to gather at annual regional and global leaders' summits, including through the East Asia Summit (EAS), APEC and even the G20.

Other public diplomacy initiatives, including delivering key speeches, policy statements and opinion pieces to influential audiences, aim to sustain and amplify the narrative. For example, during his term as Australia's prime minister, Malcolm Turnbull delivered the keynote to Singapore's 2017 Shangri-La Dialogue. India's Prime Minister Modi delivered the keynote speech the following year in 2018. Both anchored their remarks in the notion of a 'free and open Indo-Pacific'. In a bold move — presumably sanctioned by their respective political leaders — the naval chiefs of Japan, India, Australia and the United States shared the stage during the closing plenary session of Delhi's 2018 Raisina Dialogue to promote the need for wider maritime cooperation in the face of increased Chinese aggression at sea. These targeted initiatives have been supported through policy statements. Japan embedded the 'free and open Indo-Pacific' strategy within its foreign policy in 2016. Australia's 2017 *Foreign Policy White Paper* refers to the Indo-Pacific as a neighbourhood, 'in which adherence to rules delivers lasting peace, where the rights of all states are respected, and where open markets facilitate the free flow of trade, capital and ideas'. India's Prime Minister Modi has also confirmed the Indo-Pacific as the regional framework for India's foreign and defence policies.[31]

US President Donald Trump played an essential role in further raising the profile of the Indo-Pacific narrative. His repeated reference to US aspirations for a 'free and open Indo-Pacific' during an extended tour to the region in 2017 captured media headlines throughout South-East Asia. Trump's Indo-Pacific rhetoric was reinforced through the US National Security Strategy and subsequent renaming of the US Indo-Pacific Command (from the US Pacific Command). These developments were reported as significant, because they represent 'a specific vision for a rules-based order in one of the world's most dynamic regions' — an order that is seen to be 'increasingly under duress

---

31   Rahul Roy Chaudhury, 'Modi's Vision for the Indo-Pacific Region', *IISS Analysis* (2 June 2018).

from an assertive and ambitious China'.[32] Importantly, however, these shifts in US positioning reflect positively on the sustained and consistent messaging by Japanese, Indian and Australian leadership over the previous decade. In his keynote speech to the Shangri-La Dialogue, Australia's Prime Minister Malcolm Turnbull hinted at the significance of such leadership coalitions, noting that:

> Now in this brave new world, we cannot rely on great powers to safeguard our interests. We have to take responsibility for our own security and prosperity while recognizing we are stronger when sharing the burden of collective leadership with trusted partners and friends. The gathering clouds of uncertainty and instability are signals for all of us to play more active roles in protecting and shaping the future of this region.[33]

In contrast to Chinese President Xi's sweeping efforts to set and control the narrative of China's rejuvenation at home and abroad, Prime Ministers Abe, Modi and now Australian Prime Minister Scott Morrison have sustained a targeted messaging campaign aimed firmly towards strategic publics and opinion leaders. The 'Indo-Pacific' narrative hasn't won mainstream popularity. Nor is it intended to. Rather, for these leaders the intent is to see the language and underpinning principles of the 'free and open Indo-Pacific' embedded in the policies of nations and institutions across the region in order to counter, or at least to manage, China's rising influence. Ensuring US policy uptake of the Indo-Pacific was a significant win, one that might be credited in particular to Shinzō Abe. However, integrating the Indo-Pacific narrative into the policy of regional institutions, especially ASEAN, presents a more significant challenge for the traditional and public diplomacy skills of regional leaders.

The ASEAN Way

South-East Asian leaders are thus caught in the middle of the emerging Indo-Pacific contest. Yet the leadership style for these leaders is marked by an aversion to prominence beyond their national boundaries. For many, addressing the multiplicity of internal policy issues while managing fractured domestic constituencies fosters an inward gaze. Indonesia's President Joko Widodo is such an example. Elected in 2014 on the promise of a 'bottom–up,

---

32   Jeff M. Smith, 'Unpacking the Free and Open Indo-Pacific', Commentary, *War on the Rocks* (14 March 2018).

33   Malcolm Turnbull, Keynote Address, 16th IISS Asia Security Summit, Shangri-La Dialogue, Singapore (3 June 2017).

people-centred approach' to policy-making and governing, President Widodo (affectionately known as 'Jokowi') has been consumed by the need to engage with and appeal to domestic audiences. Ellen Huijgh suggests that Jokowi's engagement with external audiences occurs as a result of so-called 'intermestic' policy considerations, rather than a deliberate outward focus.[34]

It is a theme that resonates elsewhere. Malaysia's recently appointed Prime Minister Mahathir bin Mohamad, no stranger to the regional or global stage, Philippine President Rodrigo Duterte, whose popular appeal within the Philippines remains surprising to the outside world, and Cambodia's increasingly authoritarian Prime Minister Hun Sen all present similarly inward-looking approaches. Indeed, leaders from the South-East Asian region appear ambivalent about engaging with publics on the regional or global stage. Nonetheless, each of these leaders plays an instrumental public diplomacy role, contributing to the optics and reputation of their nation, including through the conduct of their leadership at home.

More important for South-East Asian leaders is the role of collective leadership that is demonstrated through their commitment to ASEAN, as a regional institution and platform for strategic diplomacy. Despite their different political persuasions and approaches, South-East Asian leaders are consistent in their calls for ASEAN centrality, to the point that it tends to dampen any overt public diplomacy aspirations that they might harbour as individuals. As a multilateral organization supported by a formal secretariat, ASEAN engages in public diplomacy activities across various layers of the institution to help 'bring understanding about its policies and activities to [the] regional and international community' and to 'get its people involved in regional issues and the community-building process'.[35] On both counts ASEAN achieves uneven levels of success.

For South-East Asian political leaders, the opportunity to engage visibly as regional leaders hinges on ASEAN summitry, which includes ASEAN leaders' meetings alongside a range of other related forums, including the East Asian Summit — a leadership summit that is strikingly Indo-Pacific in reach and composition.[36] The geography, history and anatomy of ASEAN have seen a particular style of leadership emerge through the summits. The so-called 'ASEAN Way', marked by 'mutual consultation' and 'consensus-building',

---

34 See Ellen Huijgh, 'Indonesia's Intermestic Public Diplomacy: Features and Future', *Politics & Policy*, vol. 45, no. 5 (2017), p. 763.

35 Zhikica Zach Pagovski, 'Public Diplomacy of Multilateral Organizations: The Cases of NATO, the EU and ASEAN', *CPD Perspectives* (June 2015), p. 17.

36 Today the East Asia Summit draws together member nations of ASEAN, plus China, Japan, the Republic of Korea, India, Russia, the United States, Australia and New Zealand.

reflects ASEAN's 'preferred methods for managing disputes and moderating differences', accompanied by a distinct ASEAN discomfort with 'adversarial approaches'.[37] From a public diplomacy perspective, this model promotes a welcome façade of political unity across the Indo-Pacific region. Resulting communiqués give little away; 'couched in opaque diplomatic language', they tend to 'gloss over complex issues and choose not to make public that which governments consider to be too sensitive'.[38]

While ASEAN has proven itself to be a robust platform for dialogue for more than 50 years, it is nonetheless an elite model of regional governance, which reflects inherent vulnerabilities in the current climate of geopolitical contest. Concerns that China is seeking to leverage economic influence to split ASEAN unity are increasingly well founded.[39] At the same time, Japan, India and Australia have all increased public diplomacy efforts towards the grouping, including through high-profile annual summitry,[40] youth leadership, education and sporting initiatives[41] and joint statements emphasizing shared interests in a 'rules-based Indo-Pacific that [...] embraces key principles such as ASEAN's unity and Centrality, inclusiveness, transparency and complements ASEAN's community building'.[42] The core message being delivered suggests that 'ASEAN sits at the heart' of the Indo-Pacific.[43]

Although captivated by the Indo-Pacific discourse, South-East Asian nations have taken some time to warm to it. For some, the narrative raises uneasiness about their own positioning within the region and appears dismissive of the enduring notion of ASEAN centrality. China's concerns about the Indo-Pacific as a form of strategic design have found resonance in South-East Asia. As Singapore's Prime Minister Lee Hsien Loong acknowledged, ASEAN would accept the Indo-Pacific construct provided that the end result is 'an open and inclusive regional architecture, where ASEAN member states are not forced to

---

37   Sultan Nazrin Muizzudin Shah, 'ASEAN and Asia–Pacific Peace and Prosperity', address delivered to ASEAN–Australia Dialogue, Sydney (18 March 2018).

38   Shah, 'ASEAN and Asia–Pacific Peace and Prosperity'.

39   Huong Le Thu, 'China's Dual Strategy of Coercion and Inducement towards ASEAN', *The Pacific Review* (15 January 2018).

40   Swaran Singh, 'India and ASEAN Look to Each Other to Balance China's Rise', *South China Morning Post* (18 January 2018); Richard Heyderian, 'Is Australia Set to Join ASEAN as China's Assertiveness Grows?', *South China Morning Post* (26 March 2018).

41   Joint Declaration of the ASEAN–Australia Special Summit: The Sydney Declaration, Sydney (14 March 2018).

42   Chairman's Statement at the 21st ASEAN–Japan Summit, Singapore (14 November 2018). It is worth noting that centrality is spelt with a capital 'C' in the official declaration.

43   Julie Bishop, Address to the Asia Society, New York (8 March 2018).

POLITICAL LEADERS AND PUBLIC DIPLOMACY IN THE INDO-PACIFIC   195

take sides'.[44] While most nations across the region have a 'shared interest in preventing China's domination, [...] they all have complex interdependent relationships with China, which they need to maintain in a reasonable state of equilibrium'.[45] An Indo-Pacific narrative that either excludes or seeks to contain China is a difficult pill for ASEAN leadership to swallow. Finding a way to bring China into the Indo-Pacific discourse would be helpful to ASEAN.

Indonesia's former Foreign Minister Marty Natalegawa, an advocate for ASEAN leadership, argues that the quiet diplomacy and public ambiguity of ASEAN leaders no longer offer a sufficient model, particularly in the face of the twenty-first-century geopolitical contest. In his view, 'ASEAN cannot afford to be a passive bystander to these geopolitical shifts', but 'must demonstrate leadership — thought leadership' that will contribute to the shape of the evolving order.[46] ASEAN's reluctance to play a more prominent leadership role, including through public diplomacy, in the key debates of the region points to the potential for strategic drift and irrelevance in the twenty-first-century strategic re-ordering. While Thailand takes on the mantle of ASEAN chairmanship in 2019, it is unlikely that the current trajectory will change.

Conclusion

The geopolitical realities of shifting power and contest in the Indo-Pacific region highlight the strategic public diplomacy role for political leaders — engaging publics, both at home and abroad — in coming decades. The objective — to shape a regional order that is favourable to national interests — provides a consistent, underlying motivation. Yet, as highlighted through this paper, asymmetries and variations arise in the approaches taken by political leaders towards public audiences. Although unsurprising, these distinctions are significant when viewed against the backdrop of regional fault lines emerging between autocratic and democratic systems of governance.

When cast against the backdrop of strategic re-ordering, it becomes clear that President Xi's intent is to advance China's 'New Era' of rejuvenation, while framing the political agendas, institutions and practices that will ultimately shape the future Indo-Pacific region. Xi's firm hold on the levers of power,

---

44   Seow Bei Yi, 'Principles of Japan's Indo-Pacific Strategy Align with Singapore, ASEAN Priorities', *The Straits Times* (14 November 2018).

45   John McCarthy, 'Correspondence', *Australian Foreign Affairs*, no. 4 (October 2018), p. 121.

46   Marty Natalegawa, 'Leadership and Regionalism in Southeast Asia', 2018 Asia Lecture, Griffith Asia Institute, given in Brisbane (28 November 2018).

alongside broad strategies to build China's profile and the endorsement of subversive offshore influence tactics, may prove effective. Political actors and publics across the region are attracted to China's offering, particularly when it comes with the promise of economic gain. China's sheer size and weight as 'the biggest power in the history of the world'[47] means that any form of pushback brings risks.

Nonetheless, Xi's ambitious pursuit of absolute control at home and of unprecedented influence on the global stage provides the touchstone against which other political leaders across the Indo-Pacific region are calibrating their own public diplomacy roles. The middle and emerging regional powers of Japan, Australia and India are working separately and together to engage strategic publics in values-based discourse about the Indo-Pacific. Spearheaded by the enduring efforts of Japan's Prime Minister Shinzō Abe, the intent is to leverage strategic public opinion in ways that will maintain US engagement in the region and dilute China's influence, while enticing China's compliance with the international rules-based order. The Indo-Pacific narrative and its underpinning principles provide a strategic opportunity for middle and small powers, including those of South-East Asia, to shape the shifting order in ways that remain conducive to their interests. Maintaining consistent and coherent messaging will be a significant challenge, especially as two of the three leaders — Modi and Morrison — face elections during 2019.

By contrast, South-East Asian leaders continue to shy away from overt and outward-looking public diplomacy leadership, preferring to orient their gaze around 'intermestic' concerns. Together, South-East Asian leaders have established a successful pattern of collective, consensus-based leadership via ASEAN. For decades, the institution has provided a robust platform for strategic diplomacy, reinforced by regular leaders' summits. Yet the ASEAN model is under pressure, faced with the increasingly dominant and disruptive rise of China. ASEAN members, and the political leaders that represent them, appear to have limited capacity for thought leadership in the face of the current contest and may thus end up caught in strategic drift and subject to the influence of others.

As public diplomacy takes a more strategic turn, practitioners and scholars must be attuned to the public diplomacy role of political leaders in shaping critical narratives — through their words and deeds — delivered at home and abroad. The challenge is not only to keep pace with, but to anticipate the future political debates, and to engage leaders in consistent, creative and, where appropriate, collective messaging that resonates with influencers,

---

47   Lee Kwan Yew, quoted in Allison, 'What Xi Jinping Wants'.

opinion-leaders and ordinary publics alike. Complacency is no longer a viable option. In the contested and multipolar Indo-Pacific, public diplomacy, particularly when exercised by political leaders, is undeniably strategic — establishing the narrative, setting the agenda and promoting the rules that will underpin the emerging regional order. From a national interest perspective, the stakes could not be higher.

Caitlin Byrne
is Professor and Director of the Griffith Asia Institute at Griffith University, Australia. Her research into public diplomacy and soft power, particularly in the Asia–Pacific region, is recognized internationally and has been published in journals including the *Australian Journal of International Affairs, The Hague Journal of Diplomacy, and Politics & Policy*. Byrne consults regularly with federal and state government stakeholders on public diplomacy strategy design and implementation. She is a Faculty Fellow with the University of Southern California's Center for Public Diplomacy.

Index

Abe, Shinzō   45, 189-190, 192, 196
Abu Ghraib   11
Active Measures Working Group   20
Adler-Nissen, Rebecca   107, 115
adversarial diplomatic relationships. *See* hostile nations, public diplomacy and
aesthetics, role of   111-112
affective polarization   67, 69, 70-71, 79
Afghan-Americans   59
Ager, Dennis   121
Albright, Madeleine   161
algorithms, role of   10-11, 12, 88, 91
Alliance Française (AF)   121, 123
Allison, Graham   188
Al Qaeda   158, 163, 164
Amaq (IS news agency)   158
Amazon   87
Ambassador for Digital Affairs   96
American exceptionalism   42
American Ireland Fund   53
American Irish Historical Society   53
American Jewish Committee   53-54
amplifier effect   113
Anderson, Benedict   120
Anglo-German model of public engagement   26-27
Anholt, Simon   29, 30, 124
Anholt GfK Nation Brands Index (Anholt)   29
The Annals of the American Academy of Political and Social Science (journal)   3, 143
anti-democratic movements   81. *See also* hostile nations, public diplomacy and
Arab Spring   55
Arab Uprising   148-149
Araud, Gérard   45-46
Ardern, Jacinda   111-112
Argentina   40, 110
Armenia   146
Arquilla, John   10
ASEAN   183, 184, 192-195
Asia Silicon Valley Development Plan   97
al-Assad, Bashar   92

Association of South-East Asian Nations (ASEAN)   183, 184, 192-195
Astana Film Festival   31
athletes, role of   47, 138
Atta, Mohamed   159
Atwood, Margaret   34
audience: domestic   13-15, 23-24, 26, 41, 48-50, 107; unmotivated   75, 77
augmented reality (AR)   86, 87, 88
Aung San Suu Kyi   184
Australia   18, 183, 184, 192, 194, 196
authoritarianism   149. *See also* hostile nations, public diplomacy and
authority, skepticism of   15, 40

Bad News (social media game)   80
Bahrain   67
Baidu   97
Baltic nation MFAS   93
Bastille Day   46
Beccalli-Falco, Ferdinando "Nani"   94
Belt and Road Initiative (BRI)   177-178
Bennett, W. Lance   113
Berger, J.M.   157
Berlin Wall   8
Berridge, Geoffrey   146-147
Bhatia, Kartika   159
big data, role of   9, 10-11, 86, 91, 98
bilateral hostile nation relationships   136, 146
bin Laden, Osama   154, 163
bin Mohamad, Mahathir   193
Birthright Israel   52
Bjola, Corneliu   23, 90
Black Crows (television series)   165
Black Lives Matter   47
Bloom, Mia   157
Boko Haram   90
Bolsonaro, Jair   40
Borat: Cultural Learnings of America for Make Benefit Glorious Nation of Kazakhstan (film)   31
Bosnia-Herzegovina   62
Boston Review (journal)   22

INDEX

branding, national   27-29, 30-31, 37, 44, 59, 123-124, 188-189
Branson, Richard   131
Brazil   40, 177
Brexit referendum   48, 49
"Bring Back Our Girls"   90
Britain   30, 34, 97, 111-112, 164; British Council   26; British Foreign & Commonwealth Office (FCO)   92-93
British Broadcasting Corporation (BBC) World Service   19, 26-27
BBC Russian Service   31
Bruce Gregory   138
Building Welcoming Communities Campaign   55
Bush administration   13, 14
Bymanm, Daniel   156

Callick, Rowan   188
Cambodia   193
Cambridge Analytica   114
Canada   44-45, 74, 102-103
Cardozo, Elsa   39
Castells, Manuel   59-60, 126, 127, 130
Castro, Fidel   139
celebrity role of   42
Center on Public Diplomacy (CPD)   3
Central European University   24
Central Foreign Affairs Commission (CPC)   172-173, 175
Chadian diaspora   60
Chalabi, Ahmad   57
Chávez, Hugo   39, 139, 141
China   1-2, 4, 46-47, 75, 147, 151, 169-181; ASEAN and   194; Belt and Road Initiative (BRI)   177-178; Chinese characteristics, importance of   171, 172, 174-175, 180; counterbalanced by other Indo-Pacific nations   190-192; cultural exchange   138, 173, 177-178; cultural self-confidence   175-176; disinformation from   67, 72; global initiatives shared by   177; media, resource allocation for   142; nation branding in   188-189; "New Era" narrative   195-196; public diplomacy spending by   187; "public," use of

term in   170; sharp power, use by   16-20; Xi Jinping   172, 174, 175-176, 178, 183, 187-189, 195-196. *See also* Indo-Pacific region, public diplomacy in
China Model of public diplomacy   169-181; Indo-Pacific influence   183; institutionalisation variable   171-172, 173-174; party diplomacy   172, 179; power structure variable   171, 172-173; trends forecast for   173-178; as "Whole-Nation System"   172, 179
Chinese companies, in Silicon Valley   97-98
Chinese diaspora   52, 53
Clash of Civilizations theory   118
climate change   77, 118, 130-131
Clinton, Hillary   17-18, 52, 54
Clinton–Bush Haiti Fund   55
coercion, role of   7, 17-18, 162, 194
cognitive biases   76, 77, 78
cognitive diversity   118
cognitive exhaustion   72-73, 79
Cold War   15, 17-18, 32, 113, 171
collaboration, role of   2, 129-130, 132
colonialism   123
Columbia Broadcasting System (CBS)   44
Commonwealth Summit   111-112
communication   2-3, 92, 130, 146; changes in   109, 125-126; dialogic   111; digital   84, 85-89; strategies   12-13, 130, 132; telecommunications, role of   62-63
communism: communist governments 148-149; Communist Party of China (CPC)   170-173, 175, 177, 179-180, 187
Comprehensive and Progressive Trans-Pacific Partnership   46
Confucius Institutes   19 46-47, 128, 170
Congress for Cultural Freedom   18
Constantinou, Costas   127, 128
constructivism   86, 144
Copenhagen climate talks in   130
Coptic Christians   53-55, 61
Coptic Orphans   61
Cornut, Jérémie   37
corporations role of   95

INDEX

201

corrective messaging   67, 68, 70-71, 77-78, 81, 114

counter-terrorism   108, 155, 157-167; creating narratives in   162-165; public diplomacy's relevance   165-167; recruitment   157-165; religion and   161-162; social media messaging   157-158, 164, 166-167; socio-economic issues of   158-160

country of origin (COO)   53-55, 56-57, 58-59, 60-62

country of residence (COR)   53-55, 58, 60-62

credibility, role of   10-12, 16, 20, 26-27

Crimea   66, 71-72, 91

Cuba   94, 138, 141, 149

Cull Nicholas   21, 24, 38, 46

cultural diversity   118-120, 125-132; leveraging of   118-119, 125, 129, 132

cultural exchange   46-47, 80-81, 138, 141; China   138, 173, 177-178

culture   4, 8, 42, 118-132; boundaries of   124-125; cultural filters   14; cultural unification   120; globalization and   125-126, 131-132; Maori   111-112; popular culture, role of   47; public diplomacy and 118-119, 126-127, 132; state-centric diplomacy and   119-125, 132; textual-oriented   85-86

Current Time (website)   71

Czechoslovakia   30

data-driven interactions   83-84, 87

decentralization   9-10

democracy-based programmes   144

democratic and non-democratic states' relationships   135, 144, 146, 149-152. See also hostile nations, public diplomacy and

democratic institutions, loss of confidence in   81

Democratic National Committee   18

democratization   40

denationalization   43-44

Deng Xiaoping   138-139

Denmark   96-97, 98

Der Derian, James   127

Deutsche Welle (DW)   26-27

d'Hooghe, Ingrid   171, 187

diaspora diplomacy   3, 52-63; definition of   55-57; future of   61-63; public diplomacy and   52, 57-61, 63; scope of   52-55

The Difference (Page)   118

Digital Age   94

digital diplomacy   4, 22-23, 83-100, 102-116; digital communication   84, 85-89; digital tools, use of   79, 103-104, 108-110; domestic digital diplomacy (DDD)   4, 84, 85, 89-94; emotion, role in   109-112, 115-116; future of 112-116; identity and emotion in 105-109, 115-116; Silicon Valley diplomacy   84, 85, 94-99

digital emotional intelligence (DEI)   88-89

digital information warfare   113, 115

digital literacy programmes   93

digitization   89, 94

diplomacy: actor-centric   131, 132; bilateral   98-99, 129; consular services   47-48; cosmopolitan 126-127, 128; cultural   123, 175; digital tool use in   103-104, 108-110; face-to-face   92-93; golf, use in   45; hetero-diplomacy   127; homo-diplomacy   127; humanity-centered   119, 126-132; index   29; issue-based   61-62; local offices, role of   47; mediatisation of   110-111; multilateral   94-95, 98-99, 129, 130, 151; paradox of   49-50; party diplomacy (China)   172, 179; of the peoples   39; ping-pong   138; Silicon Valley   9, 84, 85, 94-99; societisation   1-2; state-centric 119-125, 128-132; sustainability 126-127; whole-of-government   136, 149, 150, 152. See also diaspora diplomacy; digital diplomacy; public diplomacy

diplomatic failure   41

diplomatic representation, evolution of 94-95

diplomatic sites   125-126
disinformation   23, 37, 65-81, 87, 91, 93;
    campaigns   11-12, 66-67, 70-72, 89, 92,
    105, 113-114; countering of   31-32, 66,
    70-71, 73-74, 77-78, 79-81; digital   93,
    105; emotion, role of   68, 72-73,
    112-116; frequent exposure to   75-76;
    identity-grievance campaigns   66,
    67-69, 70-71, 79; incidental
    exposure   66, 75-77, 77-78;
    information gaslighting   66, 71-73,
    73-74, 79, 80-81; lack of control   72-73.
    See also fake news; hostile nations,
    public diplomacy and; propaganda
disintermediation dilemma   42-43
domestic audience   23-24, 26, 41, 47-50, 107,
    123
Dubai Expo   34
Duterte, Rodrigo   40, 184, 193
duty of care   48

echo-chamber reasoning   114
Edelman Trust Barometer   27
Edney, Kingsley   171
education, role of   62, 79, 138, 162, 178
Egypt   53-54, 55, 61, 139
Einstein, Albert   35
Eisenhower, Dwight   8
Elizabeth, Queen of England   111-112
Élysée Treaty (1963)   28
embassies   98-99, 137, 151
emotion, role of: in digital diplomacy
    109-112, 115-116; emotional
    connection   128; emotional
    contagion   104-105; emotional
    content filters   79; emotional
    dampening tools   79-80; emotional
    framing   86; emotion as
    evidence   114; identity and   105-109,
    115-116
engagement by deed   25
*Engagement: Public Diplomacy in a Globalized
    World* (Welsh and Fearn)   24
Entman, Robert M.   141-142, 143
Ernst & Young Ethiopia   61
Estonia   32
ETAPA   96

Ethiopian Commodities Exchange   61
Ethiopian diaspora   59, 61
Ethiopian Intellectual Property Office   59
European Football Championship   30
European Union (EU)   37, 40-41, 43, 60, 62;
    External Action Service's
    Disinformation Review   32;
    Parliament   43
exchanges, virtual   80-81
Expo 2017   31, 34

Facebook   13-14, 19, 67, 96, 109-111, 114, 143
Factcheck.org (website)   80
fake news   91, 93, 112-113; countering
    31-32, 80; emotional elements
    of   10-11; fake images   114;
    hostile governments, use by   17, 19,
    23; on social media   11, 69, 71-72, 74,
    79-80. *See also* disinformation
Falkland Islands   110
Farage, Nigel   41
Fearn, Daniel   24
Fisher, Ali   129-130
Fitzpatrick, Kathy   127, 131
foreign exchange students   13
foreign ministries. *See* ministries of foreign
    affairs (MFAs)
foreign policy, role of   8, 23-24, 26, 31, 53-54,
    123
Fox and Friends (television show)   43
France   28, 46, 96, 120-121, 123, 187
French National Rally (formerly National
    Front)   41
The Friendly Sons of St Patrick   53
Fulbright scholarship   138
Future Library   34

Gabre-Madhin, Eleni   61
Gaddafi, Muammar   139
Garrett, Kelly   79
General Electric (GE) Europe   94
Germany   11, 15, 28, 187
Ghanem, Hafez   159
Gilboa, Eytan   11, 171
Global Britain   48
Global Community (Iriye)   126
global consciousness   128, 130

INDEX

Global Diaspora Forum   52
Global Engagement Center (GEC)   164, 165-166
Global Fund for Women (GFW)   100
globalization   1, 3, 89, 99, 125-126, 131-132
Global North   62
Global Public Goods (GPG)   127
Global South   39-41, 118
Global Ties US   80-81
Goethe Institute   26-27
Golan, Guy J.   142
Goldstein, Steve   43
Golovchenko, Yevgeniy   115
Gonzalez, Emma   114
Goodall, H. L., Jr.   164
Good Country Index (Anholt)   29
Google   86, 87, 94, 96, 97, 99
Gorbachev, Mikhail   139
Graham, Sarah Ellen   108
great-power rivalry   23
Great War (WWI)   34
Gregory, Bruce   138, 143, 150, 151
Groupe de Réflexions et d'Analyses d'Intérêts Tchadiens (GRANIT)   60
Guantanamo   11
Guha, Priya   97
Gullion, Edmund   11
Gülmez, Seçkin Barış   128

Hagel, Charles   13
The Hague Journal of Diplomacy (journal)   1-5, 47-48
Haiti   59
Haitian diaspora   54-55
hard power   17, 147-148, 153
Hartig, Falk   171
Hartmann, Mareike   115
Hayden, Craig   108
Hebrew University   34-35
hetero-diplomacy   127
Hitler, Adolf   30
Ho, Elaine   55-56, 57, 63
Holmes, Marcus   37
holographic imagery   92, 93
homo-diplomacy   127
hostile nations, public diplomacy and   4, 134-153; bilateral relationships   136; cultural exchange   138, 141;

diplomatic representation challenge   146; embassies   137, 151; governments' role challenge   135, 149-152; history and contemporary state of   136-143; isolate-or-engage dilemma   135; new public diplomacy and   136, 150, 152; NGO involvement   140-141; P2P approach   136, 140, 150-151, 152; propaganda challenge   135, 146-147; rising-expectations challenge   135, 148-149; social media and   139-140, 142-143, 149; strategic relevance of public diplomacy   135; theory challenge   143-145; traditional foreign-ministry public diplomacy and   136, 150, 152; whole-of-government diplomacy and   136, 149, 150, 152
Huijgh, Ellen   38, 193
Hungary   24, 40
Hun Sen   193
Huntington, Samuel   118
Hutchinson, John   121
hybrid media system   110-111, 112-113
hybrid warfare   16, 23-24
hyper-empowered individuals   42-43, 44

iCivics   80
identity: American   53; beliefs, role in   68; cross-national identity politics   98; emotion and, role of   105-109, 115-116, 118; identity-affirmation   70, 79; identity mediation   130, 132; in-group   70-71; layered   61; local   120; national   39, 119, 122-123, 144-145; pan-Indian   54; social   104-105; state   106-108, 109, 110, 111, 113, 115
image, national   27-28
India   40, 54, 102-103, 183-184, 189-191, 194, 196
Indicorps   54
Indonesia   14, 192-193, 195
Indo-Pacific region, public diplomacy in   4, 182-197; ASEAN and   183, 184, 192-195; Australia   18, 183, 184, 190, 192, 194, 196; Cambodia   193; "free and open" narrative   184, 190, 192; India   40, 54,

Indo-Pacific region (cont.)
102-103, 183-184, 189-191, 194, 196;
Indonesia 14, 192-193, 195;
Japan 45-46, 170, 183-184, 187, 189-190,
194, 196; Philippines 40, 184, 193;
political leadership 182-184, 186-197;
regional powers counterbalance
China 183, 184, 190-192, 196; region
defined 183n1; Singapore 194-195;
Thailand 195; United States
and 190; Xi Jinping 172, 174, 175-176,
178, 183, 187-189, 195-196. *See also*
China; China Model of public
diplomacy
inducements, role of 7, 17, 194
influence: continued influence effect 76,
77-78; Indo-Pacific 183; multi-
polar 61; religious 161-162; targets
of 63; theories of 144
information: deliberation of 78;
disarmament 32; information-
discernment education 74, 80;
information revolution 9-11, 14;
literacy 74, 77; overload 86, 87;
secrecy of 146, 156; warfare 17-20
informational learned helplessness
(ILH) 72-74, 79-80
information and communications
technology (ICT) 62-63, 103
Institute of Deep Learning 97
intelligent assistants 84, 87, 88
interconnectivity 125-126, 128-132
Interim Haiti Recovery Commission 54
International Center for Religion and
Diplomacy (ICRD) 162
International Mother Language Year (2015)
100
international organizations, role of 128
International Republican Institute 15
internet, role of 22, 62, 188
Internet of Things 9
Iran 75, 90, 98, 139, 141
Iran Nuclear Agreement 90
Iraq 11, 14, 57, 77, 154-155, 158
Iraq War 11, 14
Ireland 97, 98
IREX 74
IrishCentral (website) 53

Irish diaspora 53
Iriye, Akira 126, 128
Islam 11, 13, 67, 161, 163
Islamic State (IS) 19, 92, 155, 157-159, 162-163
Israel 32, 54, 91-93, 107, 139
Israeli diaspora 52-53, 91
Italy 18, 74

Jabado, May 163
Jamaican diaspora 56
Japan 45-46, 170, 183-184, 187, 189-190,
194, 196
Jibiki, Koya 45
jihad, global 32
Jönsson, Christer 85
Jordan 91

Kabila, Laurent 57
Kampf, Zohar 139
Kazakhstan 31, 34
Kennan, George 137
Kennedy, John F. 34
KGB 17
Kim Jong-un 139-140, 184
Kinshasa, march to 57
Klynge, Casper 96-97, 98
Korea. *See* North Korea (DPRK); South Korea
(ROK)
korowai 111-112
Kosovo 30

Laclau, Ernesto 38
language, role of 3, 81, 121
leadership 8, 149. *See also* political
leadership, public diplomacy and
"Learn to Discern" media literacy
programme 74
Leonard, Mark 12
Libya 137
listening, role of 4, 24-25, 38, 53, 87, 130
Liu Yandong 170, 178
Livingston, Steven 113
Loong, Lee Hsien 194-195
Los Angeles Diocese 55
Louis XIV 120-121
Ludwig, Jessica 17, 147
Lumpkin, Michael 164

INDEX

machine learning 87, 88
Macri, Mauricio 40
Macron, Emmanuel 20, 45-46
Malaysia 115, 193
Malkovich, John 34
Maloney, Suzanne 141
Manchester School 22
Manor, Ilan 23, 90
Maori peoples 111-112
marginalized voices, enhancement
   of 99-100
market forces 15
Martinon, David 96, 98
material exchange 54
Matlock, Jack 137
McConnell, Fiona 56, 57, 63
McDonald, Kelly 164
McFaul, Michael 40
media: broadcasting, international 13, 123,
   124, 142, 158; China, resource allocation
   for 142; counter-terrorism measures
   through 164-165, 166; credible
   outlets, decline of 75; emergent
   media 132; hybrid media
   system 110-111, 112-113; indigenous
   media 32; of Islamic State 158;
   literacy education 74, 78, 80; mass
   media 123; news media literacy
   (NML) 78, 80; press, role of the 12.
   See also social media
Melissen, Jan 37, 38, 138, 179
Melki, Jad 163
Mercer, Jonathan 30
messaging: corrective 67, 68, 70-71, 77-78,
   81, 114; dominance 109;
   inoculation 79, 80
Metzger, Geneive Brown 56
MH17 115
Middle East Broadcasting Center 165
military, role of 16, 154-155
ministries of foreign affairs (MFAS) 87, 89,
   90-100, 136, 150, 152; Baltic nation
   MFAS 93; British FCO 92-93;
   French MFA 96; Israeli MFA 91-93;
   Russian MFA 92
mis/information 98
Miskimmon, Alister 163
Mitchell, David 34

Modi, Narendra 40, 102-103, 189-191, 196
Moon Jae-in 47, 184
Moore's Law 9
Moriyasu, Ken 45
Morozov, Evgeny 22
Morrison, Scott 192, 196
Mosul, Iraq 154-155, 158
motivated reasoning 67-69
Multicultural Network of Women Workers
   for Peace (MWPN) 61-62
multinational corporation (MNC)
   employers 54
Munich Conference 30
Murrow, Edward R. 18
Muslim ban 62
Myanmar 184

narratives: alternative 77-78, 89;
   role of 48, 162-164, 184, 190, 196;
   victim 32-33
Natalegawa, Marty 195
National Democratic Institute 15
National Endowment for Democracy 15,
   17, 24
National Front (France) 41
nationalism 38, 119, 120-122, 126, 128
nation-branding 27-29, 30-31, 37, 123-124,
   188-189
nation-state, rise of the 120-122, 123
Nauert, Heather 43
Nazarbayev, Nursultan 31
Netanyahu, Benjamin 139
*The Net Delusion: The Dark Side of Internet
   Freedom* (Morozov) 22
Netherlands 87-88
networks, role of 28, 126
Neumann, Iver B. 125
New Jersey 114
The News Hero (social media game) 80
New Zealand 111-112
Nicolson, Harold 43, 156, 186
Nigeria 90
Nikkei Asian Review (magazine) 45
9/11 attacks 13, 55, 59, 123, 169-170
1984 (Orwell) 9
Nixon, Richard 138
non-governmental organizations (NGOs),
   role of 8, 15, 24, 140-141, 180

non-state actors, role of   3, 56, 87, 94-95,
    98-100, 110, 126; technological-based
    non-state actors (TBNSAS)   95-97, 99,
    100
North Atlantic Treaty Organization
    (NATO)   12, 31
North Korea (DPRK)   94, 139-140, 149, 184
Norway   34
Nye, Joseph   40, 106, 123, 147-148, 153, 164

Obama, Barack   138, 149, 165
Obama, Michelle   90
Obama administration   13-14, 41, 44, 55,
    60, 90
Oglesby, Donna Marie   130, 184
O'Loughlin, Ben   163
100 Years (film)   34
online learning technology   80-81
Open Government Partnership   96
openness, role of   4, 18, 19-20
Orbán, Viktor   24
Orozco, Manuel   58
Orwell, George   9
Oslo, Norway   34
Otero, Maria   58
Ottoman Empire   120
Oxfam America   59

Packer, George   159
Page, Scott   118
Palestine   32, 54, 91
Paris climate accord (2015)   130-131
Paterson, Katie   34
Le Pen, Marine   41, 45-46
People's War   30
people-to-people (P2P approach)   28-29,
    136, 140, 142, 150-152, 173, 175, 177-178
personalism   39, 42, 45-46
persuasion, role of   7-8
Peterson, Pete   146
Petraeus, David   155
Philippines, the   40, 184, 193
Pierre-Louis, Jean   55
Pigman, Geoffrey   120-121
Pinheiro, Paulo Sérgio   95
Pittsburgh, Pennsylvania   55
Pizzagate   17
Poland   30, 41

policy-making, role of   25-26, 108-109
political homophily   114
political leadership, public diplomacy
    and   182-197; Indo-Pacific public
    diplomacy and   182-184, 186-197;
    leaders as public diplomats   186;
    leadership coalitions   192; leadership
    summits   189, 193
Polynesian islands   128, 131
populism   4, 8, 38-50, 118, 126, 131; anti-
    diplomatic impulses and   38-40; new
    populism   24, 32-33; public
    diplomacy challenge of   43-48, 49-50;
    rise of   40-43
Portland Communications   11, 18
Post-Facto (social media game)   80
power   7; hard power   17, 147-148, 153;
    hyper-empowered individuals
    42-43, 44; sharp power   4, 16-20,
    23-24, 147-148, 153; smart power   153;
    table of power   98-99. *See also* soft
    power
"Presenting Israel" campaign   107
propaganda   11-12, 37, 91, 105, 107, 113, 135,
    146-147. *See also* disinformation
protectionism   44-45
psychological operations, military
    (PSYOPS)   16
public diplomacy: as academic
    discipline   143-144; citizen-based   2,
    28-29, 47-48, 62, 110; Cold War
    Model   171; culture and   118-119,
    126-127, 132; definitions of   1, 37, 136,
    170, 179; diaspora diplomacy and   52,
    57-61, 63; disinformation, strategies for
    countering   31-32, 66, 70-71, 73-74,
    77-78, 79-81; disintermediation
    dilemma   42-43; domestic citizens,
    focus on   23-24, 26, 41, 47-50, 107, 123;
    Domestic Public Relations
    Model   171; emotion and identity, role
    of   105-109; external/internal
    disconnect   37-38, 39; future of   1-2,
    24-25, 29-35, 37, 43-48, 49-50, 112-115;
    holistic   128-131, 132, 167; indirect
    16; investment in   187; lessons of   4,
    24, 35; mediated   141-142; new
    approach   2-3, 22-23, 136, 150, 152;

INDEX   207

new public diplomacy approach   2-3,
22-23, 136, 150, 152; Non-state
Model   171; people-to-people
approach   28-29, 136, 140, 142, 150-152,
173, 175, 177-178; populism, challenge
of   43-48; principles of   25-29, 35;
soft power, role of   10, 11-16;
transformation in governance
practices   39-40. *See also* China
Model of public diplomacy; counter-
terrorism; digital diplomacy; hostile
nations, public diplomacy and;
Indo-Pacific region, public diplomacy
in; ministries of foreign affairs (MFAS);
political leadership, public diplomacy
and; terrorism
*Public Diplomacy: Foundations for Global
Engagement in the Digital Age* (Cull)   21
"Public Diplomacy: Seven Lessons for its
Future from its Past" (Cull)   24
Pugwash conferences   138
Putin, Vladimir   24, 140
Putnam, Robert   89-90
PyeongChang Winter Olympics   47

Quadrilateral Security Dialogue ("the Quad")
190

Rácz, András   23
Rashtrapati Bhawan   103
Reagan administration   12, 15, 20, 34
refugee diasporas   62
regime behaviour change (*vs.* regime
change)   136
relational approach   128-129, 132
Religious Freedom Reports   53-54
reputational security   29-31, 37
Reputation and International Politics
(Mercer)   30
Research, Information and Communication
Unit (RICU)   164
Riad, Nermien   61
Rodriguez, Robert   34
Rogers, Ivan   41
Roman Empire   8
Roosevelt, Franklin D.   34
Roselle, Laura   163
Rouhani, Hassan   139

Rubin, Barry   161
Russian Federation   2, 24, 75; disinformation
campaigns by   11-12, 66, 70-72, 89, 92,
113-114; international political
interference   16-20, 23, 29-30, 140,
148
Russian Internet Research Agency   75
*Russia's Hybrid War in Ukraine: Breaking the
Enemy's Ability to Resist* (Rácz)   23
Russia Today (RT)   18, 142

Sadat, Anwar   139
Samuelsen, Anders   96
Schmidt, Eric   86, 94
scientific exchange   138, 178
Second Life   22
Second World War (WWII)   30, 33, 124
Seib, Philip   108
Seko, Mobutu Sese   57
selfies, role of   90, 103
semantic meaning, new   88
sentiment analysis   91
September 11, 2001   13, 55, 59, 123, 169-170
Serbia   62
Shambaugh, David   18, 188
shared identities/values approach   70-71
sharp power   4, 16-20, 23-24, 147-148, 153
Shi'a Muslims   67
Shirky, Clay   22
Shultz, George   12
signals *versus* noise, separation of   87
Sikh separatists   103
Silicon Valley diplomacy   9, 84, 85, 94-99
Singapore   31, 191, 192, 194-195
SinoInsider (magazine)   46
60 Minutes (television show)   44
Skype   92
Small Island and Developing States
(SIDS)   131
smart power   7, 148, 153
Smith, Anthony D.   121
Smith, Huston   161
social identity, role of   104-105
social informatics (SI)   84-85, 86-87, 89, 94
Socialism   175
social media   22, 35, 43; counter-terrorism
via   157-158, 164, 166-167; democratic
values spread via   149; diasporans,

social media (cont.)
use by 55, 62; as diplomatic sites 125-126, 132; emotional dynamics of 79-80, 104-105, 108, 109-116; fake accounts on 18, 19, 93; fake news on 11, 71-72, 79-80; filter bubbles 91; hostile nations, use by 139-140, 142-143, 157-158; public information on 156; rise of 10-12, 14, 103; use by diplomats 90, 103-104; victim narratives on 32-33

societisation 1-2

soft power 3-4, 7-20, 44, 46, 106-108; authoritarian governments, use by 8, 16-20, 176; counter-terrorism, use of 164, 166; credibility, role of 11; culture as 119, 123-124, 132; in digital age 87-88; as a force-multiplier 8; information revolution, role in 10-11; P2P approaches and 152; public diplomacy as key instrument 144, 145; sharp power, *versus* 147-148; strategic use of 153; by US civil society 8, 16

Soft Power 30 (Portland) 11, 18

South Korea (ROK) 47, 170, 184

Soviet Union 12, 17, 30, 32, 137, 138

Speck, Ulrich 39

sports exchange 47, 138

Sputnik (online news) 18, 75

Stalin, Joseph 141

state-building process 119

state identity 106-108, 109, 110, 111, 113, 115

Stevens, Christopher 137

StopFake (website) 31

St Patrick's Day 53

Sudan 54

Sunni Muslims 67

Sunnyvale 97

Sustainable Development Goals (SDGS) 34

Swartz, Brecken Chinn 127

Syria 62, 92, 95

Taiwan 30-31, 67, 97

Tamil Tigers 63

Tech Ambassador 96

tech-cities 96

technocognition 66, 79-80

technocracy 38

technological-based non-state actors (TBNSAS) 95-97, 99, 100

technologies, role of 1, 4, 22, 66, 79-81, 125, 131

techplomacy 98

Teen Vogue (magazine) 114

Tehran, Iran 98

telecommunications, role of 62-63

tele-presence 92-93

terrorism 154-165; creating narratives in 162-165; military tactics to fight 154-155; prevention 155-156; recruitment 155, 157-165; religious influence 161-162; socio-economic issues of 158-160. *See also* counter-terrorism

Thailand 195

theory-driven formative and summative evaluation research 81

"30 Neighbors in 30 Days" project 55

Thucydides 30

Tiananmen Square protests 139

Tillerson, Rex 43, 165

townhall meetings, virtual 92

town twinning 28

Transfer of Knowledge through Expatriate Nationals (TOKTEN) 54

Trans-Pacific Partnership (TPP) 45, 46

Treaty of Westphalia (1648) 120-121

Trethewey, Angela 164

trolls, internet 19, 23

Trudeau, Justin 44-45, 102-103

Trump, Donald 41-43, 45-46, 49, 139-140, 149, 189-190

Trump, Ivanka 47

Trump administration 11, 13, 14-15, 46, 62

Trump campaign 114

Tsinovoi, Alexei 107

Tucker, Robert 141

Tunisia 158-159

Turkey 87-88, 146

Turnbull, Malcolm 192

Twitter: campaigns 13; credibility of tweets 11; diplomats, use by 22, 44, 87-88, 90, 103, 139-140; emotion, role of 104-105, 109-112; fake news via 69, 75

INDEX 209

two-level game theory 89-90, 91-92
Tylor, Edward B. 122

ubuntu 128
Ukraine 12, 23, 29-31, 69-70, 74, 91, 115
Ullah, Haroon 161-162
United Front Work Department
(China) 189
United Kingdom (UK) 41, 48, 93, 97, 110, 187
UK Independence Party (UKIP) 41
United Nations (UN) 34, 60, 93, 95, 100, 139;
Development Programme
(UNDP) 54; Educational, Scientific
and Cultural Organization
(UNESCO) 100
United States (US) 11, 30, 34, 46-47, 97, 113;
Agency for Global Media 71; Bureau
of Educational and Cultural
Affairs 47; Central Intelligence
Agency (CIA) 18; China
relations 151, 170; Cold War 17, 18,
32; Congress 90; Constitution 114;
Copts Association 53-54; counter-
terrorism measures 160, 163-164;
cultural exchange 138, 141; diasporas,
US-based 53, 60; Embassy 54;
Foreign Service 56; Indo-Pacific
region and 183, 190; Korea and
139-140; "Made in USA" culture and
entertainment 47; North Korea
negotiations 149; Patent Trade
Office 59; Peace Corps 54;
Pentagon 16; Public Diplomacy and
Public Affairs 37, 43, 187; State
Department 13, 43, 47, 52-54, 58,
80-81; Vietnam relations 146

University of Southern California 3
"Unknown Russia" (*Current Time*) 71

Venezuela 39, 40, 139, 141
Venice Biennale 30
Vietnam 170
virtual reality (VR) 86, 88, 91-92, 98-99
visioning, role of 33-35
visuals, use of 86-87, 92, 111-112, 113-114
Voice of America (VOA) 15, 27, 142

Walker, Christopher 17, 147
Wang, Jian 37, 171
Webb, Alban 31
Wells, H.G. 34
Welsh, Jolyon 24
Westphalian perspectives 4, 120-121, 122
"We The North" campaign 44
wicked problems 118-119, 125, 130, 132
Widodo, Joko (Jokowi) 192-193
Wight, Martin 145
Wilson, Woodrow 34, 37
Wiseman, Geoffrey 42

Xi Jinping 172, 174, 175-176, 178, 183, 187-189,
195-196
Xinhua (news agency) 18, 142

YouTube 11, 71, 164
Yugoslavia 32

Zaire, former 57
Zhang, Juyan 127

Printed in the United States
By Bookmasters